Aspects of Soviet Culture:
Voices of *Glasnost'*, 1960-1990

Jelena Milojković-Djurić

EAST EUROPEAN MONOGRAPHS, BOULDER
DISTRIBUTED BY COLUMBIA UNIVERSITY PRESS, NEW YORK

1991

EAST EUROPEAN MONOGRAPHS, NO. CCCVII

PREFACE

My inquiry is one of the few aiming to discern the interdependence of literary and musical works in counterpoint with the evolving ideological issues. The comparative approach helped to elucidate the roles of writers, composers, and musicologists highly appreciated by the Soviet intelligentsia and society at large. Yet music, as a discipline, is an underrepresented area of Soviet studies in spite of the abundance of musical works of highest artistic eloquence. I traced the Soviet cultural scene roughly from the time of Stravinsky's visit to the Soviet Union in 1962 during the era of "the thaw" in the societal and cultural life. Thus, the book examines the relaxation of stringent ideological policies under Khrushchev, following the subsequent development until the introduction of *glasnost'* and *perestroika* doctrines in 1985, and leading to the end of the 1980s. The first four chapters examine ideological, cultural and literary issues in the dimensions of literary history and criticism. The next three chapters study the music and musical life in the perspective of aesthetics and cultural context. The final chapter aims to define the objectives of Soviet education from the sociological and ideological viewpoints.

About the chronology, the starting point for this book was a review paper presented at the Second World Congress of Soviet and East European Studies in Garmisch-Partenkirchen in 1980. My paper, "The Musical Culture of Yugoslavia in the Period after the Second World War," evaluated the influence of the doctrine of socialist realism on Yugoslav music, literature and art. During the postwar period Yugoslavia remained, to a different degree, in the domain of Soviet political and cultural influences.

I was personally confronted with the Soviet criticism in the journal *Sovetskaia muzyka,* the official publication of the Union of Composers. The infamous *Journalist (Zhurnalist),* criticized, in the Editorial 1982/3, the mentioned paper presented at the Second World Congress. My colleague from Germany Dr. Detlef Gojowy was also criticized in the same Editorial for his paper presented at the Congress. Dr. Gojowy pointed to the achievements of the Russian avant-garde in the early decades of the 20th century. The Editorial signed by the *Journalist,* the pen name of a Party functionary in the Union of Composers, appeared often on the pages of *Sovetskaia Muzyka*, although rebuttals were never published.

The improved flow of information after the 27th Congress of the Communist Party in 1985 concerning the literary and artistic productions, and equally the valiant efforts leading to the revaluation of the once censored cultural heritage helped to a great extent my subsequent research.

Another impetus for the continuation of my work was provided by *The Conference on the Uses of Nationalist Ideology in Russian Literature*. The Conference took place at Rice University and it was organized by Professor Eva Thompson, in 1988. For this Conference I prepared my paper "Soviet Russian Musicological Revaluations of Stravinsky's Neo-Classical Phase."

A greatly expanded version of this paper was presented at the 1989 Annual Meeting of the American Musicological Society at the University of Texas at Austin. The seventh chapter of the this book presents the revision of the Stravinsky paper.

I would like to use this opportunity to express my thanks to Professor William Kearns, Director of the American Research Center, University of Colorado and Professor Nicholas Lee, Department of Slavic Languages, University of Colorado, for their interest and support of my work. I worked in the Library of University of Colorado in 1987 using the splendid collection of Soviet periodicals, and benefited from the discussions with my longtime colleagues. Professor Benjamin Stolz, Head, Slavic Department, University of Michigan, was kind to arrange for my research at the Graduate Library in 1988 and 1989. I am also grateful for the research grant provided in 1990 by the Russian and East European Center, University of Illinois, and its Director, Professor Diane Koenker. I completed my present manuscript and the final checking of bibliographical sources during my stay at the Center. I would like to acknowledge the friendly assistance of Dr. Robert Burger and his staff in the Slavic Library at the University of Illinois. I am indebted to Professor Nicholas Cook, Head, Department of Music, University of Southampton, for his interest in my present work. Dr. Valeriia Egorova, Institut Istorii Iskusstv, Moscow, offered valuable insights into the Russian musical scene.

CONTENTS

CHAPTER I

IN THE VANGUARD OF *PERESTROIKA:*
IDEOLOGICAL AND CULTURAL ISSUES

In April of 1985 an important Resolution was ushered in the life of the
Soviet society. The 27th Congress of the Communist Party accepted the
policy of restructuring, as submitted in the political report of the General
Secretary Mikhail Gorbachev at the Plenum of the Central Committee.
The subsequent Resolution of the Plenum formulated the new political and
social viewpoints substantiating the concept of restructuring of the largely
centralized government, educational and cultural institutions and of the
troubled economy. Most of all, the Resolution encouraged constructive
criticism, and openness in societal relations, promoting a broad
democratization of the Soviet society. Another important stage of
restructuring was reached at the two consecutive Plenary Meetings of the
Central Committee of the Communist Party, in January and in June of
1987, sustaining the theory of revolutionary restructuring. Both Plenums
dedicated their concerted efforts to the 70th anniversary of the October
revolution, and stressed their commitments to the socialistic ideology as
formulated by Lenin.[1]

Gorbachev often reiterated in his speeches that restructuring presented,
in fact, the continuation of the historical course begun in 1917. In
particular, his speech delivered in Leningrad, on the eve of the 70th
anniversary of the October Revolution, referred to the consistent following
of Lenin's lessons and revolutionary traditions.[2]

Gorbachev's speech entitled "The Party of the Revolution is the Party
of the *Perestroika,"* had a symbolic connotation interpreting the
restructuring as the perpetuation of the revolutionary spirit of the

---

1. Mikhail Gorbachev, *The Party of the Revolution is the Party of the Perestroika,*
Moscow, Novosti, 1987, p. 7. Compare also B. B. Piotrovskii, V. Vinogradov et al.,
eds., "Ot Redkolegii," *Sovetskaia Kul'tura, 70 let Razvitiia,* Moscow, Nauka, 1987, p. 3–
5.

2. Gorbachev, *The Party of the Revolution . . .,* p. 8.

Communist Party. Gorbachev delivered this speech in front of a selected audience representing the political and ideological forces, including the veterans of the Party, veterans of labor and of the Civil and Great Patriotic Wars, front rank-workers and representatives of Leningrad's intelligentsia, the activists of the Party, government and economic bodies, trade unions and the Komsomol. The distinguished members of the Soviet political and intellectual elite gathered in the Marble Hall, like an ancient Greek chorus, attested to the authority of the speaker and his message.

Gorbachev clearly hoped that his speech, delivered at this festive meeting, would find a special place in the Soviet historical annals. The speech aimed to strengthen his position at the helm of the Communist Party, and provide additional legitimacy for the restructuring change helping the consolidation of the ideological forces.

This carefully orchestrated event took place on October 13, 1987, in the white Marble Hall of the famous Smolny Institute, the former headquarters of the Revolution. In the same Hall, on the night of October 24-25, 1917, Lenin announced that the initial tasks of the Revolution have been accomplished. Gorbachev's pilgrimage to the same Hall, seventy years later, symbolized his adherence to Lenin's legacy and Party's ideology.

Gorbachev started his speech by honoring the memory of Lenin as the leader of the October Revolution. The present development of the new crucial stage of revolutionary restructuring was carried out in the spirit of the October Revolution. He described this stage of renewal as the turning point in the history of the socialist state.[3]

In his speech Gorbachev aimed to strengthen the historical conscience of the nation by linking the past with the new unfoldment. *Perestroika* was perceived as unsettling for some members of the Party and citizens alike, and the unprecedented changes seemed to undermine the established principle of socialism. In addition, the process of restructuring progressed at a slow speed and with difficulties, causing, at times, great concern and criticism.[4]

Gorbachev extended in his speech the cordial greetings on behalf of the Central Committee of the Communist Party. Gorbachev admitted that he had special feelings entering Smolny Institute which preserved the "sacred

---

3. Gorbachev, *The Party of the Revolution . . .*, pp. 3–4.

4. P. N. Fedoseev, "Istoriki i pisateli o literature i istorii," *Voprosy istorii,* No. 6, 1988, p. 4.

memory of October 1917." He trusted that his audience would share the same historical awareness transcending the present festive occasion, and achieving a deeper identification with the national past and future prospects. In his speech, Gorbachev expounded the official political views of the necessary reforms, and expressed satisfaction since the restructuring drive was gathering momentum. Over the past two years Soviet citizens have begun to show more initiative in accomplishing the great task. Gorbachev emphasized that continuing support was vital for the final success of the restructuring process.

Gorbachev was not only appealing to the minds of the Soviet people at large, he was trying to win their hearts and enthusiasm for the changes. He recounted, with obvious pleasure, his first official trip to Leningrad, after the Central Committee entrusted him with the duties of the General Secretary. The destination of the trip was not a random choice. At that time, in the spring of 1985, there was an intense search going on for ways of accelerating the country's social and economic growth. In the current stage of development, restructuring demanded from the many millions of working people civic courage, genuine enterprise, competence and application of spiritual and physical strength in order to prevent discrepancies between words and deeds. Gorbachev concluded:

"Today we are at a crucial stage of the *perestroika* when it should penetrate all spheres of our life from the material to the spiritual. The special feature of this stage is the deepening of the processes of restructuring and the drawing into them of many millions of working people, of our entire vast country. And it is for this, comrades, that we should all prepare ourselves as we consistently follow Lenin's lessons and the tradition of the October Revolution." [5]

Gorbachev maintained that the new intensive development benefited from the thorough study of history and a fresh interpretation of Lenin's postulates. The preparation for the celebration of the 70th anniversary enabled a renewed assessment of this historical period. The scrutiny of the past, he thought, justified the democratization and strengthened the restructuring and openness.

Gorbachev also aimed to redefine the role of the Communist Party as the leading force of the restructuring process. He pointed out that already

---

5. Gorbachev, *The Party of the Revolution* . . ., pp. 7–8.

Lenin envisaged the Party as a political vanguard capable of transforming the society. Gorbachev admitted that he came to realize that no transformation was possible without such a leadership capable of rallying the best forces of the country.[6]

Gorbachev knew that some members of the Communist Party were hampered by conformity and backwardness, unable to fully support the restructuring reforms. Therefore, he tried repeatedly to induce the indecisive membership, as well as his political opponents, to follow him on the new path. He hoped that the well argued clarifications provided the needed reassurance for the new policies of restructuring while safeguarding, at the same time, the essence of the spirit of the October Revolution. The introduction of restructuring and openness was a legitimate continuation of the course chartered by Lenin and his guard:

> "I would like to stress again that 1987 was a very fruitful year for us. Even by the most stringent of yardsticks, it must be evaluated as a year of great work. Indeed, if the theoretical, political and practical work carried out last year in connection with the celebrations of the 70th anniversary of the Great October Revolution had not been done, we would be now two or three steps lower in our understanding of the past and the present stage, as well as of our prospects. We have now a better knowledge of our history . . . . One cannot agree with those who suggest that we forget history or remember only a certain part of it. We now fully realize that such a point of view is unacceptable. We must have a deep knowledge of our country's history, especially in the period after the revolution. Knowing our history, knowing the causes of these phenomena, the causes underlying our country's major achievements, and knowing the causes of the serious mistakes and tragic events in our history - all this allows us to draw a lesson today as we seek to revitalize our society." [7]

The long awaited renewal of the Soviet society evolved in many levels. This renewal reflected, most of all, the fundamental importance of the fresh point of view, the new political and moral emphasis, formulated in the course of the 1980s. One of the main aspirations of Soviet society was to revaluate many notions about the present and the past and to devise prospects of socio-economic and cultural development. At this turning

---

6. M. Gorbachev, *Democratization—the essence of perestroika, the essence of socialism,* Moscow, Novosti, 1988, p. 10.

7. Gorbachev, *Democratization . . .,* p. 5.

point of history, it was recognized that the greatest value of socialistic government was its man power. The cultivation of the humanistic character of socialism became an important issue. Moreover, the affirmation of the human rights and human priorities ranked above the party interests and other related political issues. According to the candid testimony of Mikhail Gorbachev, the Soviet leaders approached this platform only after an intense political and theoretical scrutiny:

"We thought about it a lot. We criticized ourselves, and others, proposing hard and intricate questions, until we saw the reality of the present state . . . . We came to the conclusions that enabled us to reexamine what was formerly considered as axiomatic . . . . We came to the standpoint that enabled the liquidation of former political practices, moral and aesthetic norms."[8]

The new ideological and theoretical concepts of socialism, accentuated the democratization of Soviet society, as opposed to previous attention to the long range development in general, and the oversight of the importance of the "human factor," and care for the fellow man. The concept of the centralized, autocratic socialistic government, that evolved during the 1930s and 1940s, acquired an absolute and dogmatic predominance. This ideological and theoretical model of socialism was repeatedly criticized in an effort of finding new solutions to existing problems. Most of all Gorbachev advocated respect for all Soviet citizens. He thought that it would be a crime to treat an individual, or an entire generation with injustice and disrespect:

"The attitude to man, to his life and to all his work must be the most respectful and honest, especially as regards those who bore on their shoulders the brunt of struggle at the sharp turns of our history. . . . We take pride in our history, each day of it, because even when people, the glory of the Motherland, unjustly perished, even during those hard times factory workers, farmers and intellectuals worked, pushed ahead and raised the country to new heights of progress. That's why when we talk of history, we don't want to exalt or overthrow individuals, but give the people, the decisive force in history, their due."[9]

---

8. Iu. S. Borisov, "O nekotorykh tendentsiiakh v razvitii sovremennoi kul'tury",*Sovetskaia Kul'ura, 70 let razvitiia,* Moscow, Nauka 1987, p. 180.

9. Gorbachev, *Democratization . . .,* p. 26–27.

It was not always easy to introduce the new ways. Gorbachev commented that the political and ideological situation reflected well the laborious process of restructuring and the Party had often literally to lead a fight for necessary changes. The people were concerned about the various difficulties of the restructuring process and there were many fierce discussions. However, the innovative decisions of the January and June Plenary Meetings of the Central Committee of 1987 were gradually implemented. The Soviet people were supporting perestroika in a growing number. Gorbachev pointed out a remarkable development: For the first time in many decades the Soviet society was experiencing a veritable, socialistic pluralism of opinions. This fact alone was unusual and therefore, in turn, interpreted in many ways requiring additional analyses, explanations and studying.[10]

Overall, Gorbachev thought, 1987 was a successful year for the restructuring propositions. In addition, the celebration of the 70th anniversary of the October Revolution was carried out accentuating the spirit of the ongoing progressive changes. Gorbachev stressed the importance of a keen knowledge of historical development, especially of the period after the revolution: The careful scrutiny of the causes of major achievements as well as the causes of serious mistakes and tragic events in the past will allow the revitalization of Soviet society and a better development of potential assets of socialism.[11]

In January of 1988, during a meeting at the CPSU Central Committee, Gorbachev stated that the first stage of *perestroika* was completed and its second stage was beginning. The beginning of restructuring brought an evaluation of the political and economic situations and the gradual implementation of a number of improvements. During this period the theoretical assessment of the political, social and economic goals of the next phase were accomplished. The initial stage of *perestroika* took roughly two and a half years to complete. The second stage of *perestroika* was just starting, coinciding with the beginning of the year 1988. The focus was already shifting into the realm of practical realization. The new integrated economic reforms were designed to prepare a transition from

---

10. M. Gorbachev, *Revolutsionnoi perestroike—ideologiiu obnovleniia,* Moscow, Izdatel'stvo politicheskoi literatury, 1988, p. 7.

11. M. Gorbachev, *Democratization . . .,* p. 5.

the old to the new system of self management. Gorbachev noted that although a new stage was reached there were still elements of the old contained in the new. Still, some doubts persisted concerning the restructuring very likely derived from inadequate comprehension of the process itself. Some saw *perestroika* as a superficial and cosmetic effort. It presented an embellishment of the façade, or mending of the existing mechanism that worked poorly, yet managed to carry on. The new innovations were not understood well and there was an uncertainty how all these implementations will work. Others, in turn, wanted to demolish the socialistic system that was for decades perceived as false and leading nowhere. Instead, they proposed alternatives taken from the arsenal of the bourgeois liberalism and nationalism. Some other individuals displayed a radical phraseology and advocated a jump over the consecutive stages of socialistic development, ignoring the logic of *perestroika*. Gorbachev noted that the revaluation of ideological principles was always a difficult problem, yet the Soviet history abounded with similar challenging situations.[12]

The ideology of restructuring — *perestroika* - presented well the basic content and aspiration of the Soviet society during the mid 1980s and later on. *Perestroika* focused on the problems of a radical economic reform, development of democracy, moral and cultural renewal. The affirmation of a new political thought established a wish for a candid dialogue on the world scene. The necessity of preserving peace, in the view of the ever increasing potentials of nuclear war, ranked high among the concerns of the Soviet society at large.

The 70th anniversary of the October revolution was marked by a number of studies assessing the development of the Soviet socialist society and the importance of Lenin's leadership. The radical reforms connected with the reconstruction of the Soviet Society heightened the interest for the past. The recognition of historical events has an important significance for the self-orientation of people in the time of flux.

An important document of the reform movement presented the essay by Iurii Nikolaevich Afanas'ev "Perestroika and Historical Knowledge," first published in a book entitled *Inogo ne dano (There is no other Way)*. The book included, in addition to the mentioned essay, articles by influential academicians, writers, journalists, and public figures, among them Andrei

---

12. Gorbachev, *Revolutsionnoi perestroike . . .*, p. 7.

Sakharov, Tat'iana Zaslavskaia, the historian Mikhail Gefter, and the Editor of *Novyi Mir* S. P. Zalygin. This volume was edited by Afanas'ev. In retrospect, due to the acuity of perception and wealth of documentation the book was dubbed the manifesto of the restructuring.[13]

Afanas'ev very much like Gorbachev in his speech at the Smolny Institute stressed the historical ties that existed between the 70th anniversary of the October Revolution and the radical reforms of restructuring. Despite all the hardships that the Soviet society has lived through, the impulses of October 1917 had preserved the spiritual unity of the people. Afanas'ev obviously supported Gorbachev's views. Moreover, in his essay he reiterated Gorbachev's postulates about the necessity of a comprehensive understanding of the past. He even suggested concrete research topics that could elucidate the most blatant failures of the past.[14]

Thus, Afanas'ev argued that it is important to find out why the efforts undertaken by the 20th Congress of the Communist Party of the Soviet Union failed. The criticism of the Cult of Personality scrutinizing Stalin's role turned to be inconsistent. The first attempt to restructure the Soviet society and to democratize did not succeed. Therefore, it is important to rethink everything that has happened over the last seventy years. To some, this process of learning seemed horrifying; this is why in certain circles a notion to stop the search for truth has emerged. The newspaper *Sovetskaia Rossiia* published a series of publications in an effort to save Stalinism. The most significant among these publications was the infamous letter against *perestroika* by Nina Andreeva. Andreeva based her accusations on both falsification and the dogmatization of Soviet history.

Even the Soviet history textbooks were misconstrued to a great extent. The textbook for the 9th grade contained mostly fabrications, and the teachers were forced to teach this untruth into young heads. The college textbooks, especially on Soviet and Party history were burdened with the same faulty presentations. Afanas'ev argued that in the last decades the writing of textbooks remained largely in the conceptual limits of Stalin's *Short Course:*

---

13. *Michigan Quarterly Review,* 1989, p. 463.

14. Iu. Afanas'ev, "Perestroika and the Historical Knowledge," *Michigan Quarterly Review,* 1989, pp. 532–534.

"I think that if we tried collectively to answer the question 'what is historical knowledge today?,' we would come to the conclusion that there is no country in the world with a more falsified history than ours. This is most relevant to the history of the Soviet period. But not only to it. Falsifying Soviet history, historians were forced to do the same to pre-revolutionary history. . . . It is important to understand that Stalinism needed history only as a propaganda service. . . . Totalitarianism was called democracy; that which had not yet been begun was called already completed. The Stalinist regime created its own history."[15]

Afanas'ev concluded that not only courage was needed in order to solve most important problems, but also intensive scholarly research, based on the analyses of historical materials.

The Institute of History at the Academy of Science published a volume of such studies by leading historians under the title *Sovetskaia Kul'tura, 70 Let Razvitiia, (Soviet Culture, 70 Years of Development),* marking the 70th anniversary of the October Revolution and the subsequent development of the Soviet culture. The editors were well known cultural historians: B. B. Pietrovskii, Editor-in-Chief, V. A. Vinogradov, Iu. A. Poliakov, B. A. Kumanev, V. S. Lel'chuk and Iu. S. Borisov, Editor's substitute.

The Editors stated, in their brief Introduction to the volume, that a re-examination of Soviet culture was needed in the context of the general restructuring — *perestroika* of the social life in the whole country. The Editors extended their support to the resolution of the 27th Congress of the Communist Party. They understood the importance of the renewal and acceleration of economic and social growth in the USSR. The Editors pointed out the necessity of re-examination of the world- and national histories, and in particular of Soviet history. Further development of the social and intellectual life should increase even more the need for culturological explorations of the Soviet society as a whole. The Editors were in agreement with the Party's recommendations concerning the progressive and long lasting economic development. The intellectuals

---

15. Afanas'ev, ibid., pp. 539–541.

were expected to play an important role in the restructuring process supporting all areas of social and spiritual growth.[16]

The importance of the cultural heritage and its role in the profile of the contemporary society was often discussed by Soviet literary historians and writers alike. Such an historical and spiritual repository enabled the individual, or the society as a whole, to ascertain its stability and its place in the history. The cultural heritage was preserved, most of all, in the respective national traditions, systems of values, and in the national languages. The accumulated wealth of historical and spiritual experiences played an important part in all societies ancient and new alike. A number of cultural historians argued that the contemporary culture benefited from this heritage since it safeguarded a special meaning in the time of great changes.

The academician Iurii Bromlei addressed this topic in his article, "Rol' sovetskoi nauki v izuchenii, sokhranenii i rasprostranenii kul'turnogo naslediia narodov Evropy", at the Symposium on Security and Collaboration held in Budapest in 1985. The revised form of this article was published in the mentioned collection of studies dedicated to the 70th anniversary of Revolution.[17]

Bromlei explained the twentieth century as a historical period saturated, as never before, with revolutionary spirit. The social, political, economic, scientific, and artistic developments pointed to intense and dynamic growth. The comprehensive picture of the contemporary European world was to a great extent inherited from the previous epoch. Yet, this world picture *(kartina mira)* was subjected to many subsequent changes. Bromlei noticed that these multiple alterations were perceived as unsettling to many, impairing the ability to adapt to the changing world. These events fostered an increasing preoccupation with the present situation and contemporaneity, and perpetuated a desire for self sufficiency and isolationism. Such an attitude seemed to obliterate the past and weaken the interaction of the past with the present.

---

16. The editors were: editor-in-chief B. B. Piotrovskii, V. A. Vinogradov, Iu. A. Poliakov, B. A. Kumanev, V. S. Lel'chuk, and Iu. S. Borisov, editor's substitute. *Sovetskaia Kul'tura, 70 let razvitiia,* Moscow, Nauka 1987, p. 3.

17. Bromlei, "Rol' sovetskoi nauki v izuchenii, sohranenii i rasprostranenii kul'turnogo naslediia narodov Evropy," *Sovestskaia kul'tura, 70 let razvitiia,* Moscow, Nauka, 1987, pp. 297–309.

Bromlei stressed the emerging global interdependence. Earlier, the economic, social and cultural developments were modelled mainly in accordance with the specific requirements of a particular society. Such developments grew to a large degree independently although not completely cut off from other societies. Each society claimed to develop a just interpretation of its own historical and geo-political missions. Phenomena that could not be fitted into the established plans were delegated to the cultural periphery. Thus, each national culture served as a measure for evaluation of all other cultures. In Europe these tendencies formulated the notion of Euro-centrism. Bromlei declared Euro-centrist supposition as dated historical provincialism.[18]

The steady and growing interaction among the peoples of the world brought a new comprehension of the national cultures. Furthermore, it pointed to many possible variants in the development of different societies. Bromlei referred to the radical changes of the means of communication, preservation, and transmission of cultural information. People of the previous epochs had only a limited knowledge of their own past and even less information about the historical development of other people. Today, there is an unprecedented abundance of cultural information of unlimited scope. The criteria used for selection and evaluation of the available information were receiving foremost attention. In the process, two opposing tendencies emerged from the present situation: the first was the weakening of historical memory and preoccupation with the present. The past was perceived only as the preliminary stage of the current development. Such a view, from "the top down," promoted the comprehension of the present as the vantage point of the preceding historical development *(vzgliad sverhu vniz)*. Thus, a meaningful dialogue and interaction between the past and the present *(sviaz vremeni)* could not be established since the cultural heritage was not understood as a necessary link in the comprehension of the present. Bromlei pointed out that the Soviet scholars endeavored to stress the importance of the past and devoted great attention to the study of world's cultural heritage. Bromlei was obviously well aware of the danger of cultural and spiritual isolation. Such an attitude prevents a culture from seeking the necessary equilibrium inducing a crippling provincialism.

---

18. Bromlei, "Rol' . . .", p. 299.

Iu. S. Borisov, head of the Department of History of Soviet Culture at the Academy of Science, scrutinized the leading tendencies of development in the contemporary culture. He explained that the term 'contemporary culture' referred to the development that took place after the April Plenum of the Central Committee and the 27 Congress of the Soviet Communist Party in 1985. He pointed to the many changes taking place in the cultural growth, and to the encouragement of the inquisitive spirit nurturing the intellectual potentials. Borisov stated that the imperative of the new thought acquired an universal meaning, demanding a reconstruction of concrete, practical activities, and of the related theoretical postulates. Moreover, the solution of some important global problems seemed to be possible thanks to the help of the newly created gnoseological and political basis.

Borisov discerned the steady cultural growth, and the enrichment of the foundations of the Soviet society. These changes emerged slowly in the second part of the 1950s with the return of many positive accomplishments that were eradicated from the official cultural history. Borisov alluded to the former censoring of the academic curricula of high schools and universities and pertaining textbooks for literary courses. These excisions were often futile: the censored books and documents were proliferated in handwritten copies, the forbidden music and songs were recorded on tape. The widespread circulation of these literary and musical works was not only the result "of the sweetness of the forbidden fruit." The prohibition was unjustified because the "fruit" was of real and undisputed value. Therefore, the return of these works was inevitable introducing a number of literary and artistic creations that justly claimed an important place in the cultural world of the Soviet society. An analogous occurrence presented the reinterpretation of literary works that were previously analyzed in a biased and untruthfull manner such as the literary works of Dostoevskii, Esenin and even the satirical novels of Il'f and Petrov.[19]

The Academy of Science USSR, decided also to restructure its activities focusing its efforts on the processes of acceleration in the scientific, technical, and social field. P. N. Fedoseev, vice-president of the Academy of Science, reiterated that the ideology of renewal encompassed many aspects of societal life: education, economy, cultural establishment, science and world politics. The new historic phase dictated the reexamination of

---

19. Borisov, "O nekotorykh tendentsiiakh . . .," pp. 189–181.

many complex issues of the past and present, requiring theoretical clarifications of general social development, and of the intellectual life. The central issues addressed the place of man in the new social and economic development, the creative potential and training of man, his motivation for work and capacity of cognitive evaluation. The study of the system "man-machine-environment" has become an important tendency in scholarly explorations. The attention was directed, most of all, to the humanization of the working conditions and the abolishment of the prevailing technocratic approach. In addition, the preservation of the environment and rational use of natural resources became issues of central importance.[20]

Soviet historians were aware of the long lasting interdependence of literature and historical past. Many Russian and Soviet writers, in the past as well as in the present, were attracted to historical themes. A number of outstanding literary works have succeeded to preserve the impact of historical events on the lives of the generations past and present. Such works have often portrayed the general political and social implications caused by the historical happenings. Thus, the writers came to be expected to detect and evaluate with keen acuity the historical changes in the Soviet society.

The existing interdependence of history and literature was the topic of the conference arranged jointly by the History Department of the Academy of Science USSR, the Union of Writers USSR, and the Academy of Social Sciences of the Central Committee of the Communist Party USSR. The conference took place in April of 1988. The participants at the conference evaluated the current questions facing the historical sciences and literature. The topic of the conference "The Historians and Writers about Literature and History" ("Istoriki i pisateli o literature i istorii") described well the kinship among historians and men of letters. The necessity of the re-examination of the Russian and Soviet history and literature was a matter of great concern for historians and writers alike.

The key note address was given by P. N. Fedoseev, the vice-president of the Academy of Science USSR. He reminded the audience that starting from the 27th Plenum of the Central Committee of the Communist Party, the *perestroika* and the revolutionary renewal remained central issues of

---

20. P. N. Fedoseev, "Istoriki i pisateli o literature i istorii", *Voprosy istorii*, Akademiia Nauk SSSR, 1988, No. 6, p. 4–5.

the Soviet society. At the present breaking point of history, the task remained to redefine the comprehension of the past and of the present, and to explain theoretically the new phenomena of the social development. The ideology of renewal encompassed all aspects of societal life, education, economy, culture, science and world politics. The Academy of Science restructured its research programs in order to concentrate more fully on the scientific, technical and social progress and long range plans of development. In the field of economy, the improvement of management presented primary concern, in addition to the betterment of professional qualifications of workers, improved productivity and increased utilization of progressive technical and scientific methods. However, the main attention in the scientific field was addressed to the problems facing the man and the actualization of the human factor.

Fedoseev thought that the questions of history and literature have never before acquired social significance as it was lately the case, although history was always a domain of ideological struggle. The lively interest of the society at large demanded elucidation of the past as presented in historical books, in the literature, in literary criticism, and in journalistic writing. The thorough research of the historical happenings of the past and the present was dictated by the wish to preserve the truth, but equally it was an obligation of moral consciousness. The difficult repercussions caused by the gross misappropriations of the principles of socialism cast a long shadow on the Soviet society. Yet, these aberrations should be observed only as one aspect of the historical past. The great achievements of the Soviet people and the bravery during the World War II should never be tarnished.[21]

The opening paper was delivered by V. V. Karpov, the first secretary of the board of the Union of Writers. Karpov pointed out that the conference was taking place at an important moment, at the eve of the 19th All-Union Party Congress. He noticed that the historians and writers alike were taking part in the restructuring process assessing a new and truthful standpoint. The time has come to present the historical development in its entirety, eliminating blank spots, and patchwork. The study of history should corroborate the periods of the ancient and the medieval ages; the study of these important chapters of the national history was, until recently, sadly neglected. This historical knowledge would enable the

---

21. Fedoseev, "Istoriki i pisateli. . .," p. 4–5.

Soviet people, in particular the youth, to fully understand the heroic strength of their forefathers *(bogatyrskuiu silu prapradedov)*, as well as the moral fortitude of the fathers of the Soviet land, the Lenin's guard.[22] The literary historian A. I. Ovcharenko took also part in the mentioned conference. Ovcharenko reminded the participants that historians may work researching historical questions without consulting the literature. Yet, the writers, literary historians, and critics can not work in their area of expertise without the knowledge of the historical past or the present. Therefore, the men of letters were anticipating with great interest the lively and frank exchange of ideas during this conference. The clarification of many issues was vitally important. Even the new generation of men and women coming of age will benefit from this exchange of ideas.

Ovcharenko contended that his students often asked what was accomplished during the last thirty five years. Most of all the students questioned whether the newly founded Soviet society was indeed the one that the whole humankind used to dream about. However, Ovcharenko pointed out that even three years after the introduction of restructuring the answers to existing questions were constantly changing, and almost daily different answers were suggested. Ovcharenko concluded: ". . . we do not have history, and we do not know it; and if there is a history than it is the most falsified in the whole world."[23]

The new assessments of Soviet historical past were discussed by a number of writers and historians, and these evaluations reflected the emerging spirit of openness. The blank spots of the historical past and rigid interpretation of dated literary canons were scrutinized, and this attitude enabled a new creative flow that became a dominant characteristic of the literary creations of the 1980s. However, among some historians there appeared some perplexity due to unprecedented openness and critical attitude toward the past. In particular the historians of the older

---

22. V. V. Karpov, "Istoriki i pisateli o literature i istorii," *Voprosy istorii,* Akademiia Nauk SSSR, 1988, No. 6, pp. 3–4.

23. A. I. Ovcharenko, "Istoriki i pisateli o literature i istorii," *Voprosy istorii,* pp. 104–105.

generation were experiencing great difficulties in revising modes of thought and in overcoming inertia and former practices.[24]

The writers again were setting an example and led the way: their efforts in clearing the important literary works from unjust banishment, and the revaluation of once censored writers have been in the making from the early days of the thaw during Khrushchev's time. The literary journals have helped in this task by publishing controversial authors from the past and the present.

The Soviet writers voiced also their support for the elimination of existing difficulties by supporting the restructuring reforms. At the the 8th Writers' Conference, the first secretary of the Writers' Union G. Markov presented his lengthy report assessing the general situation in the cultural life. Markov suggested that the administration of the Writers' Union should speed up the introduction of necessary changes. He thought, most of all, that the contribution of the writers should not be measured with new resolutions or required attendance at various meetings, but with "talented, original and necessary books, films, plays, paintings and musical compositions, that will enrich the spiritual life of the people."[25]

The writers should try to preserve their high position in the Soviet society. The publication of truly outstanding works of talented writers should be encouraged in order to stop the production of dull literature. The Writers' Union should try to strengthen the position of Soviet literature, and organize promotion of Soviet books on a regular basis. Markov also suggested the arrangement of conferences with writers, and the establishment of closer ties with the Book Lovers' Society. Most of all the human factor should be fostered, and the Union should try to stimulate the creative work of the membership in a variety of approaches having in mind the individual qualities of every author.[26]

The Soviet writers were often criticized by their Western colleagues for following the dictate of the Communist Party. Markov refuted this notion stating that Soviet writers did not take orders from anyone since the writers considered their work as an objective necessity. The Party always

---

24. V. I. Kas'ianenko, "Istoriki i pisateli o literature i istorii,"*Voprosy istorii*, No. 6, 1988, p. 69.

25. Markov, "Nikogda ne otgorazhivat'sia ot trevog sovremennogo mira," *O partiinosti literatury*, Moskva, Khudozhestvennaia literatura, 1987, pp. 8–9.

26. Markov, "Nikogda . . .," pp. 10–11.

respected talented writers and supported their development, provided the writers showed a mature responsibility towards their work. Markov pointed to an important statement, concerning the writers, formulated in the Political Report of the 27th Congress: The Report specified that all that the Party expected from the writer was "to unveil the artistic discoveries, and the truth about life that was always the essence of true art."

Early in this century Lenin expressed an idea concerning the priority of social values over the political priorities of a class.[27] This supposition was scrutinized again in the era of *glasnost'* and pronounced as an important guideline in the shaping of political and cultural policies. Lenin's idea helped to determine the new and more liberal attitude enabling the discussions of once forbidden chapters of Russian and Soviet history.

In addition, the widening of the foundations of Soviet culture pointed to the importance of the continuity of intellectual and spiritual enrichment. The assimilation of the past was manifested in the diachronic reception of the heritage, while the synchronic reception was directed horizontally towards the contemporary achievements. The previous obstructions of these processes interrupted the evolution of culture and pointed to the futility and danger of projecting false premisses.[28]

While discussing the development of Soviet culture in the second half of the 1980s, the poet Andrei Voznesenskii acknowledged the profound changes that were taking place. The ongoing revolutionary process of restructuring, according to Voznesenskii, manifested itself in a virtual "spiritual revolution" (*dukhovnaia revolutsiia*). Suggesting for the first time the usage of this term, Voznesenskii claimed that the spiritual revolution was introduced by *perestroika,* and in turn, served well the policy of restructuring. Voznesenskii believed in the necessity of changes and asserted in an article published in the journal *Sovetskaia kul'tura* in 1987:

---

27. M. Nenashev, *Books promote an Understanding of the Restructuring Process,* Moscow, Novosti, 1987, p. 29.

28. Borisov, "O nekotorykh . . .," p. 178.

"The spiritual revolution is evolving not as a fight for life but for death; the fight of the new thinking with the still strong reactionary, inert strata of society. This is not the "cultural revolution", but the revolution of Culture."[29]

Voznesenskii, with a keen insight of a poet, expressed succinctly what many others felt: the new thinking introduced a more just and truthful assessment of the past and, equally, of current failures and shortcomings. The "new thinking" pointed as well to fresh possibilities for further betterment and growth.

---

29. Borisov, "O nekotorykh . . .," p. 185.

CHAPTER II

LITERARY JOURNAL *NOVYI MIR* AS PRECURSOR OF OPENNESS: THE ROLE OF ALEKSANDR TVARDOVSKII

The revaluation of the past, within the newly established political and cultural context of openness, was repeatedly scrutinized by a number of Soviet cultural historians, writers, and literary critics. The development of Soviet literature, starting from the mid 1950s, was characterized by a slow and strenuous process of overcoming the literary and aesthetic stereotypes. The writers pursued their explorations of reality in search for truth, yet many of the works that offered new points of view were usually placed in the archives. Some of these works, when accepted for publication, were heavily edited in order to conform with standardized content and form. The aphorism: "A post is a well edited tree," was not far from truth when comparing the original manuscript with its edited version.[1] The writers became accustomed to long periods of waiting for publications of their works. This struggle continued with varying degree of success, yet the outspoken words of poets and writers acted as catalysts of discontent. The present day mentality of openness was nurtured by the literary works of high artistic and moral standards. These works facilitated, to a great extent, the introduction of new vistas of social and political thought.

In this process, several literary journals became testing grounds for fresh ideas and played a pioneering role in supporting the new literary voices during the gradual process of democratization. On the pages of *Novyi Mir, Literaturnaia gazeta, Neva, Iunost'*, and others, some of the major novels and review articles appeared which signaled the rise of social and moral aspirations of the new historical self-analyses.

The publication of the novel *Ne hlebom edinym (Not by Bread alone)* by Vladimir Dudintsev in 1956 was among these new voices of the period

---

1. Mikhail Nenashev, *Books promote an Understanding of the Restructuring Process*, Moscow, Novosti, 1987, p. 20.

that became known as the "thaw." Obviously, the editorial board of *Novyi Mir* agreed to publish Dudintsev's novel since it possessed literary qualities and seriousness of purpose. It was a moving account of the sometime difficult predicaments of ordinary people, in many walks of life, and their tenacious efforts to fight the constriction of bureaucracy.

The first installments of Dudintsev's novel appeared in the autumn of 1956 on the pages of *Novyi mir*. The novel became the subject of controversy and it was discussed at several public meetings. Well known writers praised its honest realism, its humanity and respect for ordinary people. However, toward the end of the year the Soviet Press started printing predominantly unfavorable criticism of Dudintsev's book. Certain literary critics and writers alike declared it a pernicious and malicious distortion of the Soviet reality "trying to blacken and pull to pieces all that the Soviet people has created." Such criticism surprised the author who even considered writing a new version of the novel following the request for its publication in the West.[2]

The writer and literary critic Aleksandr Tvardovskii became a member of the editorial board of the journal of the Union of Writers USSR, *Novyi mir*, in 1950. Tvardovskii was known by many Soviet readers as the author of the poem *Vassily Terkin* . The hero of the poem was a simple soldier who fought in the many battles of World War II. In time, Terkin became a popular hero and Tvardovskii's fame as a poet was established. However, the political turmoil of the middle 1950s brought new restrictive measures and Tvardovskii was dismissed from the editorial board of *Novyi mir* in 1954. He was charged with the publication of "harmful critical articles by Abramov, Shcheglov, and Lifshits."[3]

Following the Second Congress of Soviet Writers in December of 1954, a gradual improvement of the cultural policies brought new concessions to literary life. Tvardovskii was elected to the Executive Board of the Writers' Union, together with Panova and Grossman, who also had been previously reprimanded for their liberal attitudes. In 1958 Tvardovskii became the chief editor of the journal *Novyi mir* . He continued serving in this capacity for the next twelve years. Following the introduction of

---

2. *Not by Bread Alone,* translated by Edith Bone, New York, Dutton, 1957. Preface by the author, p. 9.

3. Marc Slonim, *Soviet Russian Literature,* London, Oxford University Press, 1973, p. 296.

restrictive measures levied against literary explorations after 1964, Tvardovskii managed to preserve the progressive, democratic character of the journal. However, Tvardovskii paid the price for propagating literary liberalism and at the Twenty-third Party Congress his name was dropped from the list of candidates to the Central Committee. *Novyi mir* continued to appear unscathed by the changes until Tvardovskii was relieved from his editorial duties in February of 1970.[4]

Tvardovskii understood the role of literary journals, in the tradition of Belinskii's interpretation, as the media that fosters an engaged and passionate exchange of ideas. As the chief editor of *Novyi mir*, Tvardovskii supported the new voices of Soviet literature and encouraged a lively discussion between the writers and the reading public. The featured articles in *Novyi mir* often discussed contemporary literature. Almost every new literary work of importance written in the 1960s had been serialized in *Novyi Mir*. At times, the discussion turned to the revaluation of the Russian literary heritage that frequently became the cause of heated polemics on the pages of this journal.[5]

Tvardovskii strongly supported the publication of Bulgakov's literary heritage. In the mid 1950s some of the Bulgakov's theatrical plays were reprinted. Bulgakov's unfinished masterpiece, *Master i Margerita (The Master and Marguerite)* was published in 1967. The play delighted and enthralled Soviet readers with its lively and fantastic satire, and eventually became an intrinsic part of the literary scene.[6] Most of all, Tvardovskii encouraged fellow writers and critics to write freely about their assessments of current events and literary achievements. He believed that the improvement in social conditions and in freedom of thought, emergent during the late 1950s and early 1960s, was not sufficiently used by fellow writers and critics alike.

In his address at the Twenty-first Congress of the Communist Party USSR on January 27, 1959, Tvardovskii argued that the Soviet literary production was characterized by a prevailing inertia. Soviet writers seemed reticent about innovations and greater objectivity, as if avoiding possible adverse repercussions. The language of contemporary novels was

---

4. S. Chuprinin, "Pozitsiia, Literaturnaia kritika v zhurnale 'Novyi mir' vremen A. T. Tvardovskogo 1958–1970 gg.", *Voprosy literatury,* No. 4, 1988, Moscow, p. 6.

5. Chuprinin, "Pozitsiia . . .," p. 3–5.

6. Slonim, *Soviet Russian Literature,* p. 301 and p. 346.

drab, the composition exhibited an unimaginative structure, and the literary characters lacked life. It appeared as if the writers did not have anywhere to turn for help. Clearly, the editors of various journals did not discuss the new works with the writers or offer constructive criticism. Tvardovskii stressed that literary criticism comprised an essential part of Soviet literature. The role of criticism was important and the critics should strive to implement solid criteria in evaluation of contemporary literary works.[7]

Most of all, Tvardovskii felt that the writers were not fully using the existing favorable cultural and political climate to comment on the long awaited changes, or to discuss the past historical events. He reminded his colleagues about the splendid literary works left by the great Russian writers. As an example he discussed Tolstoi's assessment of the Napoleonic war and the Russian victory of 1812. Tolstoi's rendering of these historical events were entwined with the lives of Russian people, their individual fate and patriotic calling. His visions of peoples' willingness to serve the higher goals of liberation and of the grandeur of their accomplishments left a profound influence on the creation of national consciousness. Tolstoi's impressive images of peoples' brave and honorable efforts - the true patriotic spirit that moved them - could never be recaptured in textbooks filled with dry historical data.[8]

Tvardovskii, in his capacities as the editor and as the literary critic of *Novyi mir,* provided an example of perseverance and quiet dignity. He introduced fair and unfaltering editorial policies that gave an unifying trait to the body of published works. The so called "novomirskaia proza," selected and published during his editorial tenure in *Novyi mir,* implemented high professional and artistic standards. However, his editorial policies never became a unified voice that would attempt to level the writers' personalities and erase their individual characteristics. The editor, and his associates, did not enforce a monolithic, and unified concept of literary criticism, or encourage a blind following of literary advice dispensed from the editors. Tvardovskii and his board favored a pluralistic approach and this spirit was reflected in the polemics that evolved at first between the journals *Novyi mir* and *Oktiabr.* Later a

---

7. A. Tvardovskii, *Stat'i i zametki o literature,* Moscow, Sovetskii pisatel', 1963, p. 203.

8. Tvardovskii, *Stat'i . . .,* p. 195.

similar exchange of ideas occurred between *Novyi mir* and *Molodaia gvardiia*, as well as between *Novyi mir* and some other journals. The general atmosphere of the early 1960s resembled to another "thaw." *Novyi Mir* published, in a serialized form, the widely read memoirs by Erenburg, *Years, People, Life*. Erenburg wrote with admiration about Picasso, Braque and Matisse, the artists declared as "modernists" and therefore not acknowledged by Soviet authorities in the field of cultural policies. Erenburg also wrote about Pasternak and Tsvetaeva, Mandel'shtam and Babel, reappraising the unfavorable literary criticism of their individual poetic credos that placed these writers in isolation. The publication of the novel *One Day in the Life of Ivan Denisovich* by Aleksandr Solzhenitsyn was another memorable achievement of the editorial board of *Novyi mir* headed by Tvardovskii. The novel had a great political and literary impact due to its subject matter. For the first time in Soviet literature the truth was told about concentration camps filled with imprisoned Soviet citizens. The publication of Solzhenitsyn novel had to be authorized by Khrushchev after an astute intervention of Tvardovskii. At that time, Solzhenitsyn was virtually unknown, yet the publication of his work aroused new hopes among liberals. During 1964 and 1965 many new recollections and factual reports of Stalin's terror were told.[9]

Tvardovskii continued the dedicated editorial work and published a total of 138 issues of the journal during his tenure. This splendid record presented an impressive accomplishment. With the passage of time, Tvardovskii's achievement as the chief editor of *Novyi mir* gained increased respect and acknowledgment. After the period of regressive cultural policies in the mid 1960s and 1970s, the policy of openness brought a revaluation of Tvardovskii's contribution. Recently, several well written articles have elucidated Tvardovskii's participation in the shaping of the Soviet literary thought during the prime of his life.

The critic Iu. Burtin, who served as a member of Tvardovskii's editorial board, wrote an interesting article titled, "I nam uroki muzhestva dany" ("And we received lessons in courage").[10] Burtin portrayed Tvardovskii's role in the cultural life during a difficult time of Soviet history. In addition, the critic S. Chuprinin discussed the impact of *Novyi*

9. Slonim, *Soviet Russian Literature*, pp. 332–336.

10. *Oktiabrr'*, 1987, No. 8, p. 197.

mir on the Soviet literary thought in a well documented review article published in *Voprosy literatury*.[11] Evgenii Sidorov devoted much attention to Tvardovskii by tracing his influence on the Soviet literary life, and on his contribution to the changes ushered into Soviet society after the spring of 1985.[12]

Tvardovskii was a distinguished example of courage during a repressive period that did not officially sanction the criticism of the established ways, repeatedly thwarting the growing discontent. In spite of the limitations imposed on him and on the literary thought, Tvardovskii did not tolerate suppression of truth. His unwavering stand has brought him, in retrospect, highest marks. The pages of *Novyi mir* safeguarded a wealth of information that reflected the interaction of the journal with various institutions, censors, Union of writers, and readers alike.[13]

Tvardovskii endeavored to evaluate a newly submitted work in accordance with its literary value. He judged, most of all, the ability of the writer to portray reality truthfully, as well as the validity of the artistic concepts and stylistic mastery. The works that did not possess true literary qualities, Tvardovskii described as 'nominal.' The 'nominal' category referred to the usually ephemeral content of the work, or the superficial necessity or urgency of the topic. The 'nominal' value often aimed to impress with the title of the book or its chapters due to name recognition or topicality of the subject matter. These qualities were declared as 'nominal' in the final assessment of a literary work.[14]

The editorial board, headed by Tvardovskii, recognized justly the potential greatness of the new literary voices, unknown at the time. When the stories of V. Astaf'ev were published in a little known Siberian journal, his contribution was recognized as "one of the powerful and remarkable works of contemporary Soviet prose." The literary debuts of many young writers were greeted on the pages of *Novyi mir*. Among these, then unknown writers, were V. Bogomolov, V. Fomenko, F. Abramov, Iu.

---

11. Chuprinin, "Pozitsiia . . .," pp. 3–47.

12. Evgenii Sidorov, "The Wind of Change," *Soviet Literature*, 1988, No. 1, pp. 112–116.

13. Chuprinin, "Pozitsiia . . .," p. 4–6.

14. *Novyi mir*, 1965, No. 1, p. 18; quoted after Chuprinin.

Kazakov, Iu. Davidov, Ch. Aitmatov, K. Vorob'ev, V. Konetskii, V. Belov, and V. Rasputin, among others.[15]

Novyi mir occasionally published books that did not present true literary value. The books *Brat'ia Ershovy (The Brothers Ershov),* and *Sekretar' obkoma* (The Secretary of the Obkom), by B. Kochetov; *Rodnik u berezy (The Spring at the Birch),* by N. Shundik; *Belyi svet (The Wide World)* by S. Babaevskii; proved to be works of 'nominal' value, according to the Tvardovskii's classification. Yet, the editorial board agreed on the publication of these works in order to point to a literary trend that still existed and catered to the personality cult. These novels served well to illustrate the displaced, humiliating servility that obstructed truthful presentation of historical facts. Therefore, such books were quickly recognized by the majority of reading public as a dated and false tribute to dictatorship. The denigrating content of these books, dubbed deftly and scornfully on the pages of the journal as 'obsequious content' ('reptil'no soderzhanie'), posed more harm to the memory of the 'people's father' and 'choryphaeus of all sciences,' than the outright criticism and harsh words of more subtle works.[16]

The journal repeatedly addressed the historical period ruled by Stalin's iron fist and his heirs. The pitiful heritage of this period was reflected in the established hierarchy of values and social attitudes. These residues lingered in the ideological and artistic concepts of literary works, propagating the restrained and mistrustful relations among the people and people's attitudes towards various governmental bodies.[17]

The editors understood well that it was easier to change the people's comprehension of Stalin's role, and his repressive policies, than to change the established world outlook, the philosophy of life and the social conduct of Soviet citizens. These demoted stereotypes were accepted not only by veterans of Stalinist policies, but equally by a massive number of the Soviet population. The journal aimed to help the process of demystification not only of literary works with backward point of view, but equally of the attitudes that produced such denigrating concepts. All these efforts were conducted in order to hasten the process of intellectual liberation of the Soviet people.

---

15. Chuprinin, "Pozitsiia . . .", p. 9–10.

16. Chuprinin, "Pozitsiia . . .", p. 13–14.

17. Chuprinin, "Pozitsiia . . .", p. 15.

These were the reasons that led to the writing and publication of the
literary reviews based often on the dychotomy of the old and the new,
contrasting the prejudices of Stalinism with the importance of honesty and
trust. Such an example was presented in the review of Mikhail Bulgakov's
Zhizn' gospodina de Mol'era, (The life of Mister de Moliere) written by
V. Lakshin and published in *Novyi mir* in 1963. In his review, Lakshin
chose to center his evaluation around the role of the artist and a despotic
government. Lakshin also reviewed Bulgakov's play *Master i Margarita
(The Master and Marguerite)* in 1968, and used this opportunity to discuss
the motive of social anguish and ways of overcoming these debilitating
feelings.[18]

The literary reviews, essays and literary criticisms published in *Novyi
mir* during Tvardovskii's time often showed the interdependence of
aesthetics, ethics and politics. Although some reviews and literary
criticisms discussed only the artistic merits of literary works, the majority
of reviews were written in an educational vein. Guided by the desire to
serve the people, the literary evaluations in *Novyi mir* acquired moralistic,
tendentious, and gnoseological overtones. That is why some critics, such
as S. Chuprinin, compared the engaged spirit of literary criticism as
practiced in *Novyi mir*, with the period following the Twentieth Congress
of the Communist Party of USSR in February 1956, marking the new
social and political era. Chuprinin drew another parallel by comparing the
positive changes in the Soviet society in the course of the 1960s with the
period of Chernishevskii and Dobroliubov who tried to abolish the
ideological residues of serfdom. [19]

Most of all, Chuprinin thought that it should be remembered that
Tvardovskii's courageous and unfaltering stand helped the formulation of
the concept of "moral realism" *(nravstvennego realizma)* and "stoic ethos"
(stoicheskogo etosa) that served as a model for many compatriots during
the 1970s and 1980s.[20]

The subsequent editors and collaborators of the journal *Novyi mir* did
not forget the lessons of bravery taught by Tvardovskii. The engaged
dialogue, that Tvardovskii was trying to cultivate, was revived again with
the beginning of the changes introduced after 1985. In this process *Novyi*

---

18. Chuprinin, "Pozitsiia . . .," p. 17.
19. Chuprinin, "Pozitsiia . . .," p. 18.
20. Chuprinin, "Pozitsiia . . .," p. 47.

mir served as a veritable flagman of the new openness and restructuring efforts. The role of *Novyi mir* in the ongoing restructuring process was discussed by F. F. Kuznetsov, director of the the Institute for World Literature of the Academy of Science USSR. Kuznetsov presented his views at the joint conference of historians and writers that took place in April of 1988. Kuznetsov pointed that the popularity of the journal has grown immensely and the numbers of readers have multiplied; *Novyi mir* is presently publishing more than one million copies per issue. Even other journals had large printings and were approaching the record set by *Novyi mir*.[21]

It behooves one to remember that the famous Russian journals *Sovremennik* and *Russkoe slovo*, the most respected and influential publications of their time, were published in three to five thousand copies. Presently, the journal *Novyi mir* reaches many more readers. The journal truthfully depicts the revolutionary changes of the renewal of the Soviet cultural life, thus influencing and supporting expectations of further development. According to Kuznetsov, Soviet literature has attained an unprecedented prestigious place and now plays such an outstanding role in the intellectual and social life that, in all probability, was never the case before.[22]

Most importantly, Tvardovskii left his mark as a fine poet and as such he was recognized as the creator of the beloved Vassily Terkin, a brave young private, typifying the young, common man fighting the Germans in World War II. Tvardovskii wrote a sequel to this war-time poem, following the hero in his adventures after death. The poem presents an anti-Stalinist satire describing the established hierarchy of the other world as ruled by bureaucratic absurdities, secret police, and stupid censorship. Copies of *Terkin in the Other World* were circulated in Moscow for two years, and one of its versions was reproduced by the journal *The Bridges* which was published in Munich. Finally, the decision was made to print it in *Novyi mir*. Later the poem was staged in one of the Moscow theaters and performed in front of capacity audiences for two years.[23]

---

21. "Istoriki i pisateli o literature i istorii", *Voprosy istorii*, 1988, No. 6, p. 27.

22. Ibid.

23. Slonim, *Soviet Russian Literature*, p. 338.

However, it was Tvardovskii's last major poem *Po pravu pamiati (By the right of memory)* that he wrote shortly before his death which brought him the accolades of his fellow writers. The poem, written in the late 1960s, was shelved for a long time and was simultaneously published in two journals *Novyi mir* and *Znamia* in 1987. The fact that the poem was published testified to the favorable changes in the social climate: it seemed as if the times have finally caught up with Tvardovskii's outspoken and bold stand.[24]

The publication of the poem propelled Tvardovskii's name alongside the greatest Russian and Soviet writers, and brought him the unequivocal admiration of the Soviet literary community. Tvardovskii was praised and included, by several literary historians, in the same poetic category along with Pushkin, presenting a part of the "golden fund" of Russian poetic thought.[25]

Tvardovskii's confessional poem was written in the form of a monologue displaying epic breadth. Highly autobiographical, the poem *By the right of memory* recounted Tvardovskii's own life and tragic fate of his father who was branded as a "kulak" (wealthy peasant) in the 1920s. The young Tvardovsky, together with his parents, faced eventually forced deportation to the northern Urals. The loss of dignity was harder to bear than the hardship of the expulsion and collectivization of his parents earthly possessions. Worst of all, the stigma of a compromised father followed his sons. Tvardovskii wrote about the humiliation of the branded new-born sons that the new Soviet government continued to prosecute as social outcasts:

> Fate treated all as equals
> Under the same law:
> The son of a kulak and the son of a commissar,
> The son of a commander or a priest ...
> Babies were branded as foes from birth,
> But the country never seemed
> To have enough branded sons.[26]

---

24. Slonim, Ibid.

25. Mikhail Nenashev, *Books promote understanding* . . ., p. 4.

26. Quoted after Sidorov, "The Wind of Change," p. 115.

The poetic language of this poem is straightforward and unadorned, permeated with deep compassion. The poem is written in a clear and sober vein, as if to settle accounts that have not been cleared before. Tvardovskii wrote with the feeling of the responsibility of preserving the truth, that haunted his memory. Obviously, Tvardovskii was aware that his personal recollections had a historical and universal importance: he witnessed the fate of his generation and his own experience personified the fate of many. The almost forgotten shameful history was relived many times over by countless others who did not have a chance to speak out. He was speaking for all of them, in order that the truth, although belated, be known and not forgotten.

Tvardovskii could not accept the admonishment of some concerned public figures who advised, in the aftermath of Stalin's death, to forget what is now the past: "They tacitly bid us to forget, forget . . . ." Many thought that the past memories of suffering should not be retold in order to prevent the distress of the uninitiated. In addition, such testimonies could provide the ammunition for the ideological adversaries. Therefore, the unhappy past and the sad memories should be buried. Tvardovskii thought that the conscious concealment of historical facts perpetuated potential harm. To pretend that the dictatorship never happened, posed real danger because people would fail to learn from the lessons of the past. Tvardovskii firmly believed that, "Only untruth is damaging, only truth is profitable".[27]

By right of memory presented the final chapter of Tvardovskii's epic saga of his country. His previous works *The Muravia Country, A House by the Roadside, Vasili Terkin, Terkin in the Other World* and *Horizon Beyond Horizon,* depicted the sweep of the revolutionary events and people's valor during the World War II. In his last work, *By the right of Memory,* he aimed to describe the once hushed pages of Soviet history — those associated with the reprisals during the Stalin's dictatorship. Tvardovskii felt the responsibility to tell the truth about the events that were, until recently, left out of the official Soviet historical assessments of this period. He could not tolerate amnesia and the policy of covert or overt attempts to gloss over history.

Tvardovskii believed that the consequences of the difficult past could only be overcome in an atmosphere of openness, of restored democratic

---

27. Sidorov, Ibid, p. 115.

principles in government and social life.   Conscious concealment of the historical truth presented the worst type of social pessimism and Tvardovskii knew the value of genuine optimism.

According to the poet, the important thing was not what Lenin would have said if he could see the Soviet people today, but how the people passed the judgement on themselves, to the best of their intellectual and spiritual ability.   However, it should be remembered that todays children will eventually judge their parents.   Therefore, the making of history in the Soviet state should be, ideally, a matter for the whole people.   Every conscious citizen should be responsible for everything that takes place in his or her country.   Tvardovskii explained that this was what Lenin bequeathed, and in this sense "the son answers for his father", and the father for his son.[28]

Many younger and older writers alike have understood well Tvardovskii's literary and moral bequest.   Tvardovskii, at the end of his life, was thinking of the many who have suffered silently during their lifetime; he also thought of the coming generations.   Tvardovskii's last poem, *By the Right of Memory*, recounted the shameful events in order to guard the future generations from similar hardships.   Most of all, the poem preserved the brave voice whose calling inspired others to pursue this poet's unfinished mission.

---

28. Sidorov, "The Wind of Change", p. 116.

CHAPTER III

SOVIET LITERATURE IN THE 1960S AND 1970S: A PROLOGUE TO *GLASNOST'*

The literary historian Aleksandr Ovcharenko compared the impassioned search of the writers for truthful portrayal of reality and their probing into the depth of social issues, during the last twenty years, to the brave exploration of the space. The writers launched a number of magnificent works and their efforts could be compared to the launching of sputniks: The literary works of Rasputin, Belii, Trifonov and others, served well such an exploratory mission. These works attracted great attention and prepared gradually the emergence of the ideology of democratic openness and restructuring in USSR.[1]

In retrospect, the literary historians and critics agreed that the gradual renewal of Soviet literature started in the course of the 1950s. The Second Writers' Congress in 1954 provided a much needed forum for the deliberations about the state of Soviet literature and the path of the future development. The participants took the initiative for evaluating many complex notions about the present and the past social realities. The Second Writers' Congress remained to be remembered as the turning point in the process of the renewal of Soviet literature. The ensuing unfoldment was marked by a keen awareness of the changed literary policies and was dubbed as "the contemporary phase" of Soviet literary thought.[2]

The importance of individual contributions and achievements became an issue of foremost concern. The human problems came into the foreground and established its priority over all other questions. The literary works showed a growing awareness of the supreme significance of the individual contribution to the society. The writer Daniil Granin in his novel: *Idu na grozu (Into the Storm)*, expounded the importance of the man as the

---

1. A. I. Ovcharenko, "Istoriki i pisateli o literature i istorii,"*Voprosy istorii,* Akademiia Nauk SSSR, 1988/6, p. 105.

2. *Sovremennaia russkaia sovetskaia literatura,* "Vvedenie," Eds. A. G. Bocharov et al., Moscow, Prosveshchenie, Vol. I, 1987, pp. 5–6.

highest value in any society. Everything should exist for the man and he should be not understood as a means but as an end in himself. Granin's heroes in the novel argued, against worn out slogans about higher societal goals. Soviet citizens were asked to work for the future, and to be prepared to make sacrifices if they were called on to do so. Many demands were made for the sake of progress and the pursuit of personal fulfillments was labeled as a self serving capacity of "individualism." Granin spoke about the uniqueness of human endeavors and life's fleeting quality since no one will be able to live on this earth again. Human life is precious and can not be reversed:

"... What do you think a man is — an end or a means? ... But can't you see that man is an end in himself? Man is the highest good, everything exists for him. Neither you nor I will ever live on this earth again. We only exist once... When a man lives in the present he does more for the future because he's more human."

These words sounded the new awareness of the value of human life opposing the dismal cliches about the necessity of perpetual sacrifices for the sake of a better future.[3]

Interestingly enough, similar thoughts about the value of human life and its ephemeral nature were reflected in Gorbachev's speech delivered some twenty years later at the meeting at the Central Committee of the Soviet Communist Party with the heads of the mass media, ideological institutions and artistic unions. The meeting took place on the 8th of January, 1988. Gorbachev, like many concerned intellectuals, was well read and informed about the questions and dilemmas discussed in literary works. He stressed the necessity of safeguarding the integrity of the men and women in the Soviet society :

"Recall our history — how ready our people were to make self sacrifices. This must not be forgotten. But this must not be abused either .... We live on this earth but once. The attitude to man, to his life and to all his work must be the most respectful and honest, especially as regards those who bore on their shoulders the brunt of struggle at the sharp turns of our history. We must not allow an individual, or

---

3. Daniil Granin, *Into the Storm*, (*Idu na grozu*), Moscow, Progress Publisher, 1965, p. 304.

an entire generation for that matter, be treated with injustice and disrespect. That would be a crime."[4]

Very likely, that Gorbachev's respect for human dignity was fostered by a similar insight of the writers acknowledging the essential role of many unknown individuals sustaining the power of the Soviet society. Their selfless efforts and sacrifices were taken for granted. The interest of the writers for the men and women in many walks of life became increasingly apparent in the course of the 1960s and 1970s. The new literary characters were not treated as cogwheels in a well adjusted social mechanism, but rather as purposeful members of the society. The writers asserted the wisdom of the common people and the dignity of the working men. These new literary personages were often described as "little men" or "common men"[5] The writers Chingiz Aitmatov, Grigorii Baklanov, Aleksei Arbuzov, Viktor Astaf'ev, Vasil Bykov, Aleksandr Iashin, Nikolai Voronov, Boris Mozhiaev, Vitalii Semin, Viktor Rozov, among others, praised the accomplishments of these people treated unjustly with misunderstanding and neglect.

Chingiz Aitmatov pointed out that it would be more just to describe these worthy characters simply as men that have finally attained due recognition. These people have discovered their own worth. They also attained their own perception of reality while contemplating "the secret beauty of the world" in which they have been living for millennia.[6] Aitmatov himself wrote about the necessity of appreciating the lives and deeds of common people. In his story "Pervyi uchitel" ("The First Teacher"), written in the early 1960s, the one time pupil at a country school in Kirgiziia remembered her first teacher, whose efforts in the once backward village were not recognized, and posed the question: "When did we loose the capability to honor the simple man, in the manner Lenin used to honor him?"[7]

---

4. Gorbachev, Mikhail, Democratization — the Essence of Perestroika, the Essence of Socialism, Moscow, Novosti, 1988, pp. 25–26.

5. I. Dedkov, "Literature and the New Way of Thinking". Dedkov's article was first published in 1987 in Kommunist and subsequently reprinted in *Soviet Literature*, No. 5, 1988, p. 154.

6. Ch. Aitmatov, "Time to speak out," *Soviet Literature,* No. 5, 1984, p. 143.

7. Ch. Aitmatov, "Pervyi uchitel'," Moscow, Detskaia literatura, 1988, p. 91.

Many Soviet writers turned their attention to these individuals since they felt that their valuable, yet unpretentious contribution to the society was not duly appreciated. In addition, the literary works projected a polemical attitude towards the idealization of societal life and personages, pointing to the contradictions and difficulties of contemporary existence. During the mid 1960s, the writer Vitalii Semin tried to clarify the preoccupation of the writers with subjects that were declared by critics as "trivial life stories". Answering the *Novyi Mir* questionnaire on Gor'kii, marking the 60th anniversary of the October Revolution, Semin stressed that writers have always shared a concern about human predicaments. He spoke about Maksim Gor'kii and his ability to reveal great meanings in the most trivial life stories. To his mind, the most striking thing about Gor'kii's work was the unfailing interest possessed by ordinary people. Sometimes, the things 'uninteresting' swelled to such an extent that what remained to be presented as 'interesting' was not credible. As a result, a strange assurance emerged that uninteresting things were already surpassed.[8]

In his story "Seven people in our house", Vitalii Semin depicted a working-class suburb, the characters, the daily work, talk and memories of its inhabitants. The story was published in 1965 in the literary journal *Novyi Mir*, whose editor Aleksandr Tvardovskii understood well Semin's viewpoints. The story received, by large, denigrating reviews. Apparently, the critics thought that the inhabitants of this bleak suburb were insignificant and 'trivial'. The younger personages were portrayed as rough, miserable and even cruel. The critics never thought that the lives of these young people and women might have been different if they grew up in peaceful times and if their fathers and husbands come back from war. The central character was a courageous woman, Mulia, a factory worker, possessed by her love of work. Determined to hold out, Mulia was aware that the work was tough and weakening her health: "It's killing me, this work, but I can't do without it." This realistic portrayal of people's attitudes was opposed to the idealization of many heroes and heroins in the novels that followed the stereotyped formulas of socialist realism. The so called 'production novels,' depicted the work in factories as an ennobling act, building the body and strengthening the soul. In reality, many middle-aged women and men who lived through the war,

---

8. Dedkov, "Literature . . .," p. 151.

their health weakened by war-time sufferings, continued to discharge bravely their duties. Like Mulia, they wanted to work and continue a productive life, but all the same knew the true cost of their hard labor. The critic Igor Dedkov was attracted to the literary work of Vitalii Semin. Dedkov wrote, in retrospect, about the process of changes manifested in the Soviet literary thought following this development from its start in the 1960s. He pointed out that the literary works, introducing a fresh point of view, were not easily accepted at first. This was the case with the story "Seven people in our house" by Vitalii Semin. The story, Dedkov thought, presented one of the best pieces of Soviet literature of that time. Yet, Semin was described by the critics as a 'pseudo-realist' and his story received harsh reviews. The story was declared as petty, trivial and dull. The literary critics, at that time, upheld precepts which were based on a strange preference given to 'elevated' characters over 'common' ones. Dedkov stressed that he did not want to reproach anybody for mistakes made decades ago, or describe the consequences of some similar critical reviews. He wanted to acknowledge that many were taken aback by the critic's strange, haughty non acceptance of the realities of life.[9]

Similarly, in Victor Rozov's play *The Traditional Meeting,* Lida — a secondary character — is a quiet woman who works as bank clerk in the polar region. It seemed as if the critics were alarmed that the playwright failed "to give due attention to the real hero of Soviet society, who is not only capable of performing heroic deeds, but constantly performs them." In comparison, Lida's "trivial mission in life", did not seem significant. Surely, the critics' thoughts soared over the expanses of human life; an ordinary human face could not be appreciated justly from such a height. The criticism sometimes sounded very accusing as if attempting to silence the simple, yet truthful voices.[10]

In addition to Vitalii Semin and Victor Rozov, many writers shared similar concepts about the man, his role in the making of history, his mission in life, his place in society. The agreement of their viewpoints and their approaches were noticeable in the choice of subject matter and the implied social criticism. Dedkov quoted among these writers the names of Fedor Abramov, Aleksandr Volodin, Grigorii Baklanov, Aleksei Arbuzov,

---

9. Dedkov, "Literature . . .," p. 150.
10. Dedkov, "Literature . . .," p. 151.

Vasil Bykov, Aleksandr Iashin, Nikolai Voronov, Boris Mozhiaev, among others.

The scope of "things uninteresting" was growing. New works emerged portraying life stories of ordinary people and the harsh circumstances they had to overcome. However, the critics tried to explain to the authors that reality itself and the artistic reality had two aspects: the superficial "appearance" and the hidden substance. Things may look ugly at first sight, but inside there was a perfect harmony: everything was balanced and taken care of. Appropriate measures have been introduced to eliminate callous attitudes, while tyranny never really existed. Dedkov concluded that these critics, acting in the name of socialism, democracy, and culture, hampered society's true progress toward those same goals. Nevertheless, the writers understood that the well-being of men and women, the rank and file of the society at large, were of central importance. The neglect of the due respect and attention to these worthy individuals upholding the intricate web of life was examined repeatedly in many literary works:

> "It must be said that the new way of thinking had its beginning in the works of those who sought to follow the complex and contradictory realities of life, history and people's destinies. "Some may wonder whether I do not diminish the role of science and philosophy by over-rating the influence and potential of art. But it was exactly literature that, in the 60s and 70s, placed in the center of the world 'man of no consequence', the 'little man' or in other words, man of the people." [11]

The best novels and stories emphasized man's individual and subsequently his historical destiny trying to provide answers to some basic questions. Yet, the answers were far from being rosy, since they were concrete by their very nature. Dedkov reiterated the well known postulate of socialist realism by asserting that the cornerstone of genuine art is the objective reflection of reality. The new way of thinking was based on a realistic approach but cleared from the mist of demagogy. Realism in literature relied upon knowledge, accurate historical memory and a new sensitivity. Blank spots in history needed to be scrutinized, in order not to repeat same mistakes again. This new thinking emerged in opposition to the factors that hampered the development and produced stagnation. Such

---

11. Dedkov, "Literature . . .," p. 153.

were the stifling of initiative, the obstruction of talents and the parting of those who died in sorrow and bitterness.

Dedkov was concerned with the concealments of injustice during Stalin's time. Therefore, he understood well the question posed by the writer Iurii Trifonov: "Do we need to remember?" Trifonov formulated this question in his novel *Vremia i mesto (Time and Place)*, published in 1981. Trifonov pondered the necessity of reviewing an epoch of the not so distant past. The wrongs cannot be undone and the children whose fathers perished have themselves become elderly people. As the bitterness of years passed, it seemed to him that all the sufferings must be remembered, since facts should not be suppressed. Otherwise, it would mean that the Soviet literary thought lacked the courage and conscience by pretending that things which occurred "never really happened."

Dedkov concluded that Trifonov's question: "Do we need to remember?" — was already answered. A number of recently published works aimed to complete the blanks of the historical past. Sometimes these works laid too great an emphasis on revealing previously unknown historical facts in the wish to safeguard a truthful account of the past. Literary accounts of historical events were always more impressive than the dry historical chronicles. Literature portrayed history through the lives of individual people, uniting objective and subjective accounts of events, displaying knowledge and imagination.[12]

The new way of thinking promoted a new sensitivity and emotional depth that was reflected, at its best, in the books such as *The Executioner's Block* by Aitmatov, *Tashkent* by Matevosyan, *The Commission* by Zalygin, *The Cathedral* by Gonchar. These books were united by a common aspiration in picturing people's destinies, successes and failures, happiness and unhappiness against the background of historical events. Dedkov agreed with Vitalii Semin that there will be always a certain resistance which any writer must overcome if he is to deserve that name. It would be hard to think that a time will come when no courage, dedication or risk-taking will be required of writers. Only cheap success could be possible without serious involvement, but that is not the road of true literature.[13]

12. Dedkov, "Literature . . .," p. 156.
13. Dedkov, "Literature . . .," pp. 155–6.

The Revaluation of the Literary Heritage

The changed and more truthful assessment of the early development of Soviet culture helped to change the comprehension of the Russian and Soviet literary heritage, and equally of the foreign literature. The names of many prominent writers have been returned to the Soviet literary fund from the unjustified estrangement, and their previously censored literary works were restored to their rightful place. These changes emerged slowly in the course of the last thirty years, starting from the mid 1950s. The process of the liquidation of these unjust eradication continued steadily although the progress was slow, and marred with contradictions. At first, it brought the rehabilitation of the eminent personalities, pioneers of the socialistic culture such as I. E. Babel', V. E. Maierkhold, academician N. I. Vavilov and others. Thereafter followed the revaluation of the legacy of writers and artists labeled as "fellow-travellers" *(poputchitki)*, among whose were M. A. Bulgakov, M. I. Tsvetaeva, and Andrei Belyi. The third group of rehabilitated personalities encompassed major writers such as I. A. Bunin, who did not understand the revolution and preferred to live in emigration.

The publications of works of foreign writers was resumed, including those not published before, like Hemingway, who nevertheless enjoyed great popularity. Thus, his novel *For whom the Bell Tolls* was eventually translated into Russian and published. All of these brought the present day revaluation of important works, that although written in a different epoch, became an intrinsic part of the contemporary culture. Such position was reserved formerly only for the contributions of writers considered to be the literary classics. The spirit of openness pointed not only to the introduction of changes in the present cultural and literary life, but was extended to the revaluation of the past.

In addition, many unjust decisions were reversed. In February of 1987, Boris Pasternak was reinstated posthumously as a member of the Union of Soviet Writers. Pasternak was excluded from his former membership to the Union in 1958. The publication of his monumental novel *Doctor Zhivago* was finally permitted. During 1986-1987 the literary works of N. Gumilev, V. Nabokov, and V. Khodasevich were published as well as the two volumes of the works of the theatrical director and critic Mikhail Chekhov.[14] Many literary critics, writers and reading public alike thought that the time has come to reinstate the poet Velimir Khlebnikov to his permanent place in the Russian literature. It behooves to remember that Khlebnikov admonished his fellow poets, members of the futuristic movement, that it was necessary to reconsider the true priorities, since it is always important to know one's identity. Khlebnikov exclaimed, "My ustali byt' ne nami", ("We are tired of not being ourselves") which may very well serve as the motto for writers of any period seeking their identification.[15]

It was Maiakovskii's lighthearted pronouncement about Khlebnikov that stubbornly continued to conceal the true character of Khlebnikov's contribution. Maiakovskii declared Khlebnikov as "the poet's poet" stressing, as it were, Khlebnikov's elitist attitude. The misunderstanding of Khlebnikov's position caused the prolonged silence that overshadowed his poetry. The publication of Khlebnikov's *Tvoreniia* finally changed this wrongful situation. The favorable reception of this volume proved that Khlebnikov was not appreciated only by the initiated few. The lively reaction of the public and critics alike showed convincingly that his work attracted a huge following.[16]

The reading public was reminded of some overlooked yet valuable clarifications formulated by Khlebnikov concerning the literary heritage. Khlebnikov, as a Russian poet, found the roots of his spiritual heritage in the Russian poetic tradition and, equally, in the poetic treasury of distant Asian republics. He pointed to the existing affinity of the Russian culture to the poetic tradition of the Asian nations and helped to establish the "Asiatic" layer of Russian culture. Khlebnikov protested against the exclusive Western orientation of the Russian avant-garde at the beginning of the century, in order that the Russian poets do not became "the imitators of Western voices". His criticism of the irrational urge of Euro-Centrism ushered in the important notion of equality of Western and Eastern

---

14. Iu. S. Borisov, "O nekotorykh tendentsiiakh v razvitii sovremennoi kul'tury," *Sovetskaia kul'tura, 70 let razvitiia,* Moscow, Nauka,1987, p. 181.

15. Aleksandr Baigushev, "Opyt sozidaniia," *Molodaia gvardiia,* No. 12, 1988, pp. 234–235.

16. Baigushev, "Opyt . . .," p. 234.

cultural traditions that became eventually the common aspiration of the multinational Soviet state.[17]

The acknowledgement of the great importance of the work of B. Eikhenbaum, in the field of literary history, and criticism, brought the publication of his theoretical works. Eikhenbaum was for a long time considered a formalist, and he was also judged as an elitist. Therefore, the importance of his theoretical work was degraded due to the primitive and wrong interpretation of his postulates. After his youthful attraction to formalism his mature works reflected a balanced world outlook. His works were translated in many languages and enjoyed great popularity abroad.[18] Subsequently, Eikhenbaum has been reinstated as a literary scholar in his own land, and his best known works have appeared in new editions.

The New Publishing Policies

The revaluation of the literary heritage was greatly encouraged by the changes in the publishing industry. Many previously censored authors were published again. The restructuring of the publishing policies gave also to the Soviet writers greater freedom, and much needed additional support in their literary quests. This change became apparent with the arrival of the historian Mikhail Nenashev at the helm of the highest publishing authority. Nenashev, a former professor of history, has been heading the USSR State Committee for Publishing, Printing and the Book Trade since February 1986. Nenashev believed that the books promote, at its best, the desired understanding of the restructuring process. He contended that the books, as the most valuable cultural assets, should be protected.

Nenashev himself always treated books "with awe and reverence" since the books were, in his youth, the principal source of learning and intellectual growth. Born in 1929, he grew up in a village during the years of World War II. Under these difficult circumstances, Nenashev developed a deep appreciation for books ". . . as a man made miracle. The book links the past with the present and has a dramatic impact on the future. It enables man's accumulated experience to be passed from

---

17. Baigushev, "Opyt . . .," p. 234.
18. Baigushev, "Opyt . . .," p. 235.

generation to generation."[19] The books, in the process of restructuring, advanced the renewal since the books introduced the new, yet also relied on the cultural wealth which mankind has produced and continued to produce. The reconstruction drive, along the path of democratization, increased the bold quests, truthful appraisals and innovative solutions. The books acted as a mighty weapon in the renewal of the Soviet society.

The Soviet Union was traditionally known for its avid readers. The Russian literature played, from its inception, a great social role as in no other country anywhere. Russia's literature of the 18th-19th centuries was never belles-lettres only: it was permeated with revolutionary spirit, invariably carrying social messages and commitments to solving injustices. Nenashev thought that, at the present time, the political books were of major importance. The accelerated comprehension of the current societal changes depended precisely on the topicality of such publications and their timely appearance. The participation of writers in this process was of paramount importance for both the people and the country. Again, Nenashev thought that the writers should be pioneers in this cause. He very likely derived this conclusion from the historical role of writers in Russian society and their frequent involvement concerning the well being of the people.

Lately, Nenashev observed, several important literary works have dealt with the historical questions of Stalin's rule, the collectivization of farming, the World War II and the difficult postwar period of rebuilding of the war-ravaged country. Literary works by Karpov, Aitmatov, Bogomolov, Tvardovskii, Bek and others dealt with these subjects in one way or another. Any attempts to embellish history and to ignore injustice, would arouse distrust among the younger generations. However, the Soviet society's interests were not entirely concentrated on the past. What the Soviet people lacked presently were straightforward, and militant books about the revolutionary changes taking place in the country. Although the Soviet society was determined to carry through the changes, the restructuring process was evolving in a complicated, contradictory and uneven manner.[20]

---

19. Mikhail F. Nenashev, *Books promote an understanding of the restructuring process,* Moscow, Novosti, 1987, p. 2.

20. Nenashev, *Books* . . ., p. 18.

Nenashev praised the Book Institute carrying on the Soviet cultural policies with distinction. The Book Institute was initially founded at the Petrograd University and continued, over the years, to serve well the reading public. The Institute endeavored to study the publishing policies and the reader's needs, relying in such research on furnished data from libraries, schools, book stores and readers responses. Based on a scientific analyses of these data, the Institute aimed to help the editorial policies in order to match more adequately the readers' interests. In addition, the assistance of sociological research determined not only the readers' current requirements and needs, but helped also in projecting future needs. The Institute assessed following necessary informations: what books are read and how, what are the publishing priorities, and what are, if any, necessary adjustments in book circulations.

The practice of artificial concealment of certain authors and their books hampered the literary and social advancement in USSR. Nenashev warned that there existed another undesirable extreme which must be avoided, when many once neglected authors were represented as the most important link of the cultural and literary life. Soviet literature has its "golden fund", and the works of Maksim Gor'kii, Mikhail Sholokhov, Sergei Esenin, Aleksandr Tvardovskii, among others, can not be replaced. However, Nenashev pointed out that a list of authors was drawn, whose books were, for one reason or another, published rarely. This list comprised 60 names: Leonid Andreev, Anna Akhmatova, Mikhail Bulgakov, Vladimir Vysotsky, Boris Pasternak, among others. Their books will be brought out by the central publishing houses and included in the special series *Nasledie (Legacy)* [21].

In spite of all these efforts, book publishing was still lagging behind the requirements of the present time. Restructuring, in respect to book publishing, meant democratization and a new awareness in book policy planning and titles selections. Difficulties not withstanding, over the past seventy years an impressive publishing and printing complex has been created. Over 83,000 titles of books and brochures were brought out annually in a circulation of over two and a half million of copies. In addition, the Soviet Union led in publishing translations of foreign literature. Each year over 2,000 works by foreign authors were published in a total of some 173 million copies. The most popular authors were:

---

21. Nenashev, *Books* . . ., p. 4.

Ernest Hemingway, Georges Simenon, Somerset Maugham, Andre Maurois, Pablo Neruda, William Faulkner and Herve Bazin. There is a plan underway to publish the 45-volume *Library of United States Literature,* a collection ranging from the chronicles of the 17th and 18th centuries to the present.[22]

However, the gap between the relatively slow book publishing, and a swiftly developing society was widening. It seemed to him that the readers were inundated with all sorts of hackwork which was written faster and regrettably published more promptly than genuine literature. What was even more unpardonable was the delayed publication of scientific or socio-political literature. All these delays were caused by the neglect of the existing scientific and technological improvements in printing and book manufacturing. The laser type-setting, high speed automated presses in color, and conveyor lines were widely used in world book printing elsewhere. Nenashev thought that there was a long way to go before an advanced position in Soviet printing industry was reached.[23]

In spite of all existing difficulties, thanks to rising living standards, books were becoming commonplace items in people's homes. The recent poll showed that 52.7 percent of Soviet families have libraries of 200 or more books. Books cost less in Soviet Union than comparable books in Europe, except in the case of encyclopedias or art books. Nenashev expressed his concern that although, paradoxically, books remain in great demand, the reading itself was receding, giving way to other pastimes. He quoted the observations made by Soviet sociologists: at present, the Soviet society gave its citizens the opportunity of spending a mere 11-14 percent of the average life span at work. A young person has 120-150 free days a year, yet regrettably the young and the old alike have not been reading more.[24]

However, book sellers, librarians and sociologists have some books in short supply since there existed a shortage of certain categories of books. The first list of one hundred titles has been drawn and these much needed books should be published within the next five to ten years. This list included various reference books, encyclopedias, teaching aids, socio-political works and children's literature. Recent publications included the

---

22. Nenashev, *Books* . . ., pp. 7–10.
23. Nenashev, *Books* . . ., p. 8.
24. Nenashev, *Books* . . ., p. 12.

three-volume selected works by Aleksandr Pushkin: it came out in a
circulation of some eleven million copies which had no precedent in the
world. The first volume of selected works by Vladimir Maiakovskii had a
print run of six million copies. Works by Mikhail Lermontov, Fedor
Dostoievskii, Lev Tolstoi, Anton Chekhov, Maksim Gor'kii, Sergei Esenin
and others, will also be issued in large editions.[25]

Nenashev was aware that talented writers produced unique manuscripts,
and he believed talent to be invariably an unique endowment. The
manuscripts, when accepted, were often heavily edited and stereotyped in
order to conform with a standardized content and form. On the other
hand, the ten thousand members of the Writer's Union did not produce
uniformly high quality works. The membership of the Union included
quite a few who overestimated their abilities. According to the publishers'
evaluations, their books were not good enough to come out in mass
editions. Nenashev thought that there was much truth in these remarks.
During the 1986 Writers' Congress much was said about the mediocre
literature cramming book stores. But no one specified a single book of the
mediocre range. Therefore, such works were jokingly declared as "the
most secret literature."[26]

As a relatively new development, the Soviet theaters and cinemas
presented plays and films with critical messages, although it took usually a
long time for such works to reach the audiences. However, Nenashev
pointed out that it did not suffice to discuss only negative occurrences.
The criticism can only be effective when constructive, and ". . . when
shortcomings are fought, not merely talked about . . . . It should be not
forgotten that however sharply the social, political and economic problems
were criticized today, this awareness helped to continue along the
chartered path."[27]

The Revaluation of the Role of Mikhail Bulgakov

The neglected literary heritage, in particular the contribution of
Mikhail Bulgakov, was on the mind of many literary critics, writers and

---

25. Nenashev, *Books* . . ., p. 14.

26. Nenashev, *Books* . . ., pp. 20–21.

27. Nenashev, *Books* . . ., pp. 3–4.

historians. A renewed interest in Bulgakov's works gradually emerged in the course of the late 1950s. The organizers of various conferences, symposia and literary editions tried to rectify the existing situation. The re-examination of Bulgakov's heritage continued steadily and was gaining in momentum.

The literary critic Alla Kubareva pointed out that Bulgakov wrote equally well prose works and great theatrical plays. He depicted with a keen insight the revolutionary and the post revolutionary times, providing unique testimonies of this turbulent period of Soviet history. Yet, his valuable literary creations were returned, in part, to the Soviet people only during the 1960s with the new editions of his selected works. Kubareva concluded that the memories of the lessons from the past should serve as valid guidelines for the present and the future. The spiritual followers of the RAPP, she argued, were still causing harm, not only by hindering the proper reception of Bulgakov's legacy, but equally by influencing the essence of the literary life itself.[28]

In 1972 the Soviet Writers' Union Commission for the Literary Heritage of Mikhail Bulgakov was officially formed. The critic Aleksandr Ninov took an active part in the promotion of literary works that were not previously duly acknowledged. He participated also in the preparation of the literary event dedicated to the discussion of major works of Mikhail Bulgakov. *Bulgakovskie chtenia* took place in Leningrad in 1986 and concentrated mainly on Bulgakov's ties with Soviet literature during his formative years, as a young artist, in the 1920s and 1930s. Ninov thought that Bulgakov was presently much better understood as a major figure of Soviet literature than some three decades ago. Ninov concluded, with obvious pleasure, that the existence of a solid theoretical foundation should safeguard Bulgakov's definite place in Soviet literature.

Ninov singled out the scholars who have dedicated their work to the study of Bulgakov 's literary output and participated in the *Readings of Bulgakov's Works* in Leningrad in 1986. He mentioned the names of Iu. Babichev, V. Gudkov, Ia. Lur'e, A. Smelianskii, and others. Ninov added that the number of young researchers, interested in the study of Bulgakov's legacy, was constantly growing. The recollections of Bulgakov's contemporaries: K. Paustovskii, P. Markov, V. Kataev, S. Ermolinskii, A.

---

28. Alla Kubareva, "Mikhail Bulgakov i ego kritiki," *Molodaia gvardiia*, No. 5, 1988, pp. 246–247.

Faiko, V. Toporkov, E. Sheremetaev, among others, have been recorded. These recollections preserved many important data pertaining to the writer and his biography.[29] Bulgakov's works attracted the interest of literary historians abroad. Ninov reported about the Bulgakov's Symposium in Italy. The Symposium was organized in 1984 by professor Eridano Baccarelli, who was the director of the Institute of Eastern Languages and Literature at the University of Milan. Ninov was impressed by this memorable event that testified about Bulgakov's impact on the literary world. Baccarelli, who specialized in the Russian literature of the 19th and 20th century, wrote a monograph on Bulgakov.

Obviously, Bulgakov's work transcended the period of the emerging Soviet state and literary thought of the 1920s and 1930s, at the time when he took active part in the cultural life and wrote his major works. Bulgakov's dedication to his mission as a writer testified to the sense of importance of his own work. This keenly felt obligation helped him to overcome many tribulations during a difficult period of the new Soviet society. His literary legacy withstood the unjust criticism of his zealous contemporaries, followers of the ideology of proletarian culture, members of the LEF and RAPP organizations.

Ninov justly thought that Bulgakov's personal commitment was well described in Pasternak's poem "Noch' " ("The Night") :

> Ne spi, ne spi, rabotai,
> Ne preryvai truda,
> Ne spi, boris' s dremotoi,
> Kak letchik, kak zvezda.
> Ne spi, ne spi, khudozhnik,
> Ne predavaisia snu,—
> Ty—vechnosti zalozhnik
> U vremeni v plenu!

> Do not sleep, do not sleep, but work,
> Do not interrupt your work
> Do not sleep, but fight the slumber,

---

29. Aleksandr A. Ninov, *Skvoz' tridtsat' let,* "Mikhail Bulgakov i sovetskaia khudozhestvennaia kul'tura," Leningrad, Sovetskii pisatel', pp. 423–424.

Like the flier, like the star,
Do not sleep, do not sleep, artist,
Do not let the dreams to prevail—
You are the hostage of the eternity
Held captive in time to come![30]

Pasternak understood the high principles of a whole generation of poets, whose members were Bulgakov and Pasternak himself. These poets were oriented towards future, wishing to transcend human limitations and create many new works in a steady stream, as quickly as possible.

Ninov pleaded that the approaching one hundred years of Bulgakov's birth, in May of 1991, should be properly observed as a milestone of national culture. This event should be celebrated with the increased interest in the study of Bulgakov's literary legacy. The publication of his collected works would present the best remembrance of Bulgakov's splendid contribution.[31]

Bulgakov's theatrical plays prompted a lively discussion of the critics and public alike. A number of well written articles commented various aspects of Bulgakov's works. Alla Kubareva wrote about the impact of Bulgakov's work and the criticism that it received, during his lifetime, by the politically biased critics. She acknowledged the fact that Bulgakov's literary heritage was steadily gaining grounds in spite of many decades of its absence in the Soviet cultural life. The banishment of his work was the result of the critics, supporters of the artistic policies of the RAPP. The unjust criticism created a truly tragic situation; a major writer was excluded from the Russian and Soviet literature, and the literary fund was robbed for decades of his valuable contribution. Kubareva stated that during the 1920s and 1930s around 300 negative reviews were published about Bulgakov's works. Among theses critics, followers of the RAPP policies, were the names of Averbakh, Rodov, Lelevich, Mustangova, Nusinov and many more. They placed Bulgakov's work on the other side of the barricades under false assumptions affixed to his works.[32]

Bulgakov's work continued to attract attention and the 1980s brought new publications of his literary oeuvre. Bulgakov's special talent enabled

---

30. Ninov, "Mikhail Bulgakov . . .," p. 437; transl. of the poem by J. M.-Djurić.

31. Ninov, "Mikhail Bulgakov . . .," p. 437.

32. Kubareva, "Mikhail Bulgakov. . . .," p. 247.

him to discern life's tribulations by raising such conflicting situations to the level of artistic generalization. He was able to inject in his works references of events or personalities that were easily recognized by his contemporaries. In his play *Master and Marguerite* Bulgakov left portraits of the general secretary RAPP, L. Averbakh, and the critics Litovskii, M. Kol'tsov, and others. In addition, Bulgakov's plays encompassed, invariably, complicated philosophical problems, political battles, literary happenings, theatrical intrigues, as well as many of life's hardships and glorious moments.

Having in mind the complexities of the political and social events during Bulgakov's lifetime, Ninov recognized rightfully that for a truthful comprehension of Bulgakov's work, the historical facts should be scrutinized in order to understand the inherent discrepancies and dilemmas of this period. Bulgakov identified with the hard choices that the life dictated to his fellow men. Bulgakov followed to a certain degree Gor'kii's example by extending his support to the much maligned intellectuals. However, some events captured in his literary work were intentionally described in such a manner that, in order to understand, the reader had to decipher the hidden meaning.

Taking into account readers' growing interest in Bulgakov, a new goal was set of publishing Bulgakov's *Collected Works* in 1989-1990. Aleksandr Kareganov, the chairman of the Soviet Writers' Union Commission for the literary heritage of Mikhail Bulgakov, introduced successfully the Collected Works into the publication plan of the publishing house *Khudozhestvennaia literatura*. The total of this edition was planed to be 200,000 copies.[33]

The course of Soviet literary development starting in the late 1950s and later on leading to the 1960s and 1970s pointed gradually toward greater independence from established canons. The tradition of moral and ethical awareness, the search for justice and truth, have occupied the creative minds of the Soviet society. The 1980s brought the issues of political, personal and creative freedom into the mainstram of the Soviet societal thought, enabling a fresh revaluation of the literary heritage. Many previously censored works brought valuable, timeless messages linking the past with the present —*"sviaz vremeni."* The strengethening of the collective memory provided, as well, a much needed support for the

---

33. *Soviet literature,* 1988/7, pp. 159–160.

ensuing literary and artistic explorations of the evolving historic changes leading to the new century.

CHAPTER IV

THE RISING ROLE OF JOURNALISM

The changing of the Soviet political and cultural life, and the greater freedom of expression spurred an accelerated rise of the journalistic genre. One of the most valuable new aspects of journalistic writing was reporting on the change of attitudes instigated by restructuring - *perestroika* and related activities. This new mentality, ushered in with the evolving changes, was also reflected in the journalistic reports describing personal experiences of the people involved in these processes. Valentin Chikin, Editor-in-Chief of the newspaper *Sovetskaia Rossia*, pointed out that his paper published a series of stories featuring Soviet citizens, in many walks of life, taking prominent part in the restructuring process. Chikin pleaded with professional writers to help, in order that many new stories could be written. Some writers agreed to help, such as Ivan Vasil'ev and Vladimir Sitnikov. Yet, many writers were far more concerned with publishing some of their works written fifteen or twenty years ago that they could not publish before. As a consequence, they passed unique opportunities of exploring the changed viewpoints and current aspirations of their contemporaries.[1]

Chikin's call for added collaboration of writers pointed to the vastness of available material for publication. It seemed that the journalists alone could not handle all the documentary material so vital for the support of the restructuring changes and grass-root efforts of the people from the many walks of life. The large membership of some eighty three thousand people was apparently not able to record all the valuable testimonies capturing the characteristic spirit of the time. The Union of Journalists, a strong organization uniting the working men and women of the Soviet

---

1. Gorbachev, *Democratization -the Essence of Perestroika, the Essence of Sotsialism,* Moscow, Novosti, 1988. Discussion following Gorbachev's speech, p. 38.

press, television, radio broadcasting and news agencies was founded in
1959.[2]

In due time, the efforts of the journalist Ivan Vasil'ev became
increasingly noticeable. His many articles, reports and presentations
dealing with various topics and problems of general concern were
recognized and he was awarded the Lenin prize in 1986.[3] The award of
the highest prize to Vasil'ev pointed also to the importance of journalistic
writing as an inalienable part of the new political and cultural course. This
fact elevated the rank of journalism, and its role in the rebuilding process
of the Soviet societal life.

Some well known writers and public figures were delighted with the
spirit of openness and freely expressed criticism in an ongoing, and lively
dialogue. In 1986, Viktor Rozov wrote an article for the prestigious
Literaturnaia gazeta, stating that the recent development of openness has
gone beyond his dreams. He never thought that he will live long enough to
see such changes. The newspapers, and the theatrical performances did not
resort to the figurative terms of the proverbial Aesopian language: the
criticism was expressed right in the face and up front. Rozov marveled at
the "wondrous words" expressing truth and nothing but the truth. Rozov
concluded. "I cannot believe my ears nor my eyes."[4]

The new freedom, Rozov argued, should generate action and not only
words. Like many others, Rozov realized that personal opinions were
important and he felt the need to voice his own remarks. His attention was
directed towards some of the pertinent everyday problems facing the
Soviet society. In a freely flowing narrative prose, adopted by many
writers as a new form of personal recollections and evaluations, Rozov
pointed to some undesirable occurrences, hoping to kindle the necessary
actions and corrections.

Rozov, as a writer and dramaturge, considered the man to be the
primary force in the course of further development. Yet he acknowledged
the fact that the struggle for overcoming the existing deficiencies may be

2. Albert Likhanov, *We are all responsible for our children,* Moscow, Novosti Press
Agency, 1987, p. 15.

3. "Memorable events in the history of Soviet literature 1917–1987," *Soviet Literature*,
No. 11, 1987, p. 192.

4. Viktor Rozov: "Nachat' s sebia," *Literaturnaia gazeta*, No. 19, 7 May 1986,
reprinted in *Lichnoe mnenie,* Eds. G.Markov et al., Moscow, Sovetskii pisatel', 1987, p.
295.

conducted in different areas of technological enterprise, as for example in
the heavy industry, machine building and in the construction business.
However, Rozov ascertained that the perfecting of human nature presented
a great challenge as the most difficult task. He recalled, as an example, the
powerful performance of the well known actor Arkadii Raikin on the stage
of the *Teatr estrady*. As usually, Raikin satirized human faults, pettiness,
narrow outlooks, drunkenness, and loutishness. The public was enthralled,
and the applause turned into a standing ovation. Rozov was impressed with
Raikin's performance since it touched everybody's heart. The audience
also seemed exceptionally perceptive and good natured. Yet, everything
changed as soon as the lights were turned down. The people, like a mob,
started galloping down the aisles and stairs. They charged towards the
exits as if someone have pulled the fire alarm. Rozov concluded that the
essence of human nature remained to be a closed book.[5]

Moreover, Rozov strongly believed that the arts have an educational,
cognitive and aesthetic role to play, in addition to the most important
ability to project, as it were, the underlying harmony of the universe.
Therefore, he thought that the dramatic theater influences most of all the
emotional nature of the human being. The unforgettable characters in the
dramatic works of Euripides, and Shakespeare personified some of the
eternal emotions well known to men and women from the primordial time
to the present. The overused, stereotyped phrase "Let us create the new
man" referred often to the implementation of desirable moral qualities in
the make-up of the young Soviet citizens. Such task presented an
enormous challenge, and Rozov thought that it is still easier to launch the
space ship into the cosmos than to create an ideal human being.

The newly bestowed adulation for the moral rectitude of the long
neglected "little people" presented the tribute to the desirable qualities that
were hard to cultivate. Therefore, Rozov advanced also the field of
education as the top priority of the Soviet society at large. The solutions
of key problems and the important advancement of the Soviet society were
only possible if the better part of the people had an education and shared
the high moral principles. Rozov hoped that the wish for betterment will
continue to guide the humankind, and that the joy of victories shall
transcend the sufferings and tribulations.[6]

---

5. Rozov, "Nachat' s sebia," pp. 296–297.
6. Rozov, "Nachat' s sebia," pp. 300–306.

Writers and critics alike felt rightfully that their literary work facilitated, to a considerable extent, the introduction of *perestroika* by raising the consciousness of fellow men. The writers nurtured the spirit of ethical and moral awareness and contributed their share by addressing the existing problems and shortcomings of the Soviet society. In their literary and journalistic works they often revealed candidly the dramatic conflicts and contradictions permeating the Soviet life in all its levels. They portrayed the events of everyday life and asserted the validity of human priorities.[7]

The spirit of openness influenced a growing respect for the written word voicing the new freedom of expression. As a result of changed editorial policies, allowing a greater freedom in the exchange of ideas, the circulation of all major literary journals was increased. Thus, in 1988 *Novyi Mir's* circulation has more than doubled, that of the *Druzhba Narodov* has gone up five times, and that of the *Literaturnaia Gazeta* - by 700,000 copies. In January of 1988, at a meeting of the CPSU Central Committee with the heads of the mass media, ideological institutions and artistic unions, the First Secretary of the Board of the Writers' Union Vladimir Karpov pointed out that the circulation has soared not only because the editors promised to print "hot and sensational stuff." However, Karpov conceded that such a promise might have influenced some subscribers. On the other hand, many readers wondered whether the artistic standards of all that was recently printed were high enough, and expressed concern about the emergence of a new time-serving system in literature. The readers did not appreciate works that contained a few words on Stalin's purges and some other negative phenomena used only to force through some 300 pages of mediocre writing. He singled out two books *The Children of Arbat* and *Robed in White* as topical and interesting writing, but questioned their artistic standards.[8]

The secretary of the Writers' Union G. Markov recognized, as well, in his report at the 8th Writers' Congress in June of 1986, the importance of the personal participation in the restructuring process. The immediacy of articles possessing the verve of the journalistic writing had great merits in this respect. Never before the participation of writers, in solving various

---

7. Evgenii Sidorov, "The wind of change", *Soviet Literature*, 1988, No. 1, p. 112

8. Vladimir Karpov discussing Gorbachev's speech, M. Gorbachev, *Democratization — the essence of perestroika, the essence of socialism,* Moscow, Novosti Press Agency, p. 47.

problems and answering questions of general interest, was as highly visible.   The writers contributed articles on many topical issues that were published in leading papers and periodicals such as *Pravda, Izvestiia, Komsomol'skaia pravda, Trud, Sovetskaia kul'tura, Literaturnaia gazeta* and others. The writers participated also in panel discussions broadcasted on radio- and TV stations. The issues discussed covered a wide range of interests such as ecology, agronomy, pedagogy, morality, urban planing, international politics and economy. The engaged voices of many writers helped to accelerate the social and economic progress and improve various facets of societal life.[9]

Markov discussed the journalistic writing as a genre that was steadily gaining in importance. Markov thought that everybody would agree that the rising role of journalistic writing was due to the growth of socialistic democracy, and new openness. The well written articles helped the renewal of many spheres of societal life. Most of all, Markov thought that the press remained a mighty weapon of the Party and, equally well, an influential former of an engaged and active literary thought.   The journalistic writing helped, according to Markov, the Communist Party to lead in the accelerated growth of social and economic development.[10]

The critic and literary scholar Iurii Surovtsev noted that the 1980s brought into the center of many polemics and discussions the role of journalistic writing. Papers with journalistic topics were presented at the writers' conferences as well as in books dealing with topical issues concerning the literary life. The journalistic genre was steadily gaining in social prestige. Another prominent characteristic was the infiltration of journalistic traits in various other literary genres. In particular, the presentations of unresolved human problems and intricate topics, in some literary works, approached the immediacy and verve of the journalistic style. The journalistic thrust influenced the creation of a more effective and truthful prose. Surovtsev quoted as an example for this statement the works of Valentin Rasputin *Pozhar (The Fire)*, Evgenii Evtushenko's *Fuku*, V. Astaf'ev's *Pechal'nyi detektiv (The Sad Detective Story), Ch.*

---

9. G. Markov, "Nikogda ne otgorazhivat'sia ot trevog sovremennogo mira, ot zhizni nashego naroda," *O partiinosti literatury*, Eds. G. Gudozhnik et al., Moscow, Khudozhestvennaia literatura, 1987, p. 30.

10. Markov, "Nikogda . . .", p. 30.

Aitmatov's The Executioner's Block, and *Svoi khleb (One's Own Bread)* by Iurii Chernichenko.[11]

However, Surovtsev was aware that journalistic writing was not always appreciated: The ongoing discussion in the Soviet literary press concerning the role of journalistic writing merited attention. Surovtsev reminded that it was Plekhanov who pronounced: *"The artist is not a publicist. He does not reason, he depicts" (Khudozhnik - ne publicist. On ne rassuzhdaet, a izobrazhaet.")* Plekhanov thought that the artists depicting the class struggle should recreate as well the thoughts and feelings of the main heroes of a literary work. Plekhanov expressed this thought while discussing Gorkii's play *Vragi (Enemies),* and stressing Gorkii''s ability to project an objective psychological make-up of characters.[12] Yet, Surovtsev thought that in order to fully comprehend the journalistic writing one must examine the creative process in general. Surovtsev was aware that many critics approached this topic, and he reviewed briefly several papers published in the Soviet press. Most of all, Surovtsev agreed with an earlier pronouncement by Egor Isaev who declared the immediacy of a journalistic approach to be the very spark that embodied the basis and the core of all literary work, no matter what genre such work would eventually represent. The directness of journalistic observation, in its essence, presented the first incentive and the first decisive step in the creative process.[13]

Some critics, like Aleksandr Chakovskii, saw the common ground of journalistic and literary works in the union of "the reason and the heart". This unity was presented, at its best, in some works of such great authors as Pushkin, Dostoevskii, Tolstoi, Hemingway and Mauriac. Turgenev in his *Zapiskakh okhotnika (Diary of a Hunter)* was not afraid to implement journalistic traits, in descriptive and declarative statements as the voice of reason. The purity of the novelistic genre was not debased by Turgenev's critical and candid observations of social injustice. In a similar fashion, the poetry of Nekrasov did not loose its appeal due to the inclusion of "prosaic" elements. The journalistic approach was not only utilized in

11. Iu. Surovtsev, "V mire pisatel'skoi publitsistiki" *O partiinosti literatury,* Moscow, Khudozhestvennaia literatura, 1987, p. 115.

12. Surovtsev, "V mire . . .," p. 116.

13. Surovtsev, "V mire . . .," p. 117.

novels with political connotation but equally in other literary forms, in particular if the author wanted to directly address the reader.[14]

Surovtsev referred further to the article by Vitalii Korotich, published in *Pravda,* discussing the role of journalistic writing. Korotich stated that a journalistic article presented not only an open discussion as an exercise of verbal clarification: it presented the views of a socially engaged writer. Such writer did not only report but projected also an artistic transformation of his personal perception of reality. However, Surovtsev stressed that journalism was mainly characterized, by the public at large, as an open communication of one's views in pamphlets, articles, or sketches discussing unresolved questions, mostly as a direct discourse with the readers, radio listeners or the television audiences.

Presently, the majority of writers, did not juxtapose the "presentation" ("izobrazhenie") with "reasoning" ("rassuzhdenie") as diametrically opposed. The novels of Konstantin Simonov proffered such an amalgamation of journalistic and creative elements. Simonov succeeded to weave together the free flow of imagination, and psychological finesse with the acuity of journalistic observations. The critic Aleksandr Krivetskii understood well the essence of Simonov's work; in his analyses of Simonov's *Trilogy* he pointed to the impressive achievements of the writer in broadening the avenues of artistic quests.[15]

Surovtsev approached again the discussion about the journalistic quality of some prominent Soviet literary works, in an interview about the problems facing the Soviet literature. According to Surovtsev the journalistic quality was not only present in the literary essays, in which it has been effective for a long time, but it was equally noticeable in some recently published prose works. He explained the term "journalistic quality" as an engaged and civic-minded attitude coupled with artistic and psychological finesse. This kind of journalistic writing was exemplified, in his opinion, by Valentin Rasputin's *Fire,* Georgi Markov's *For the Coming Century,* Victor Astaf'ev's *The Sad Detective Story* and Chingiz Aitmatov's *The Executioner's Block.* These works were artistically poignant, offering new possibilities for truthful and complex portrayal of reality.[16]

---

14. Surovtsev, "V mire . . .," p. 117–118.

15. Surovtsev, "V mire . . .," p. 118–119.

16. "Soviet Multinational Literature Today," *Soviet Literature,* 1987, No. 6, p. 124.

Surovtsev singled out the mentioned Astaf'ev's work *The Sad Detective Story* as an exceptional, highly topical and socially concerned book. It promoted the moral good and rejected the moral evil in a passionate manner. This compelling book was enhanced by its journalistic nature, although not without some loss of its intrinsic literary nature. Surovtsev expressed his reservations about journalistic fiction: sometimes it detracted from the value of the work if it assumed a superficial tone. On the whole, the journalistic thrust made the Soviet prose works more truthful and effective.[17]

Not all the critics and writers shared the prevailing positive evaluation of the journalistic genre. The writer Eduardas Miezhelaitis expressed a different view concerning the introduction of the journalistic style of writing in literature. Miezhelaitis distinguished himself with his own literary work and became the winner of the Lenin's prize, and of several prestigious titles such as the People's Poet of Lithuania, and the Hero of Socialist Labour.

Miezhelaitis discussed the role of journalism, yet his comments were addressed against such an influence in literary works. He noted that journalism has become fashionable and in addition produced a number of superficial works of a pseudo-literary nature. Miezhelaitis thought that the term "pseudo-literature" will offend some colleagues. In truth, he had nothing against journalism and liked to work sometimes on a newspaper column. Therefore, he suggested that this term should only describe journalistic works that did not make an effort to come closer to the standards of true literature. Yet, even such works attained often enough an influential position in literary life. He compared, as an example, the theatrical art and the circus arena: The circus can hardly be called theatrical art. In fact, the interchange of the terminology would present only juggling of terms.

At present, Miezhelaitis wrote, journalism merely pecked at the crumbs from the table of literature. Journalistic articles provided plenty of facts, the truth about life, precise data, and everything else that is found in literature. Only two things were missing — depth and beauty. Most everything in pseudo-literature was produced in a hurry, for one day only and therefore its topicality was ephemeral.

Miezhelaitis pointed that he was aware of the goals of journalism and its place in the contemporary society. However, he posed several questions

---

17. "Soviet Multinational Literature Today", p. 124.

about the reasons of its present dominant position, and fashionable quality in spite of its scant arsenal of literary means. The readers were likely to grab a sports rag while a good, valuable book was gathering dust on the shelf. Perhaps, literature was lagging behind journalism, since it had lost topicality and failed to satisfy the reader. The other possibility was the attitude of the reader towards literature who became somewhat lazy and unaccustomed to think. The more complex the problems, the greater the strain they produce; It seemed as if everybody preferred a quick solution and an uncomplicated and easy life. Miezhelaitis thought that these were the reasons why journalism, the radio, and the TV fitted the demand. These forms of mass communication tackled many problems in a prompt and easily comprehensible, if somewhat trite manner. Real literature, on the other hand, stimulated deeper thoughts and bared the human soul.

Apparently, the reader did not like such thorough examinations that exposed them to the glaring light of truth. Journalism outlined only the outward image of the man, skimming the surface of the sea of life and avoiding storms. Miezhelaitis concluded that these were the reasons for popularity of pseudoliterature. Yet, he repeated that he was not against journalism, especially good journalism, but only against protectionism and dominant positions into which journalism was lately thrust.[18]

Art must not and should not be obliged to amuse and console. Such a role is suitable for pseudo-art: show business, the circus, the radio, the television, and to some extent, the cinema and mass literature of a special kind. These shows go together with the daily bread, and easy entertainment. The centuries old catchword, *Panem et circenses,* is still effective. Miezhelaitis finished his *Monologue* with a plea:

> "I therefore ask you all, I beg you: let us not demand from art what it is incapable of giving. Let us not distort the essence of art and its significance. Art searches for an answer to the riddle of Destiny, the riddle of Being, the riddle of Eternity, the riddle of History. These are the only categories with which art operates. Art directs the eternal drama of Life and Death. Art keeps up the temperature of spiritual fire. Finally art solves the most difficult problem of all, the problem of Man. Art keeps up our concern with life. Everything else art farms out to business, advertising, the circus. I know no other art." [19]

---

18. Eduardas Miezhelaitis, "Monologue the Third", *Soviet Literature*, 1987, No. 2, pp. 101–102.

19. Miezhelaitis, "Monologue the Third", p. 112.

The poet Evgenii Evtushenko had a different opinion about the role of journalism, and posited that the rise of journalistic writing had a rightful place in Soviet society. He felt that a brisk journalistic assessment could generate the support of many against undesirable occurrences in a society, such as neo-fascism, racism and spiritual terrorism. Evtushenko believed in open discourse and became an avid supporter of journalistic writing. He wrote many journalistic articles and shorter poems capturing the essence of an adroit confrontation with issues of general concern:

"Journalistic writing—is not a genre,
Journalistic writing—is the relationship with reality
Journalistic writing—is the active relationship with the reality, when the author, as a citizen, is not concealing his position, but projecting it straightforward, without fear of consequences." [20]

Evtushenko thought that the fresh wind of openness brought the freedom to create, but not only in the field of literature: It gave the freedom of creation to the whole people. The new spirit of openness respected the personal opinions of many individuals since the collective standpoint of a people consisted of the sum of personal opinions of many. The power of personal opinions presented the lever of democracy. All the members of the society should be equally responsible in front of history. Their personal opinions are confluent, and merging like streams, into one single opinion of the people. Already the writer Andrei Platonov expressed succinctly, at one time, this thought: "Without me, the people are incomplete."

Evtushenko recalled the time when the role of one person was exaggerated, and the role of others was demoted. Many felt unimportant although performing conscientiously their duties comparing their contributions to the functions of "small screws" in the engine of history.

Evtushenko recalled that not long ago, one opinion, often incompetent, regulated not only the major interior and exterior policies, but also biology, linguistics, cybernetics, music and literature. Other opinions, even from leading specialist in the field were ignored, or even declared to be against "the opinion of the people." Therefore, Evtushenko pleaded for

---

20. E. Evtushenko, "Tochka opory," pp. 3–4; quoted after E. Sidorov, *Evgenii Evtushenko*, Moscow, Khudozhestvennaia literatura, 1987, p. 198.

democracy and participation: personal opinions should not only remain
words. The writer talking at the literary conference about the dangers
facing the ecology of the northern regions and its rivers, Soviet speaker at
the international conferences for prevention of nuclear disasters, scientist
fighting the pseudo scientific research — all these people exemplified the
individual responsibilities in front of historical challenges. Evtushenko
thought that the efforts of providing foodstuff in abundance, building of
beautiful bridges, producing important scientific discoveries, writing fine
books and enchanting theatrical shows helped to unify the opinions of the
Soviet people. These noble efforts transcended the boundaries of the
Soviet lands and contributed as well to the congeniality of the whole
humankind.[21]

A large role in the environmental issues has been played by writers and
journalists, who took initiative and discussed many urgent ecological
topics. There was a growing fear about the survival of the whole
humankind, and the already threatened environmental balance and
existence on earth. Many prominent Soviet writers took actively part in
international conferences and forums aimed at protecting the mankind
from ecological and nuclear disasters.

The writer Chingiz Aitmatov believed that the supreme and most
pressing task of literature was to foster a better moral climate, which was
as important as concern for environment:

"We had previously treated the Earth egoistically, with complete unconcern,
believing that it is its duty to feed us, slake our thirst, cloth and defend us, without
asking anything in return . . . . Now that we have penetrated the space, we have
suddenly realized, with a feeling of pain and tenderness beyond expression, that it also
needs to be protected . . . . The image of the Earth — cradle of humanity — as a
blue star as seen by the cosmonauts, is extraordinarily human and poetical."[22]

The survival of the mankind from the dangers of war and nuclear
weapons were on the mind of many writers, political and cultural leaders.
The poet Ivan Savelyev wrote the *Poem of insanity,* although he feared that
the poem will be read by no one, if his premonition of impending disaster
would materialize. He feared that the people of this earth would succumb

21. E. Evtushenko, "Lichnoe mnenie," *Lichnoe mnenie,* Eds. G. Markov et al.,
Moscow, Sovetskii pisatel', 1987, pp. 5–11.

22. V. Korkin, "Time to speak out", *Soviet Literature,* 1984, No. 5, pp. 146–147.

as victims of wrongful decisions. Therefore, he decided to describe the apocalyptic vision of the terrible annihilation of the "crazed humankind" that loomed large in his thoughts perpetually tormenting him. It seemed that after such nightmares he would lie in his bed "half living and half dead", in spite of the blinding sun rising in the morning. The fear would come over him again, and the same dreadful imagery would unfold while he was awakening:

> Those cries return in me, full of pain.
> I am like Earth, all round, far and wide,
> I'm crazily stuffed with rockets inside.
> And all of them are set at "Start." . . .[23]

However, the emerging tendencies of global interdependence and international collaboration evolved seemingly parallel to the resurgence of national self awareness. The deepening of self reliance and rediscovery of national values, as unforgrarded in the manifold emanations of folk and artistic tradition, appeared to provide the needed reassurance of the unique national entity. At times, the corroborations of national sentiments helped to provoke, serious confrontations among various ethnic, religious and cultural entities. These occurrences were widespread, beleaguering several multinational countries, including USSR. The increased preoccupation with the changing world impaired sometimes the ability for adaptation projecting the wish for isolation and self-sufficiency.[24] Amidst the preponderance of these issues, the writers, journalists and historians alike were aiming to project the validity of a pluralistic approach, recognizing the right for existence of different points of view. The respect for democratic principles seemed to assure the possibility of a meaningful dialogue, both on a national and international level.

---

23. *Soviet Literature*, 1985, No. 8, p. 128. Translated from Russian by Walter May.

24. Iu. V. Bromlei, "Rol' sovetskoi nauki v izuchenii, sokhranenii, i rasprostranenii kul'turnogo naslediia narodov Evropy," *Sovetskaia kul'tura, 70 let razvitia,* Ed. B. B. Piotrovskii, Moscow, Nauka 1987, p. 299.

CHAPTER V

SOVIET LITERARY LIFE IN THE 1980S:
THE CHANGING ROLE OF SOCIALIST REALISM

The doctrine of socialist realism, introduced officially at the First Writers' Congress in Moscow in 1934, has continuously influenced the artistic policies and viewpoints of Soviet writers, editors, and publishers alike, acquiring a dominant role in Soviet cultural life. A number of literary historians, and critics have repeatedly aimed to corroborate the validity and vitality of this artistic doctrine. The many advantages of this ideological orientation were, in the view of these literary arbiters, the bequest of Soviet writers to world literature. The inherent richness of this method, introduced by Gorkii, Maiakovskii and Sholokhov, and the impact of literary works such as *Zhizn' Klima Samgina,(The Life of Klim Samgin) Tikhii Don,(The Quiet Don) Khorosho,* and *Kak zakalialas' stal' (How the Steel was Forged)* embodied the principal innovations of Soviet literary thought.[1]

While the literary histories and textbooks were upholding socialist realism as the official doctrine, serious criticism of this doctrine was transmitted, for a long time, by word of mouth. However, in 1988 some Soviet literary journals have published several articles challenging the established position of socialist realism. Polemical discussions and questioning of the inherent values of socialist realism appeared in printed form in *Oktiabr, Literaturnaia gazeta* and *Novyi mir.* [2]

Observed from a vantage point, socialist realism provided, most of all, a common ground for the creation of the multinational Soviet literatures. The various Soviet nationalities followed different paths in their literary and artistic development while departing from the patriarchal spirit of their respective folk cultures. Over the years, the accelerated literary

---

1. A. G. Bocharov, "Vvedenie," *Sovremennaia russkaia sovetskaia literatura,* A. G. Bocharov and G. A. Belaia, Eds., Moscow, Prosveshchenie, vol. I, 1987, p. 4.

2. *Novyi mir,* 1988, No. 9, p. 142.

62

development brought the various national literatures to the level of contemporaneity. This literary fund comprised some seventy national literatures that emerged as a broadly defined entity, sharing many basic aspirations and concerns, in spite of the different languages and diversities of their respective national traditions. The critic and writer Chingiz Guseinov stated that at the time of the 8th Writers' congress in 1986, the members of the Writers' Union wrote in seventy-eight different languages.[3]

In the period of Stalin's rule, dogmatic adherence to the doctrine of socialist realism often served as a shield for mediocre works, hiding their lack of true literary qualities. The established criteria provided, as it were, predictable paradigms serving as a blueprint for the rapid proliferation of such works. However, the torrent of unimaginative novels served as a backdrop for the appearance of some exceptional works, testifying to the underlying strength of the realistic stylistic orientation.

In retrospect, many writers were bemoaning the lack of courage among the critics and writers alike. In particular, the older generation of writers stressed that the absence of a brave voice of just criticism was still deeply felt. The writer Veniamin Kaverin posited in 1987 that even the present introduction of openness did not change the situation to a substantial degree: No one seemed to fit the historic role of Belinskii. Kaverin did not dispute that there were many talented critics actively evaluating the current issues of literary life. However, their attitudes, published work, and literary pronouncements did not display the courage and clarity of vision that Belinskii's once had.[4]

While accepting the general ideological framework of socialist realism, the Soviet writers aimed to preserve their unique national contributions, as their gift to the humankind. Their literary works repeatedly explored the legacies of their national traditions, and these repositories provided the writers with a keenly felt ethical, moral, and artistic judgment, that although autochthonous, was in its essence universal.

The path leading to the present understanding of the complex social and moral issues of modern humanity was not an easily traveled one. The writers increasingly addressed their attention to the psychological profile of human nature. In an effort to probe deeper into the complexities of

3. Ch. Guseinov, *Etot zhivoi fenomen*, Moscow, Sovetskii pisatel', 1988, p. 12.

4. V. Kaverin, "Vzgliad v litso," *Lichnoe mnenie*, Ed. G.Markov et al., Moscow, Sovetskii pisatel', 1987, pp. 342–343.

human existence, many writers examined the fragility of the subsistence on earth and the inherent moral obligations to the human community at large. The ability of the human spirit to surpass given limitations and provide solutions of importance, was recognized as an individually shared human endowment.

Yet, the past was not forgotten and the revival of the splendid world of legends, stories, and folkloristic idioms enabled a renewed appreciation for life on earth, in all its magnificent versatility. The safeguarding of this common cradle of humankind, and the rising concern for the environment, already threatened by carelessness, became one of prime concerns of writers and scientists alike. These aspirations were manifested in the proclamation of the International Forum for a Nuclear Free World held in Moscow in 1987: "It is not the 'fatherland that is in danger', it is man himself, the crown of existence." The risk of nuclear warfare was perceived as the main problem, among many other serious global issues facing humankind.[5]

The poet Andrei Voznesenskii took part in the forum, and expressed his deeply felt concern in an impressive poetic vision. He explained that his poem's genesis was contained in the symbolic connotation of the current historic date: "I was overpowered by the symbolism of numbers (similar to Khlebnikov) of the present calendar year 1987, its foreboding annihilating progression, reminding of the countdown of seconds before the cosmic start. Was this the killing of culture? Of Humankind? Where are we heading?"

1987

... Chto za smysl letit nad vsem,
Ubyvaiushchii schet tsifr?
Desiat, deviat, vosem', sem' ...
Start? Vzryv?

... Desiat', deviat', vosem', sem' ... —
antischetchik pobezhal,-
Forman, Pushkin, Budda, Zen,
Skoro l' vremia obez'ian?

5. Iu. S. Borisov, "O nekotorykh tendenciiah v razvitii sovremenoi kul'tury," *Sovet-skaia kul'tura, 70 let razvitiia*, Ed. B.B.Pietrovskii, Moscow, Nauka 1987, p. 179.

Stroit khramy Gerostrat
Nitsshe govorit: "Bog zhiv!"
V kom iz nas taitsia start?
V kom iz nas taitsia vzryv?

. . . Zapreshchennykh izdaem
Ot "Zhivago" v serdtse shchem'.
Skol'ko ikh eshcho imen?
Desiat'. . .Deviat'. . . Vosem'. . . Sem'. . .

Medlenno v buran bor'by
blizitsia svobody sen',
Kak dorozhnye stolby —
"10", "9", "8", "7". . .

1907

. . . What is the meaning above all of
The disastrous count-down?
Ten, nine, eight, seven. . .
The start? The explosion ?

. . .Ten, nine, eight, seven. . . —
the counter broke away in a run,—
Forman, Pushkin, Budda, Zen,
Will the monkey's rule set in soon?[6]

Herostrat is building the temples
Nitzsche is proclaiming: "God is alive!"
Who among us is harboring the start?
Who is harboring the explosion?

---

6. In this verse Voznesenskii was very likely alluding to the sculpture that Lenin kept on his writing desk in his study at the Kremlin. It presented a monkey examining the human skull. The monkey was perceived as the sole survivor after the annihilation of the human race.

. . .
We are publishing the ones previously censored
From "Zhivago" to the heart of the oppressed.
How many more names are there ?
Ten. . . Nine. . . Eight. . . Seven . . .

Slowly, in the blizzard of fighting
Victory's sheltering arm is nearing,
Like the roadside poles—
"10," "9," "8," "7" . . .

The participation of the poet at the Forum, and the poem itself left a deep impression on the Soviet intellectual thought. Voznesenskii's poem was interpreted not only as a reflection of discrepancies permeating present day life, but also as a characteristic indicator of contemporary culture and the heightening of social and ethical consciousness. More important, these conceptual aspects of the poem pointed to the humanistic tradition of the poet's national culture as an inherent part of the culture of all humankind.

Soviet literary historians asserted that the works written in the 1970s and 1980s did not, in fact, abandon the doctrine of socialist realism, or replace the "aging" *(ustarevshii realizm)* with the "new" *(novii realizm)* realism. The realistic stylistic orientation was enhanced by the new imaginative and creative approach.[7]

The writers, reexamining the past, approached a hitherto less explored layer of their national cultures. There occurred a veritable revival of the mythological themes, and of the phantasmagoric elements. The Kirghizian writer Chingiz Aitmatov explained the power of mythology as an immense primordial poetry of the human spirit, with its unique courage and optimism. He thought that the revival of mythological themes presented the effort of modern man to try, with the help of literature, to find his place in the world, in history, and in nature:

---

7. A. Bocharov, G. Belaia, and V. Vozdvizhenskii, "Dvizhenie prozy semidesiatykh-vosmidesiatykh godov," *Sovremennaia russkaia sovetskaia literatura*, Vol. I, p. 116.

" . . . in other words he is engaged in self-quest in order to become capable of fulfilling man's duty to be man by assimilating the spiritual culture of all mankind and feeling his affinity to the past and future."[8]

The writers introduced phantasmagoric, mythological, and associative references, incorporating literary collages as an intrinsic part of their own work. All these innovations pointed, in fact, to the vast creative possibilities of the realistic style. The prose works often explored the diachronic context of current literary thought: the present was entwined with the past, touching the projection of the future. The writers' preferences for a specific genre underlined further the unique artistic interpretation of the thematic scope and concept of a literary work. The chosen genre introduced, in addition, the memory of its own genesis, since the genre, according to Bakhtin, incorporated simultaneously the old and the new, preserving the past within its ongoing mutations. However, Soviet critics pointed out that the present variety of literary genres escaped canonical interpretation and easy classification, bordering often on ambiguity.[9]

Yet, this new richness of literary content and form was spurred by still another introduction from the past: The revaluation and subsequent introduction of the works of longtime censored writers and artists whose contributions to Russian and Soviet literary and artistic heritage had, to a large degree, been ignored. In particular the legacy of M. Bulgakov, M. Tsvetaeva, I. Bunin, A. Belyi, among others, motivated the fresh examination of the multifaceted literary past.[10]

Veniamin Kaverin noticed the beginning of a new literary period starting with the publication of Bulgakov's *Master i Margerita (Master and Marguerite)*. It seemed as if a fresh breath of air had been blown into literary life. Bulgakov's work pointed to the possibility of inclusion of fantastic elements that transformed the comprehension of everyday reality into a recurring miracle. The possible meaningful historical parallels of the past with the present surprised the readers and influenced the literary thought. Bulgakov's novel generated a new self-awareness. For years, everybody trusted that literature had a higher commitment of supporting

---

8. "Time to speak out," Chingiz Aitmatov interviewed by literary critic Vladimir Korkin, *Soviet Literature*, 1984, 5, pp. 149–150.

9. Vvedenie, *Sovremennaia russkaia sovetskaia literatura*, Vol. I, pp. 6, 112–116.

10. Borisov, "O nekotorykh . . .," p. 181.

just causes. In reality, most literary works were only superficially engaged in fostering such goals and therefore remained shallow.[11]

In addition, the introduction of Bulgakov's works engendered interest in writers that cultivated a similar artistic credo. The tradition of phantasmagoric literature was revived and led to a re-examination of the works of Sukhovo-Kobylin, Saltykov-Shchedrin, Senkovskii, and Velt'man. Soon enough the new heirs of this literary genre emerged: Vl. Orlov, Nina Katerli, Tat'iana Tolstaia.[12]

The academician Dmitrii S. Likhachev discussed Bulgakov's influence in an article, with the characteristic title "Trevogi sovesti" ("Warnings of the Conscience"). He reminded the readers that in 1967 Bulgakov re-entered literary life as the author of the novel *Master and Marguerite*, with its biting and delightful satire. Very likely, the appearance of the novel was followed with trepidation by some critics expecting an adverse reaction. These fears were not justified, and instead, Likhachev concluded, society received a splendid work "that is not working against us, but for us." Bulgakov's satire was necessary, as was the sharp criticism of vices, as well as the delightful distraction and humor. Likhachev urged that the unpublished works of Bulgakov, Akhmatova and Zoshchenko should be submitted to the press along with the unpublished works of Andrei Platonov that are currently being scheduled for publication. Likhachev obviously thought that the writings of Bulgakov, Akhmatova, and Zoshchenko should not be considered secondary to any other literary works. In addition, the archives housing unpublished works should be opened and the books that have been shelved for years returned to the people. The unfair mistrust was hurting the dignity of everyone.[13]

Gradually, literary journals began publishing manuscripts that had been gathering dust in the archives. This decision was a wise one, and the newly published books were steadily raising the level of literary culture and generating in turn a greater interest in the development of the contemporary literature. The dull and boring works that had lowered literary standards were losing grounds. The introduction of the neglected

---

11. Veniamin Kaverin, "Vzgliad v litso," *Literaturnaia gazeta*, No. 25, 18 June 1986; reprinted in *Lichnoe mnenie*, Eds. K. N. Selikhov et al., Moscow, Sovetskii pisatel', 1987, pp. 341–342.

12. Kaverin, "Vzgliad v litso," p. 342.

13. D. S. Likhachev, "Trevogi sovesti," *Lichnoe mnenie*, Moscow, Sovetskii pisatel', 1987, p. 46.

literary heritage restored the memorable past. Slowly, the theory of people's inability to judge literary creations has been discredited.[14]

The literary works created during the past two decades reflect well the amalgamation of the old into the new. Moreover, many writers turned their attention to a renewed exploration of their respective national roots. These writers were, at the same time, fulfilling one of the important prerogatives of socialist realism, defined as *narodnost'*, by cultivating close ties with the people's inventive genius.

From the very beginning, the Soviet government paid great attention to the preservation of folklore. The national heritage of oral epic and lyric poetry, the tales, legends and various customs, dances, and songs, of all Soviet republics, were treated equally as a respected cultural wealth. The state universities and national academies founded or expanded existing institutions for the research and preservation of folk culture. Regular field expeditions were set up, and tales, folk songs, and dances were recorded with great care. During the 1920s and 1930s the planning of systematic recordings of folklore was headed by the prominent ethnographer Iu. M. Sokolov. Sokolov organized numerous research expeditions encompassing the whole territory of the USSR.[15] In addition to the established curricula at the university level devoted to the study of folklore and folk music, many folklore societies and clubs were set up. These societies, founded at schools and factories alike, offered courses in folk dancing and folk music. The professional and amateur folk dance ensembles enjoyed great popularity, and took frequently part in national and international concerts and competitions. During the 1980s folk music and folk dancing achieved increased popularity, and the membership in these ensembles increased markedly.[16]

The national tradition, the deeply embedded ethical and moral values, as well as the rich imagery, metaphors, and symbolic connotation of epic and lyric poetry and folk tales, provided unique threads for the weaving of outstanding new literary works. Writers in the 1970s and 1980s aimed for greater insight in portraying the many faces of their multinational country,

---

14. Likhachev, "Trevogi sovesti," p. 46.

15. E. Pomerantseva, *O russkom fol'klore*, Moscow, Akademiia nauk SSSR, Nauka, 1977, pp. 6–7.

16. A. Zakalin, "Kul'turno prosvetitel'naia rabota i ee rol' v obogashchenii dukhovnogo mira sovetskikh liudei," *Dukhovnaia sfera sotsialisticheskogo obshchestva*, Moscow, Mysl', Eds. Zh.T. Toshchenko et al.,1987, pp. 227–228.

and their works attracted the attention at home and abroad. These new works, based on the treasury of folkloristic idioms reflecting their respective past, were not treated as "exotic" aberrations but, primarily, as valid explorations of the richness of human nature. Soviet writers' interests were increasingly directed toward a better understanding of the current innovative artistic development and literary accomplishments of various Soviet republics.[17] Thus, the process of mutual enrichment of national cultures played an important part in the development of the contemporary Soviet literary life.

The parochialism of Stalin's age, the mistrust and concealed fear of the Western world, and the suppression of important chapters of the national historical and literary past were slowly fading away. The previous strict limitations instigated the wish to explore the present as well as the past with an open mind providing new evaluations of the cultural heritage. Along these lines, the period following the October revolution was repeatedly scrutinized, and the literary works written during that period were on the mind of the older and younger generations of writers and readers alike.

The increased attention to Lenin's legacy, in connection with the celebration of the centennial of his birth in 1970, was continuously supported by the official policy of the Communist party and Writers' Union alike. Lenin's works were analyzed anew, providing needed corrections of the deliberate emendations introduced by Stalin. Lenin's collected works were published in large editions, to meet the increased demand of the readers. Several writers devoted major works to Lenin's legacy by writing novels, essays, and chronicles, which eventually became part of the ongoing literary cycle dubbed *Leniniana*.. Among these writers were M. Shaginian, A. Koptelov, Dm. Ermin, and A. Voznesenskii.[18]

In the course of the 1980s the literary theoreticians and writers aimed to corroborate, in particular, Lenin's principle of the dialectical relationship of nationalism and internationalism. Love of one's native land would not preclude the appreciation of distant, foreign lands and people around the world. To this effect, the noted academician N. Ia. Bromlei stated that the healthy development of the national consciousness was

---

17. V. Piskunov, "Avtoritet istorii," *O partiinosti literatury, Sotsialisticheskii realizm: khudozhestvenyi opyt i teoriia*, G. Gudozhnik, A. Romanov, Eds., Moscow, Khudozhestvennaia literatura 1987, p. 112.

18. Ch. Guseinov, *Etot zhivoi fenomen*, Moscow, Sovetskii pisatel', 1988, p. 179.

possible only if supported by an appreciation of the equal value of all other cultures. The contemporary man understood (or should learn to understand) his role as an heir of a national cultural tradition and equally of the cultural legacy of all humankind.[19]

The poet Rasul Gamzatov expressed these feelings well in his poems about his ancestral village, *aul*, in the mountains of Daghestan:

> I odin iz nih obetovannyi,
> Gde menia pod napev rodnika
> Veter v liuliuke kachal dereviannoi,
> Zapelenatago v oblaka . . .
>
> A drugoi moi aul v etom mire -
> Belyi svet, chto raspakhnut vsegda
> I lezhit predo mnoi na chetyre
> Storony ot aula Tsada.

> One of them is the promised aul,
> Where I listened to the spring's murmur,
> The wind rocked me on the wooden swing,
> Swaddled in clouds.
>
> The second aul on this earth-
> The wide world, always open
> Spread out in front of me in all four
> Directions from the Tsad's aul.[20]

By and large, Soviet literature did manage to uphold the special and individual features of all its multinational constituents. Chingiz Aitmatov thought that many national literatures in the Soviet Union have attained great achievements in the artistic perception of reality. The single multilingual and multinational Soviet culture has emerged without precedent in the history of man. Many nationalities followed different

---

19. Bromlei, "Rol' sovetskoi nauki v izuchenii, sohranenii i rasprostranenii kul'turnogo naslediia narodov Evropy," *Sovestskaia kul'tura, 70 let razvitiia*, Moscow, Nauka 1987, p. 299.

20. Piskunov, "Avtoritet istorii," p. 113. Russian translation of the poem by Ia. Kozlovskii. English translation from Russian by J. Milojković-Djurić.

periods of transition, departing from the patriarchal spirit of folk cultures
and epic poetry leading to the present literary development.[21]

The literary critic Iurii Surovtsev thought that the various national
literatures were like members of an extended family. During the course of
their common life these literatures were not dissolved or absorbed by any
other literary entity. On the contrary, they helped each other to display
their best accomplishments, yet remained true to their unique potentials
and originality.[22]

Another critic, V. Piskunov, had a similar point of view when
discussing the present state of Soviet literature. He stated, with a measure
of pride, that it is possible to speak about Soviet literature when discussing
the literary works of the Russians L. Leonov or S. Zalygin, the Ukrainian
O. Gonchar, the Kirghizian Ch. Aitmatov, the Lithuanian E. Mezhelaitis,
the Chukchi Iu. Rytkheu, or the Moldavian I. Drutse. All these national
literatures were participants in the creation of Soviet literature, although
safeguarding their own national path of literary development. One should
remember that prior to the October revolution, Russian literary works
approached the realistic style, while Georgian literature was in its romantic
stage, and the literatures of Uzbekistan and Tajekistan were not far
removed from the realm of their medieval poetry. Many people in
Siberia, the North, and the Far East were not even literate.[23]

In this process, the postulates of socialist realism presented writers and
artists with an ideological platform, which provided a common ground for
their respective literary explorations. Shortly after the official
introduction of socialist realism in 1934, and later in the 1940s and 1950s,
the rigid enforcement of this doctrine slowed the creation of literary and
artistic works, since every innovation had to be justified. The gradual
"thaw" of the established guidelines in the mid 1950s opened avenues to
new literary exploration, and, in turn, made possible the renewal of the
doctrine of socialist realism itself.

Assessing the very beginning of this betterment, the role of the Second
Congress of Writers in 1954 was singled out, marking the beginning of the
contemporary development of Soviet literature. After a hiatus of twenty

21. "Time to Speak Out," Chingiz Aitmatov interviewed with literary critic Vladimir
Korkin, *Soviet Literature*, 1984, No. 5, p. 145.

22. Y. Surovtsev, "Soviet Multinational Literature," *Soviet Literature,* 1987, No. 10,
p. 120.

23. V. Piskunov, "Avtoritet istorii," *O partiinosti literatury*, pp. 86–87.

years the writers convened for the second time since the formation of the Writers' Union in 1934. The Second Congress provided a suitable platform for the discussion of Soviet literature. The members of this Congress evaluated in an overall positive fashion the past achievements and projected avenues of future growth. In spite of the inherent difficulties and disagreements characterizing this turbulent period of Soviet history, several literary masterworks have been created: The fourth book of *Tikhii Don (The quiet Don)* by Sholokhov presented such an outstanding achievement.[24]

The writers were, as many times before, in the vanguard of societal development. Their literary works examined life's realities and spoke with compassion about the vicissitudes of human existence. Most of all, the writers were exploring possibilities of social and political betterment while projecting the necessity of a fresh point of view. Thus, Soviet society was gradually prepared for the emergence of *glasnost'* and *perestroika* and the resulting new outlooks.

At the same time, while opening new avenues of thought, writers became aware of a larger global interdependence. The issues of world peace and peaceful coexistence, concern for the environment, and control of nuclear power opened the door for meaningful worldwide cooperation. Aitmatov summed up these feelings well in an interview with literary critic Vladimir Korkin:

"I believe that the supreme and most pressing task of literature is to foster a better moral climate in the world, which is as important today as concern for the environment, without which there can be no normal, healthy life on earth . . . . Mankind cannot have a more important concern today than concern for peace. Can it be tolerated that, having traveled a long and difficult road, and having become aware only recently . . . of the sublimity of life in its historical movement . . . humanity would agree to self-humiliation and self-destruction?"[25]

The celebration of the seventieth anniversary of the October revolution was marked as an important milestone in the development of the Soviet

---

24. V. G. Vozdvizhenskii, and V. L. Iakimenko, "Dvizhenie prozy kontsa piatidesiatikh-shestidesiatykh godov,"*Sovremennaia russkaia sovetskaia literatura*, Vol. 2, Moscow, 1987, p. 9. Compare also, A. Ovcharenko, *Sotsialisticheskii realism*, Moscow, Sovetskii pisatel', 1977, p. 68.

25. "Time to Speak Out," *Soviet Literature*, 1984, No 5, p. 139.

nation. The Central Committee of the Communist Party organized a gala meeting devoted to the anniversary of the October revolution of 1917. At this meeting, General Secretary Mikhail Gorbachev presented his report containing an analysis of many complex issues that once faced the emerging socialistic society.[26] Gorbachev commented on the importance of the remembrance of this historical event. The theoretical, political, and practical work, carried out in connection with the celebration, has enhanced the understanding of the past and present historic stage, as well as of the prospects for Soviet society in the future. Without this work, Gorbachev claimed, such an understanding would be impossible to achieve. Gorbachev concluded that the knowledge of historical events will remain as exceptionally significant.[27]

The celebration prompted appropriate publications in honor of the October revolution. Several writers, literary historians, and critics elucidated the inception and beginning of the cultural life of the new Soviet society. Many scholarly review papers discussed the prevailing ideas formulated by writers and poets, as preserved in the literary works of the period. While discussing the societal and literary development of the past, these papers also explained the evolving new points of view and evaluations brought forth by the *glasnost'* doctrine.[28]

The literary scholar and critic V. Piskunov wrote such a review paper in observance of the seventieth anniversary of the October revolution. He understood this period as a new epoch marking the beginning of the emerging socialistic culture. Piskunov elucidated the evolvement of Soviet literature from its beginning as an intrinsic part of the unique historical development. Thus, his account, projecting a fresh point of view, served well to strengthen the viewpoints of Soviet literary historicity.[29]

Piskunov thought that the poet Aleksandr Blok understood well the beginning of Soviet society and the first major efforts to propel the revolutionary development in all spheres of societal life. The new literary

---

26. A. Butenko, "To Avoid Mistakes in the Future," *The Stalin Phenomenon*, Moscow, Novosti Press Agency 1988, p. 5.

27. M. Gorbachev, *Democratization the Essence of Perestroika, the Essence of Socialism,* Moscow, Novosti, 1988, p. 5.

28. Compare also: *Sovetskaia kul'tura, 70 let razvitia,* Akademia nauk SSSR, Otdelenie istorii, Moscow, Nauka, 1987, pp. 3–399.

29. V. Piskunov, "Avtoritet istorii," *O partiinosti literatury, Sotsialisticheskii realizm: Khudozhestvennyi opyt i teoriia,* p. 85.

works were future oriented, aiming to support the establishment of a progressive contemporaneous culture There was a feeling of competition with centuries old European civilization, and in this noble battle everything seemed possible. Blok expressed these feelings, as he addressed the nations of Western Europe in his poem "Skify"("Skiths"):

Dlia vas—veka,
dlia nas—edinyi chas.

For you—the centuries,
For us—a single moment.

The concept of speeding-up of time, of infinite energy and mobility became subject of stories and novels of A. Serafimovich, D. Furmanov, K. Fedin and L. Leonov.[30]

With the closing of the twentieth century and the approaching of a new epoch, Piskunov noticed a similar appreciation of the passage of time. There was a growing awareness of history, and many questions were on the mind of the people, such as the evaluation of the past, the fear for the fate of all humankind, and the anticipation of the future. Writers felt the rise of historic consciousness, and the poet Ia. Smeliakov wrote: *"Ostree stalo oshchushchenye shagov Istorii samoi."* (The awareness of the pace of History became more acute.)

As always, writers contributed their share in the assessment of the past and of future life on earth. Rasputin wrote the novel *Zhivi i pomni (Live and Remember)*; Iu.Trifonov, *Vremia i mesto (Time and Place)*; N. Dumbadze, *Zakona vechnosti (The Laws of Eternity)*; Ch. Aitmatov, *I dol'she veka dlitsia den' (The Day Lasts More Than a Hundred Years)*; O. Chiladze, *I vsiakii, kto vstretitsia so mnoi (And Everybody Who Meets Me)*.[31] All these works depicted, in one way or another, the historical events that influenced the human consciousness.

---

30. Piskunov, "Avtoritet istorii" p. 85. The titles of several books written at that time reflected the same preoccupation with time: *Ne perevodia dykhaniia (Without pausing for breath)* by I. Erenburg, *Vremia vpered! (Time Forward!)* by V. Kataev, *Temp (Tempo)* by N. Pogodin, *V griadushche (Days to come)* by E. Charents, and *Veka i minuty (The Centuries and Minutes)* by H. Taktash.

31. Piskunov, "Avtoritet istorii," pp. 88–89.

The authorities in the administration of cultural policies continued to encourage the writers and artists to safeguard the principles of socialist realism. Literary historians wrote often about the various aspects and stages of development of this doctrine. In 1987 a collection of studies and articles was published discussing this art doctrine: *O partiinosti literatury. Sotsialisticheskii realism: Khudozhestvennyi opyt i teoriia*.[32] Included in this book was the study of G. Berdnikov elucidating the historic First Congress of Soviet Writers in 1934. Berdnikov wrote in great detail about the participation of Soviet writers at the conference and the topics that were discussed. He also acknowledged the presence at the Congress of a number of prominent writers from the West. He discussed the emergence of the doctrine of socialist realism and declared the Soviet multinational literature as "the child of socialist realism."[33]

Soviet writers and artists were urged to follow the established practice of continuous ideological awareness. After each congress of the Communist Party, the writers' and artists' unions scheduled their own meetings or even congresses to discuss the new resolutions and methods of implementing the Party's recommendations.

True to this practice, the 8th Writers' Congress took place in June of 1986. The aim of this Congress was to evaluate the current issues of literary and political life. The conclusions reached by the 27th Congress of the Communist Party were discussed, and, at the same time, the writers extended their support for the restructuring process and the fulfillment of the twelfth Five-Year Plan.

The opening report at the 8th Writers' Congress was delivered by Georgii M. Markov, its longtime secretary. His report, under the characteristic title, "Nikogda ne otgorazhivat'sia ot trevog sovremennogo mira, ot zhizni naroda" ("Never turn away from the worries of the contemporary world, life of the people"), presented a detailed analysis of the current state of Soviet literature and its future goals. The report was published subsequently in a book containing a collection of related articles dealing with the art doctrine of socialist realism.[34]

---

32. G. Gudozhnik and A. Romanov, Eds., Moscow: Khudozhestvennaia literatura, 1986, pp. 4–44.

33. G. Berdnikov, "Pod znameniem leninskih idei," *O partiinosti literatury*, p. 62.

34. *O partiinosti literatury. Sotsialisticheskii realism: Hudozhestvennyi opyt i teoriia*, pp. 4–44.

Markov noted the widespread support for the newly established course of the Party that was directed toward accelerating social and economic development. The historic decisions reached by the Congress were also addressed by the writers who made serious propositions concerning the future obligations. The political report of the Central Committee invited the participation of writers and suggested the following guidelines:

> "The moral health of the society, the spiritual climate permeating the life of the people, is determined to a great degree by the conditions that prevail in literature and the fine arts. Our literature, reflecting the new world, at the same time participated in its formation, shaping the man of this world—the patriot, and equally, the true internationalist. Thus, literature has chosen its own place and its role in the general aspirations of the people. Yet, these criteria are also used by the people and Party to evaluate the works of writers and artists, the literature itself, and the fine arts." [35]

Markov thought that writers had as their most important task the nurturing of spiritual life. In addition, writers should help in the restructuring *(perestroika)* of people's thinking and their attitudes toward daily work, strengthening their abilities for organization and discipline. The literary works, produced during the last few years, aimed to express in a new and truthful manner the complexities, drama, and grandeur of the contemporary life of the people, although this was a goal that was hard to reach. Yet, the best works pointed to the changes in the Soviet society and thus anticipated the ideological position which the Party eventually chose.[36]

Writers were aware of many shortcomings in the every day reality of Soviet life. Literary works often described undesirable aspects and difficulties, the social and moral problems. A number of well written novels, stories, poems, and theatrical plays dealt with these issues. Eventually, these negative occurrences came to the center of public attention. Markov noted that Soviet writers, from various republics, wrote about existing inadequacies in order to wake up the public consciousness. In addition, book production and other literary activities were noticeably increased after the Plenum of the Communist Party in April of 1985.[37]

---

35. Materialy XXVII Congress of the Soviet Communist Party, Moscow, 1986; quoted after G. M. Markov, "Nikogda ne otgorazhivat'sia," *Sotsialisticheskii realizm: khudozhestvennyi opyt i teoriia,* Moscow, 1987, p. 4.

36. Markov, "Nikogda . . .," p. 5.

37. Markov, "Nikogda . . .," p. 6.

However, during the last few years, readers have complained about the dullness of many new literary works. In addition, these new prose and poetic works discussed mainly negative phenomena; there was no initiative to rectify the situation. Although Markov believed that Soviet literature abounded with talents, the new works did not succeed in creating remarkable literary heroes; the example set by the previous generation of Soviet writers was not followed, and the current literary works did not portray positive heroes in the manner of the Soviet classicists. Markov reminded the writers that these problems had been discussed before, during the 7th Writers Congress in 1981. The previous artificial embellishment of reality *(lakirovka deistvitel'nosti)*, might have spurred the opposite tendencies and preoccupation with negative occurrences at the present stage. The absence of the positive literary heroes *(otsustviia polozhitel'nykh literaturnykh geroev)* was declared pernicious. The new literary works did not change this situation to a substantial degree.[38]

It seemed as if the dividing line between real literature and pseudo-literature was disappearing. The critics apparently had lost their objectivity and praised equally the works of very different ideological and artistic values.[39] Unfortunately, the new and unusual works of talented writers often have to wait for a long time to be published. The editors, unsure of the quality of such works, asked for additional reviews in order to be able to make up their minds. On the other hand, the standardized works, those that followed the beaten path, continued to crowd the pages of journals. Markov encouraged the critics to take the risk and constructively help the writers by affirming the new works that merited attention.

Most of all, Markov admonished fellow members of the Writers' Union to respond to the requests of the Party's leadership: members should apply consistently the creative method of socialist realism and try to elevate the ideological and literary qualities of their works. Writers should be in close touch with the life of the people in order to be able to influence the life itself. Markov reminded that the challenges of the time, current events, and the intuitive voice of the people's consciousness, remained invariably the eternal quests for writers to pursue.[40]

Markov pointed out, with just pride, that currently eighty-six monthly journals were published according to the schedule, in addition to sixteen

38. Markov, "Nikogda . . .," pp. 24–25.

39. Markov, "Nikogda . . .," p. 6.

40. Markov, "Nikogda . . .," p. 7.

literary magazines that appeared once in a year, with a combined circulation of over twelve and one half million copies. The publishing house of the Writers' Union alone published five hundred titles yearly, with a circulation of five million copies. About one third of the published books presented translations from various languages of the USSR.

In assessing the present achievements of Soviet literature, Markov singled out the Russian contemporary novel, the Russian historical-revolutionary novel, and the Russian story. The critics wrote, with good reason, about the rise of the historical novel. This genre was favored by a large number of devoted readers and the following writers of historical novels were gaining in importance: D. Balashov, P. Zagrebel'nyi, T. Kaipbergenov, O. Chiladze, I. Guseinov, Ia. Kross, V. Chivilikhin, among others. Latvian writers excelled in theatrical plays and enjoyed great popularity among the theatergoers. The writers in the Ukraine, Georgia, Azerbaidjan, and Moldavia, Markov thought, produced remarkable achievements. All these literary works encompassed a variety of genres: from the strict documentary prose to the realm of the free literary fantasies.[41]

The literary critic Aleksandr Alekseevich Ninov also attended the 8th Writers' Congress and wrote afterward a review paper. Ninov noticed primarily the sincerity and frankness of the speakers during the conference. Such an attitude was unusual at large gatherings where everything seemed to be staged beforehand according to the accepted rituals and regulations. Ninov stressed that the outspoken discourse did not present always the ultimate truth of the matter, or deep evaluation of important and vital issues. However, a candid and outspoken communication constituted one of the essential elements of truthfulness, insight, and persuasiveness of any statement. Last but not least, the outspoken word defined its speaker with a fair measure of truth. This fact in itself was as important as the issues that were discussed.[42]

Dissatisfaction with the current literary criticism, as practiced by Soviet critics, was often cited in papers read at the Writers' Congresses, and in the ensuing discussions. The speakers discussed the deficiencies of the Soviet literary criticism, analyzing its moral and ethical content, its

---

41. Markov, "Nikogda . . .," p. 14.

42. Aleksandr Ninov, "Tri uslovia kritiki," *Skvoz tridtsat' let,* Leningrad, Sovetskii pisatel', 1987, p. 438.

polemical spirit and language. Such criticism did not generate a deeply felt influence on either the writers or the reading public.

In order to remedy the situation in the field of literary criticism, Ninov suggested a closer scrutiny of the study of Soviet literature as presented in authoritative textbooks at the university level. He reasoned that the body of knowledge contained in the scholastic literary curricula should establish the foundation of objective criticism. However, many textbooks were inadequate and far from providing an objective evaluation of many literary figures, past and present.

As an example, Ninov singled out the literary textbook *Istoriia russkoi sovetskoi literatury (History of Russian Soviet Literature)* edited by P. S. Vykhodtsev, and published by the textbook publisher Vysshaia shkola. Ninov discussed the third and fourth editions of this textbook issued in 1979 and 1986, respectively. The book represented a collective effort of a group of prominent literary specialists headed by Vykhodtsev, and was duly approved by the Ministry of Education of USSR. This book was used by students majoring in Russian language and literature. Several generations of young critics have been educated using this voluminous *History*. However, upon a closer examination, Ninov thought that the third edition of the *History* had serious shortcomings. He compared, at first, the sparse and unjustified commentaries concerning four major poets: Anna Akhmatova, Marina Tsvetaeva, Osip Mandel'shtam, and Boris Pasternak. These poets were declared to be "individualists," unaware of the social realities of Soviet life, alienated from the major achievements of their epoch. Therefore, their literary work was lacking in real and significant content, by propagating "anti-democratic and reactionary ideas."[43]

In the mentioned third edition of the *History* these poets were discussed together with an older poet, Fedor Sologub, as if these poets did not show major differences in their respective creative contributions. Most important, Sologub was a symbolist, whose works were published in the 1890s; he belonged in time and spirit to another stylistic period of the Russian poetry.

On the other hand, Akhmatova, Tsvetaeva, Mandel'shtam, and Pasternak became well known after the October revolution. In spite of the many upheavals and the complexities of a difficult social reality, these poets ascertained themselves, in time, as major literary figures. In recent years the poems of these illustrious artists have been repeatedly published

---

43. Ninov, "Tri usloviia kritiki," p. 452.

in the series *Biblioteka poeta,* and other editions. Their poetry was read and broadcasted on radio programs. Well-known actors have recited their poetry, and it was recorded on records. However, both editions of the *History of Russian Soviet Literature* seemed unaware of the steadily growing affirmation of the literary legacy of these fine poets.

The fourth edition of 1986 brought a slight correction of the previous statements concerning the four poets. Sologub and Mandel'shtam remained grouped together "with some other poets" as representatives of "individualism," sharing a backward social and aesthetic viewpoint. The name of Marina Tsvetaeva was not mentioned in this context. Instead, the poetic work of Tsvetaeva was completely omitted in the main volume of the *History.* Her contribution was briefly mentioned in the manual *(posobiia),* although her work merited a more propitious treatment. The fourth edition still lacked special chapters dedicated to prominent writers such as M. Bulgakov, A. Platonov, I. Erenburg, V. Kataev. The following writers were only briefly discussed, as if they were of minor importance: M. Zoshchenko, S. Marshak, Iu. Tynianov, L. Panteleev, V. Panova, Iu Trifonov. In addition, E. Shwarts, a fine and original writer and dramatist, was completely omitted.[44]

Ninov thought that the historic and aesthetic criteria presented in the *History* were, in many cases, distorted and dated. Both editions, declared on the title page to have been "improved and enlarged", when in fact they were anachronous with the current level of literary comprehension of critics and readers. These editions lagged some twenty-five to thirty years behind the present state of research.[45]

However, Ninov's outspoken criticism of Vykhodtsev's textbook on Russian literature prompted a polemical answer. The journal *Molodaia gvardiia* published in 1988 a review of Vykhodtsev's book that aimed to establish, on a broader level, the importance of continuity in Soviet cultural policies. According to the writers of the review, A. Ognev and A. Red'kin, Vykhodtsev's book offered a valid effort to safeguard the established points of view. It should be noted that both Ognev and Red'kin were graduates of the Philological College and recipients of doctoral and candidate degrees, respectively. Although Ninov's name was not

---

44. Ninov, "Tri usloviia kritiki," pp. 452–453.

45. Ninov, "Tri usloviia kritiki," p. 451.

mentioned, the reviewers aimed to refute some of the issues raised by Ninov.[46]

The reviewers stated the importance of preserving the fundamental literary and artistic values as established during the past seventy years of Soviet government. At the present time of increased Western propaganda, and the rising appearances of "rockers," "breakers," undesirable attitudes and discordances, it was important to remind Soviet youth of solid Soviet literary achievements. Therefore, textbooks for courses at the university level should safeguard, most of all, the established ideological postulates. The reviewers thought that the improved and enlarged fourth edition of the textbook, *History of Russian Soviet Literature* by P. S. Vykhodtsev, fulfilled such a task. The textbook presented well the most important Russian and Soviet writers and their works, and the national literary tradition and development of stylistic trends and genres.

The *History of Russian Soviet Literature* was written in compliance with the established programs for literary textbooks for universities. It was tested in the classrooms at the various Soviet universities while teaching the students. The *History* was acknowledged as a reliable textbook. However, the reviewers stated that due to the established curriculum, some writers and their works have received insufficient attention. The works of O. Mandel'shtam, M. Bulgakov, A. Akhmatova, B. Pasternak have not been discussed at length. The commentaries about these writers were precise and well defined, although briefly stated.

In addition, there remained the unresolved questions of writers I. Bunin, M. Tsvetaeva, V. Nabokov, and their literary works written in emigration, after the October revolution. The reviewers thought that, perhaps, the time had come to plan a separate textbook of Russian emigre literature. Thus, the reviewers raised another possibility in the classification of Russian literature. Their suggestion would establish two categories comprising writers who live or lived in Soviet Union, and as a separate entity Russian writers who lived abroad.

Such an approach would present a belated acknowledgment of several prominent writers who have been, in the not so distant past, unjustly ignored or slighted by Soviet literary historians. This narrow minded attitude harmed and impoverished the Soviet society and its literary fund. Many millions of readers were deprived of valuable literary accounts of

---

46. A. Ognev, and V. Red'kin, "Chetkost' pozitsii," *Molodaia Gvardiia*, 1988, No. 5, p. 280.

profound explorations of human life in all its versatility. Several of these literary works presented unique testimonies of historical events contributing to the better understanding of times gone by. The expatriate Russian writers continued their literary work with great dedication. They searched for fulfillment and inner peace in spite of the hardship of emigration which took its own special toll.

The reviewers pointed to the validity of additional chapters that have been added by Vykhodtsev in the fourth edition of the *History*. Thus, new attention was bestowed on the village poetry written in the period from 1917 to 1920. The poetry of Nikolai Kliuev, a close friend of Sergei Esenin, was introduced in one of these chapters. The passage of time has brought the necessary corrections of former omissions and the just inclusion of Kliuev's contribution into the national culture.[47]

The reviewers concluded that Vykhodtsev's literary textbook presented the Soviet youth with moral issues as well, teaching them about life and ethical points of view, observed from a vantage point of literary development. Such a healthy influence, based on true values, was much needed to counterbalance the restitution of long forgotten works permeated with individualism. The reviewer declared the exaggerated interest for such shelved works as a form of 'necrophilia'.[48]

In spite of justifications of Vykhodtsev's selections and methods of presenting several Russian and Soviet writers, Ognev and Red'kin also pointed to several shortcomings in Vykhodtsev's textbook. In fact, the reviewers discussed mainly the issues raised previously by Ninov, thus supporting, although indirectly, the validity of Ninov's conclusions. In addition, their explanation established the existing concordance of Vykhodtsev's textbook with the approved teaching plans. Hence, possible omissions were explained as part of the obviously dated, yet officially sanctioned literary classification.

In September of 1988, two articles dealing with the interpretation of the theory of socialist realism were published in the journal *Novyi mir:* E. Sergeev wrote a lengthy article under the title *"Neskol'ko zastarelykh voprosov"* (A few inveterate questions), and A. Gangnus summed up his thoughts in his article *"Na ruinakh pozitivnoi estetiki"* (On the ruins of the positive aesthetic). The writers of these articles departed from the usual positive assessments of the theory of socialist realism and voiced serious

47. Ognev and Red'kin, "Chetkost' . . . ," p. 282.
48. Ognev and Red'kin, "Chetkost' . . .," p. 280.

concerns. The Editors of *Novyi Mir* thought it necessary to provide a short introductory explanation with the statement of their own evaluation of these articles, stressing that they did not agree entirely with the points of views of the two authors. However, they considered the publication of the articles useful in view of the recent polemical discussion challenging the theory of socialist realism as the official doctrine. Very likely, in order to minimize the impact of the overall negative critical evaluation of the merits of socialist realism, these articles were published in the section dealing with journalistic topics.[49]

Nevertheless, the willingness of the editors to provide a forum for an open-minded discussion of the official art doctrine confirmed the continuation of the liberal policies of this journal. This policy was established at first by the writer Aleksandr Tvardovskii, in the course of the 1950s and 1960s, during his tenure as the chief editor of the journal *Novyi mir* was hailed as the leader of these changes and the outspoken attitude has persisted, to varying degrees, ever since.

In his article Sergeev pointed out that the theory of socialist realism lagged behind literary development causing concern among writers and critics alike. Serious criticism of this theory was discussed, for a long time, by word of mouth and remained unpublished. However, in 1988 further discussions and questioning of the specific values of socialist realism appeared in printed form in several journals such as *Oktiabr'* and *Literaturnaia gazeta*.

On the other hand, the theory of socialist realism, according to the *Literaturnyi entsiklopedicheskii slovar' (Literary encyclopedic dictionary)*, still acknowledged the importance of advancing progressive tendencies and accepted moral norms in literary works. The portraying of a positive hero continued to be mandatory in the creations of Soviet writers. Sergeev quoted a characteristic passage from the *Literary encyclopedic dictionary* stressing the importance of such a hero: "by creating the role of the positive hero, the literature projects the goals of the societal development and the road for its fulfillment," (*"sozdavaia obraz polozhitel' nogo geroia, literatura raskryvaet tseli obshchestvennogo razvitia i puti ikh dostizhenii"*). Sergeev obviously thought such a requirement was an outdated policy, although the dictionary as the authoritative reference book of literary studies published as recently as 1987, presented the latest status of the Soviet literary thought.

---

49. *Novyi mir*, 1988, No. 9, p. 142.

Soviet prose and drama depicted, indeed, a whole gallery of positive heroes. These personages were smart, possessed impeccable moral qualities, high principles, and work ethics, and were capable of making sacrifices for the good of others. Such were the heroes in *Pozhar* by Rasputin, *Plaha* by Aitmatov, *Pechal'nyi detektiv* by V. Astaf'ev, *Belyie odezhdy* by V. Dudintsev, and *Deti Arbata* by A. Rybakov.[50]

However, many literary works portrayed similar personages in a monotonous and uniform fashion. These literary characters acted often as a mouthpiece of the administration by propagating the officially sanctioned and accepted ideas. At certain historic intervals, literary works mirrored the changes brought in by new officials, as well as policies that were subsequently introduced and hailed as progressive. The dialogues and monologues in such works had a declarative character, advancing the absolutization of the supreme power. Sergeev thought that this model of power projected historical analogies with the epoches of absolutism of Ivan the Terrible and Peter I. Therefore, he thought, socialist realism should be more justly described as *administrative* rather than *socialist* due to its true character.

During the 1930s the method of socialist realism stood, in fact, closer to classicism than to the realistic style. There existed a rigid hierarchy of genres and themes: the ode was considered more elevated than the satire, or the intimate, introspective lyric. The literary themes inspired by extraordinary public events of national importance were preferred over stories of personal life; the incidents of an ordinary human life were declared to be insignificant and petty.[51] The ideal goal seemed to be the subordination of personal interests to the higher goals of the societal and public life. Sergeev posed the question: Who should be in charge of formulating the social ideals of a given historical period? Should it be the role of the artist to map the road of a people, by projecting their grievances and hopes? Perhaps, this should be the role of the sociologist and social scientist, who scrupulously investigated all the parameters of the contemporary society. Finally, such a task could also be the lot of the administrator, who is in charge of "the official position on the ideological front."[52]

---

50. E. Sergeev, "Neskol'ko zastarelyh voprosov," p. 143.

51. Sergeev, "Neskol'ko . . .," p. 145.

52. Sergeev, "Neskol'ko . . .," p. 146.

Sergeev concluded, in a conciliatory mood, that he would not like to suggest that the theory of socialist realism be forbidden or abolished, it would suffice to cancel its position as the official doctrine. The prohibition never amounted to anything, be it in the science, or in the arts.[53]

A. Gangnus in his paper "Na ruinakh pozitivnoi estetiki" discussed the emergence of the doctrine of socialist realism during the 1920s and 1930s. In his assessment of this doctrine, Gangnus thought that socialist realism did not embody an aesthetic system or creative method. Socialist realism presented a concealed religion, which supported the existence of Stalin's empire. The ministers of this religion were the officiating artists, writers, and musicians. However, the absence of talent or even of the elementary culture was not a barrier for a "creative career." It was important to fulfill the obligations, and the loyalty and devotion did not help if the desired goal was not faithfully upheld. On the other hand, talented writers, artists, and musicians were eliminated without explanation if they did not understand the importance of conformity.[54]

Gangnus discussed the input of several theoreticians of this doctrine in the course of its introduction to society, during the 1920s and early 1930s. The acceptance of party ideology *(partiinost')*, as the guiding spirit was one of the important requirements of the theory and method of socialist realism. Lenin was credited with the creation of the concept and terminology of this principle. However, Krupskaia repeatedly tried to explain Lenin's understanding of the role of literature. She argued that the identification of literature with the goals of the Party referred only, in Lenin's mind, to the political literature such as various articles and pamphlets serving the needs of the Party as a much needed propaganda.[55] Therefore, Gangnus thought that Lunacharskii misunderstood Lenin's definition of *partiinost' literatury*. Lunacharskii confused the role of the literature, and fine arts, with the engaged role of journalistic literature in political disputes, at one historical point in time.

The solution to the existing problems Gangnus saw in the free and open creative explorations of artists and scientists alike. False promises and deceptions must be abandoned in order to find a cure from the ills of the theory of positive aesthetics, and from the subjective demonism of the "philosophy of struggle." One should not forget the piles of useless books,

---

53. Sergeev, "Neskol'ko . . .," p. 146.

54. A. Gangnus, "Na ruinakh pozitivnoi estetiki," *Novyi mir*, 1988, No. 9, p. 149.

55. Gangnus, "Na ruinakh . . .," p. 158.

sculptures, and diligently painted canvases, so that these conditions never develop again.[56]

The new openness and the free, polemical spirit were supported by many writers and public figures of Soviet society at large. The literature written in 1980s reflected well the aspirations toward a more open exchange of ideas. The rising importance of journalistic writing was influenced by this new spirit of openness. Many writers turned their attention to journalistic genres since they believed that well intended criticism would help the renewal of society. The subjects of agronomy, economy, ecology, pedagogy, morality, literature, mass media, light music, urban planning, as well as other topics of public interest, were discussed on the pages of *Pravda, Izvestiia, Komsomol'skaia pravda, Trud, Literaturnaia gazeta, Sovetskaia kul'tura*, and others.

Furthermore, the inclusion of the previously censored chapters of Russian and Soviet culture became the prevailing tendency in the literary fabric of the 1980s. The writers strove for an ideal union of the past achievements with the present unfoldment, *sviaz vremeni,* the bridging of the present with the past. The revision of the historical and literary repositories helped the reinstatement of the many concealed and even obliterated faces of Russian and Soviet culture. In addition, the appreciation of the treasury of Asiatic cultures was renewed. Velemir Khlebnikov was acclaimed again as an outstanding poet who was among the first to recognize the submerged Asiatic layer of the Russian culture.[57]

The poignant question raised by the writer Iu. Trifonov, "Do we need to remember?" prompted definite, affirmative answers. Trifonov formulated this question in his novel *Vremia i mesto (Time and Place)* while pondering the necessity of reviewing an epoch of the not so distant past. As the bitterness of years passed, it seemed to him that all the injustice must be remembered, since facts should not be suppressed. Otherwise, it would mean that the Soviet literary thought lacked the courage by pretending that things which occurred "never really happened." Many literary works for a long time suppressed and unpublished, nonexistent in the Soviet literary fund, were introduced and favorably

---

56. Gangnus, "Na ruinakh . . .," p. 163.

57. A. Baigushev, "Opyt sozdaniia," *Molodaia gvardiia,* No. 12, 1988, pp. 234–235. Compare also A. Ninov, "Mikhail Bulgakov i sovetskaia khudozhestvennaia kul'tura," *Skvoz tridtsat' let,* pp. 422–437.

received by enthralled audiences. The numerous public readings, *chtenia,* of such neglected masterpieces became literary events of the 1980s.

The assurance that national and international cultures were achieving a measure of universality instigated a number of meetings of people in literature, science, and art worldwide. Many of these meetings were dedicated to the questions of international cooperation, ecology, nuclear power, and the fostering of sciences and fine arts. Such was the Issyk Kul Forum organized by Chingiz Aitmatov in Kirghizia in 1986. Among the participants from the West were the writers Arthur Miller, James Baldwin, Alexander King, Claude Simon, Yashar Kemal, Frederico Mayor, and the philosopher Alvin Toffler. Again the writers were raising their voices to protect the humankind from many existing problems. Aitmatov and the participants of the Forum believed that human life had absolute value in the same way that civilization in general had absolute value. It should be the duty of everyone to safeguard what humankind has developed over millennia:

"There are less than 5,000 days left until the end of the century and the beginning of the next millennium. Crises of a global nature and unprecedented complexity threaten the future of the human race. Undoubtedly, other more difficult problems will arise that cannot be solved by individual countries and which will require a completely new approach . . . . That is why we—writers, artists and scholars—have come here to lake Issyk Kul in Kirghizia in order to state ... our faith in human genius and its creative powers. Since the world is changing rapidly, and traditional institutions are becoming outmoded, all of us should be involved in seeking new solutions to our common problems." [58]

The closing of the 1980s reflected the courageous determination among men of letters to take part in the formation of the future. The survival of humankind will require imagination and profound understanding of the numerous problems. The writers, most of all, accentuated the need for freedom to be able "to create, to spread and teach new ways of thinking," in order to accomplish what had been thought impossible. The bold fantasies about the future of the planet were already depicted in some outstanding literary works. The joint missions of the astronauts and cosmonauts, guarding the planet, have already taken place in the novel *I*

---

58. Ch. Aitmatov, "We said what we thought," *The time to speak out*, Moscow, Progress, 1988, pp. 276–279.

dol'she veka dlitsia den' (The day lasts more than hundred years) by Chingiz Aitmatov.

The tradition of many great Russian writers, acting as the collective consciousness of their generations, seems to have taken place again raising the hope for the peaceful future of the mankind. The approaching new millennium was dubbed appropriately as the "Century of the Planet" and at the same time as the "Century of Creativity".[59]

The Soviet literary thought of the 1980s is emerging with a viable commitment to personal freedom and dignity transcending the imposed political and cultural isolation. The writers were seeking an equilibrium between the national and universal aspirations in the wish to join the mainstream of human thought.

---

59. Aitmatov, "We said . . ., p. 279.

CHAPTER VI

MUSIC AND MUSICAL LIFE IN THE USSR:
THE RISE OF GLASNOST 1960–1980

The changes in the Soviet political and social viewpoints during the 1960s spurred innovations in many areas of cultural endeavors, in particular in the literary and artistic productions. The relaxation in the doctrine of socialist realism allowed for a greater freedom of expression and a fresh examination of creative aspirations. The more liberal artistic policy enabled also a gradual revaluation of the previously censored yet notable musical works of the past. However, these changes did not instigate a radical break with the ruling doctrine of socialist realism. In the musical field the composers tried to achieve an enrichment of the existing ideological and artistic concepts. Gradually, the broadening of established views became apparent in the thematic scope of newly composed works, in the choice of musical forms, and modes of musical expression.

The Third Composers' Congress convened in March of 1962. The composer Tikhon Khrennikov, the secretary of the Composers' Union, pointed out in his report the maturing of important societal processes helping the consolidation in the musical scene. In spite of some positive development, the stagnation in many areas of the musical milieu was apparent. The prevailing backwardness of the musical repertoire and lack of creativity in many newly composed works became the topics of several discussions during this Congress. The proliferation of a stereotyped compositional style and insufficient command of the musical metier caused serious concern. All these shortcomings led to the appearance of monotonous, grey and inexpressive works.[1]

During the war- and postwar years the composers elucidated often enough the historic events touching the lives of the Soviet population at

---

1. G. V. Kon'kova, "Nekotorye tendentsii razvitiia sovetskoi muzyki 60–70-kh godov", *Muzykal'naia kul'tura bratskikh respublik SSSR,* Kiev, Muzichna Ukraina, 1982, p. 4.

large. Accordingly, the patriotic themes prevailed in the vocal and instrumental compositions, and many symphonic works were commissioned to commemorate historic events of the recent past. For such occasions, the composers chose frequently programmatic titles for their works in order to highlight the evocative spirit of these festive performances. The thematic duality, inherent in the symphonic form, was well suited to underline the dialectical dimension of the main theme of the composition and support the title of the symphony, if such was indicated. The symphonic works were preferred for such celebrations and considered as the highest forms of instrumental music attaining a supreme position in the hierarchy of genres.

In the course of time, the symphonic works revealed more and more the immediate, individual concerns and the unresolved personal quests facing the composer as well as his fellow man. The heroic themes celebrating the victories of the Great Patriotic War became less common in musical works, and other thematic circles were explored. The symphonic method and heroic themes became less prominent but not altogether forgotten.

During the 1960s and later on, the Soviet composers felt the need for advancement of the compositional technique and for the exploration of the wealth of musical achievements developed elsewhere. A number of composers aspired, most of all, for a broader interpretation of the national musical style.[2] Previously, the main criterion in assessing a new musical piece was whether it contained canonized harmonic and rhythmic formulas and well known folk tunes. The new interpretation of the national style differed from the previous stilted approach and encouraged new creative solutions. The emphasis was shifting towards modality and non triadic tones instead of triadic harmony, tonality, phrase and period structure. The melodic invention was sustained by rhythmic vitality of changing meters and asymmetrical harmonic phrases. The composers felt that these innovations helped the creative imagination and enhanced the individual musical expression.

The musical practice elsewhere proved that the issues and challenges facing the composers, could be expressed well without the application of the symphonic method. The early classical, and baroque concerto, in particular, attracted lively attention and produced a renewed proliferation

---

2. Kon'kova, "Nekotorye tendentsii . . .," p. 6.

of this genre. Many composers around the world preferred the lively dialogue of the concerto form since it encompassed a wealth of possibilities and changing modes of expression. Soviet composers showed also a great affinity for the musical forms of the early classical, and baroque era. The evolving neoclassical style helped to speed up the break with exaggerated emotionality that bordered in some compositions with sentimentality.[3] Previously, the musical style of the commissioned compositions helped to establish an academic, official and pompous musical language, using often large vocal and instrumental bodies. The neoclassical idiom was juxtaposed to the saturation of expressive means as elements of the demoted "academism" in music writing.

Moreover, the neoclassical tendency in Soviet music brought forth the needed correction in the process of stylistic clarification, displaying an objective and measured projection of the contents, lucid melodic inflections and simplified means of expression. A number of well known Soviet composers turned their attention to the conceptual aspects of the concerto form. The concerto even influenced other genres such as the symphony, compositions for chamber ensembles, and musical works for the stage. The composers introduced gradually the semantics of the contemporary musical language allowing a variety of compositional methods, while the essence of the sonata form and of the symphonic principle were maintained. Finally, the evolving changes facilitated the introduction of a newly found simplicity of the symphonic idiom. Interestingly enough, the compositions written in the concerto or symphonic form showed often a tendency for the synthesis of these two genres.

In retrospect, the role of Igor Stravinsky in the crystallization of the neoclassical orientation of Soviet music should be pronounced as decisive. After Stravinsky's official visit to the Soviet Union in October of 1962, his former status as an emigre composer hostile to the Soviet government was revaluated. Stravinsky knew that his name had been previously abused in the Soviet Union, yet he decided to accept the invitation primarily due to the evidence of a genuine need for him by the younger generation of Soviet musicians. Nostalgia had no part in the visit, Stravinsky posited, he wanted to offer a helping hand.

---

3. A. N. Utkin, "Kontsertirovanie kak muzikal'no-dramaturgicheskii metod," *Stilevye tendentsii v sovetskoi muzyke 1960–1970-kh godov,* Leningrad, Leningradskii gosudarstvenyi institut teatra, muzyki i kinematografii, 1979, pp. 64 –72.

During this visit, Stravinsky, in his conversations with the young Soviet composers, spoke about new compositional methods, and serial music. He also spoke about the past musical periods and his admiration for J. S. Bach, S. I. Taneev, and the art of counterpoint. He stressed his lifelong identification with the Russian culture and its landmarks. The journey to the places of his youth was a delightful experience: Stravinsky admired anew the classical beauty of the famous edifices of Leningrad, the surrounding countryside with the ubiquitous birch tree swaying its delicate branches. The Union of Soviet Composers arranged several festive meetings and Stravinsky was even invited to the Kremlin for an audience with Khrushchev.

Stravinsky's visit and the renewal of professional ties hastened the final acceptance of his oeuvre. Thus, his compositions, previously not performed in USSR, were gradually introduced and featured in concert-and operatic performances.

A number of Soviet composers and musicologists turned their attention to Stravinsky's impressive compositional output. Stravinsky's compositions indicated, most of all, his acceptance of the manifold influences of the musical past. In particular, the influence of the baroque era in Stravinsky's work was analyzed, and in turn, his example spurred the explorations of the baroque music by Soviet composers during the 1960s and later on.

Several Soviet musicologists evaluated the influence exerted by the compositions of Igor Stravinsky. The musicologist A. N. Utkin devoted a lengthy and well documented study to this topic stressing the importance of Stravinsky's acceptance of the baroque legacy. Stravinsky accomplished, Utkin posited, the synthesis of the concerto and partita genres. This much admired innovation was embodied most of all in his *Violin concerto*. Stravinsky's unique approach proved to be very appealing and the new concerto form became widespread in the course of time. During the late 1960s and later on the Soviet composers wrote often orchestral compositions using the elements of the concerto merged with the partita. The *Partita for violoncello and chamber orchestra* by Boris Chaikovskii could serve as an example of such creative efforts. The influence of partita was also present in several instrumental concertos such as the *Violin concerto* by Iu. Falik, and in the *Concerto for piano* by Ia. Riaets.[4]

---

4. Utkin, "Kontsertirovanie . . .," p. 74.

Furthermore, Stravinsky introduced a new concept of orchestration as an additional enhancement of the musical content. His clever selection and usage of instruments accentuated the boldness of the musical expression, and remained to exert a lasting influence. The composer Iu. Falik, was strongly impressed by Stravinsky's instrumentation of *The Soldier's Story*. Subsequently, Stravinsky's adept use of instrumental colors left its imprint, most of all, in Falik's musical score *Skomorokh (The Minstrel)*. Stravinsky's well known *Octet,* one of the earliest works in the neoclassical style, inspired the writing of a number of compositions. The *Second Chamber Symphony* by R. Gabichvadze, was prompted by the famous *Octet,* most of all by its cohesive instrumental dialogue.[5]

Among musical forms from the baroque era introduced into the Soviet music during the 1960s, the toccata had a widespread influence. Previously, during the early decades of the twentieth century, the toccata principle influenced the neoclassical compositional style in the formal and semantic aspects. Stravinsky's *Rite of Spring,* Prokof'ev's *Skith's Suite,* and Bartok's *Allegro Barbaro* connected the toccata with the theme of barbarism, the myth about the Skiths, and the archaic musical language.[6] It is intersting to note that the poet Aleksandr Blok wrote a poem about the Skiths, their primeval strength and the speeding-up of time in the fight to catch up with the development in the West.

Stravinsky associated the toccata form, at first, with the magic incantations, primeval barbarism and archaism. Later, in his music of the neoclassical style the toccata embodied the brisk, motoric movement of the baroque music. Rodion Shchedrin used the toccata form in several compositions modelled after Stravinsky's toccata concepts. Shchedrin eventually assimilated both aspects of the toccata interpretation. He defined the archaism and magical incantations as the expression of the heightened puls of life, and dynamism of the contemporary epoch. Therefore, he construed the figurative, motoric elements of the baroque with the sharp dissonant accents. Boris Chaikovskii understood the toccata movement most of all as a living connection with the distant, historical sources.[7]

---

5. Utkin, "Kontsertirovanie . . .," pp. 75–76.

6. Utkin, "Kontsertirovanie . . .," p. 77.

7. Utkin, "Kontsertirovanie . . .," pp. 5 –7.

On the other hand, in Shostakovich's tragic works toccata became the symbol of the mode of aggression and destruction. Boris Tishchenko, a former student of Shostakovich, understood the toccata in the same negative sense — witness the toccata movements in his very successful *First cello concerto*, and similarly in the *Concerto for flute and piano*. The sinfonia concertante was another neobaroque form used by Soviet composers. This formal concept stressed the lively instrumental dialogue and the concerto spirit of the whole orchestral score, with a lesser emphasis on the role of solo instruments. As an example of the sinfonia concertante could serve the *Sinfonia Robusta* by Boris Tishchenko, full of festive energy and sparkling instrumental virtuosity.

In addition to the return of Stravinsky's compositions the seldom performed and almost forgotten works of Prokof'ev as well as Shostakovich were "discovered" again, and slowly introduced in the concert halls and compositional curricula. The musicologist G. Sh. Ordzhonikidze remembered the scarcity of sources regarding the compositional output of Sergei Prokof'ev in the early 1950s. As a student at the Moscow Conservatory, he became interested in Prokof'ev's work, but was unable to find in the book-stores a single monograph or scholarly article concerning Prokof'ev's works. Many years later, in the atmosphere of the new openness, he wrote about this infamous situation of apparent neglect of Prokof'ev's musical legacy.[8]

Eventually, in the course of the 1960s and later on, the complete works of Sergei Prokof'ev were returned to the musical fond. His role was declared as essential for the new path promulgating many innovations. The works of both Stravinsky and Prokof'ev were often discussed while discerning their individual creative personalities and their respective affinities towards the musical heritage. Stravinsky's oeuvre testified to the propitious influence of the musical past, most of all of the baroque era. In Prokof'ev's compositional approach, the clarity of the classical musical idiom was appreciated distinguishing both the role of the composer and the musical tradition that inspired him.[9]

The Ukrainian composers Evgenii Stankovich was influenced to a great extent by Prokof'ev's distinctive musical language. Prokof'ev's short and

---

8. G. Sh. Ordzhonikidze, "I. Nest'ev — uchenyi, kritik, publitsist," in I. V. Nest'ev, *Vek nyneshnii i vek minuvshii,* Moscow, Sovetskii kompozitor, 1986, p. 3.

9. A. N. Utkin, "Kontsertirovanie . . .," p. 6.

lucid themes presented a form of musical aphorism that was much admired and emulated by the younger generation of composers.

Stankovich was a student of the renown Ukrainian composer and music pedagogue B. N. Liatoshinskii. Upon his graduation in 1960, Stankovich took active part in the renewal of the Ukrainian music during the 1970s and 1980s. He proved to be a prolific composer and his works were appreciated by the critics and public alike. On of his early works was the *Symphonietta* was written in the neoclassical style preserving the classical formal scheme. Stankovich aspired for a direct and objective communication of the musical content. In addition to Prokof'ev's influence, the *Symphonietta* paid homage to the musical heritage of J. S. Bach. Stankovich included a quotation of the *Prelude* in d minor, in the form of a musical collage, from Bach's*Wohltemperiertes Klavier* .[10]

In December of 1962 a major work by Dmitrii Shostakovich his opera *Katarina Izmailova,* was staged again in its revised form. The first version of his opera entitled *Lady Macbeth of Mtsensk,* composed between 1930-1932, was first performed in 1936 and received denigrating reviews. The operatic score was characterized by the critics as "chaos instead of music." The opera and its libretto were severely censored by the highest political authorities and the work was not performed during Stalin's time. In 1959 Shostakovich's opera was staged in Germany by the operatic company *Deutsche Oper am Rhein* at Düsseldorf/Duisburg.[11] This performance very likely instigated the preparation of a new staging in Soviet Union in 1962. Shostakovich made a few revisions that he himself described as minor in nature. The performance was received with great enthusiasm by the public and critics alike. The critics came to recognize *Katarina Izmailova* as the first great Soviet opera, and perhaps even as the greatest since *Pique Dame* by Chaikovskii.[12]

In the same month, Shostakovich's *Thirteenth Symphony,* written in the form of a symphonic cantata, for baritone solo, bass chorus, and orchestra was performed for the first time. Each of the five movements

---

10. V. Moskalenko, "Evgenii Stankovich," *Muzykal' naia kul' tura bratskikh respublik SSSR,* Kiev, Muzychna Ukraina, 1982, p. 97.

11. Detlef Gojowy, "Schostakovichs neue Kleider," *Osteuropa,* Stuttgart 1987, p. 510.

12. Schwarz, *Music and Musical, Life in Soviet Union 1917–1970,* New York, Norton, 1973, pp. 370–371.

presented a setting of a poem by Evgenii Evtushenko. Evtushenko voiced his criticism in an ironic and oblique way referring to the difficult Stalinist past. The titles of the poems were retained in the symphonic score: *Babyi Iar* proclaimed poet's outspoken criticism against anti-Semitism; *Humor* celebrated the irrepressible stamina of a people; *At the store* paid tribute to women who ploughed and reaped and managed somehow to feed the family; *Fears* depicted forebodings engulfing the human existence; *Career* was a tribute to Galileo and the non-conformist man. The *Symphony* was received by a standing ovation rarely witnessed before.[13] However, another opera by Shostakovich *The Nose,* composed in 1928, was not unfrozen by the "thaw". The chamber music style, musical declamation and grotesque portrayal of personality did not find an easy approval by the authorities. *The Nose* was eventually included in the operatic repertoire. The performance of *The Nose* during the Prague Festival in 1981 received excellent revues.

An important role in the musical development during the 1960s and 1970s played the performances of the compositions by Arnold Schönberg, Anton Webern and Alban Berg. The innovations of the composers of the New Viennese school, in particular Webern, influenced to a great extent the younger generation of Soviet composers in the course of the 1960s and later on. The remarkable composer Sofia Gubaidulina credited Webern's innovative compositional approach as the major influence in her creative development. The composer Al'fred Shnitke became interested in Webern's role as a composer, and as a historic figure. Therefore, he decided to translate into Russian a selection of Webern's letters in order to inform the Soviet readers about this remarkable man and his work. The interest for twelve-tone music was cultivated, most of all, by Philipp Herscovici, a former student of Webern, who gave private lessons to both Al'fred Shnitke and Edison Dennisov. Herscovici emigrated from Austria to the Soviet Union following Hitler's Anschluß of Austria in 1938. Both Shnitke and Dennisov were known as proponents of innovative ideas and of the contemporary compositional thought.[14]

In addition, the composers Bela Bartok, and Olivier Messian among others, were slowly introduced in musical programs and lecture halls alike.

---

13. Schwarz, *Music and Musical Life . . .,* pp. 366–367.

14. Detlef Gojowy, "Schostakovichs neue Kleider," *Osteuropa,* Stuttgart 1987, p. 517.

Bartok's unique style of concertant symphonism was emulated by a number of composers. The revaluation of the contribution of these masters gave a new insight into the realm of compositional possibilities. Consequently, the creative aspirations and musical language of Soviet composers were greatly enriched and for the first time the twelve-tone system, aleatory music, sonority, and pointillism were freely discussed and analyzed.

Gradually, in the course of the late 1960s the situation in the musical field was greatly improved with the arrival of a new generation of composers. Many of these young musicians were former students of well known masters such as D. Shostakovich, A. Khachaturian, D. Kabalevskii, B. Liatoshinskii, K. Karaev, A. Balnchivadze, Iu. Iuzeliunasa, and others. The music critics and the public alike showed great interest for the young composers. The names of Sergei Slonimskii, Boris Tishchenko, Sofia Gubaidulina, Edison Dennisov, Andrei Eshpai, Valerii Gavrilin, and Rodion Shchedrin became well known, among others. Their compositions testified to a high level of professionalism and the questions of insufficient preparation and accomplishment became obsolete.

The circumstances in the musical field continued to improve. The subsequent changes in the ideological policies enabled performances of the Russian, Soviet and Western composers not featured often enough in musical programs. On the eve of the Fifth Composers' Congress in 1974, Tikhon Khrennikov summed up the improved situation by stating that literally in all Soviet republics — federal and autonomous — the quantitative growth in the ranks of young professionals went hand in hand with the qualitative achievement.[15]

The neoclassical style continued to be cultivated and the compositions written in the neoclassical style showed a wide range of expressions: from light and humorous views of the dance movements of the suite, and the vocal settings of the madrigal to aleatory music. The selection of suitable instrumental colors, and the choice of formal concepts provided additional evidence of the neoclassical stylistic orientation. Some of these avenues were explored by B. Kutavichius in the *Little partita* for flute and harp. The composition *Dialogues* for ensemble of old instruments by Iu. Shirvimskas projected a similar affinity. The *Dialogue* for violin and clavecin by Iu. Karlson showed a congruent approach stressing the contrasting instrumental colors. In the *Madrigal Suite* for an instrumental

---

15. Kon'kova, "Nekotorye tendentsii . . .," p. 4.

ensemble by the Moldavian composer B. Bitkin, the polyphonic vocal
texture was adapted to the instrumental treatment. The *Madrigal* for voice
and chamber ensemble by A. Zograbian was steeped in the classical
simplicity and austerity of expressive resources.[16]

The much sought neoclassical repertory was cultivated by the newly
created vocal and instrumental ensembles specializing in the performance
of the old music. Andrei Volkonskii founded and conducted the old-music
ensemble "Madrigal," and, when required, played harpsichord. Some
highly original and versatile ensembles addressed their efforts equally
towards the propagation of contemporary music written in the neoclassical
idiom. This was the case with the well known "Chamber Music Ensemble"
of the Association of Composers of Ukraina.

The neoclassical tendencies permeated many compositions and were
manifested in many different manners. Thus, the form of the concerto
grosso served as the archetype in the creation of several outstanding
compositions such as the *Sinfonia da camera* by Ia. Ivanov; the *Concerto
grosso* by B. Arpov; the *First Symphony* by V. Sil'vestrov; *In Modo
classico* by R. Karlson, *Sinfonia per archi* by A. Grinup, and the *Second
Symphony* by G. Vagner. At times, various neoclassical forms were
coupled with the folklore traditions. As an example for these endeavors
may serve the *Partita for string orchestra* by M. Skorik, the *Suite for flute
and string orchestra* by Iu. Ishchenko, the *Partita* by P. Vasks, and the
Concertino for chamber orchestra by I. Gadzhibekov, among others.[17]

Elements of neoclassicism can be also discerned in the use of collages as
a pointed reference expressed in an epigrammatic and laconic way. The
composers used collages as a specific comparison of different time periods
where the past retained the ideal category as a measure for the
contemporaneous reality. Boris Chaikovskii used collages reminiscent of
the musical themes of Mozart, Beethoven, Bach, and Schumann in his
Second Symphony.[18]

At times composers chose mythical and archetypical literary texts to
stress the universality of human quests and responses to life's tribulations.
The human actions, conflicts, and passions were often observed in the
context of the the cultural and historical realities. Shostakovich, in the last

---

16. Kon'kova, "Nekotorye tendentsii . . .," pp. 22–29.
17. Kon'kova, "Tendentsii razvitiia . . .," pp. 20–21.
18. Kon'kova, "Tendentsii razvitiia . . .," p. 16.

decade of his life, turned to the poems of Dante, Shakespeare, Michelangelo, and Marina Tsvetaeva extolling the common nature of human experiences. Most importantly, the composers often chose the literary texts of previously censored Russian poets and playwrights for their musical compositions. The beauty of these almost forgotten verses and their poetic and human messages resounded anew, enhanced by the musical setting. The composers helped in their own way the revaluation of the literary heritage, and the restructuring of the cultural scene.

Sergei Slonimskii showed a great affinity for the poetic messages from the poets past and present. In his compositions he strove to find the best suited musical setting for each poem. Slonimskii was among the first composers to turn his attention to the poetic world of Anna Akhmatova, and Osip Mandel'stam. In the course of the 1970s, he wrote two cycles of poems underlying the lucid clarity of thoughts and rich imagery of these two writers. Slonimskii composed the *Four poems* with the poetry by Mandel'shtam and *Ten poems* using the poems by Akhmatova.[19]

The musical setting of these poems suggested the composer's comprehension of the content. Thus, Mandel'shtam's poem "O, nebo, nebo" was interpreted in a form of a recitative, the swiftly moving vocal part accompanied by chord formations reminiscent of bell sonorities. The poem has a character of an epigram. Mandel'shtam discussed the inability of the poet to express the vastness of the world, and to became a part of it. The single word is unable to express the poets thoughts since the word itself is only a shadow of the true meaning defined in a context*(slovo-ten)*. Mandel'shtam often imported that the poet often tried to record the existing world of sounds swarming above him. "Nezhnee nezhnogo" is conceived as a romance filled with elated expressions of thanksgiving since the poet has succeeded in creating a new work. Slonimskii created a musical rendition that captured the quiet resolution at the end of the tormenting process of creation. The third song "Muzykant" projected association with the distant and unpredictable events. The introduction consisted of a recitative leading to a march like melody as if dictating to the poet to sing in order to overcome fear and anxiety, "Kakaia toska shchemiashchaia, Kakaia beda striaslas'. . . . A v nebe tantsuet zoloto,

---

19. A. L. Porfir'eva: "Russkaia poeziia v vokal'nykh tsiklakh S. Slonimskogo 70 godov," *Stilevye tendentsii v Sovetskoi muzyke 1960–1970 godov*, Leningrad, Leningradskii gosudarstvennyi institut teatra, muzyki i kinematografii, 1979, p. 33.

Prikazyvaet mne pet'," ("What an oppressive sorrow, what a misfortune occurred, . . . And in the sky dances the golden sheen, Ordering me to sing.") That is why the poet chose the march movement to project the necessity of going on in spite of the feeling of helplessness. "Ia slovo pozabyl" ("I forgot the word") is a monologue lamenting the difficulties in capturing the initial grasp of the words that were forgotten and impossible to fully remember and reconstruct. Mandel'shtam's poetical idiom seemed to suggest to the composer a neoclassical musical language, rooted in harmonic, melodic and rhythmic clarity and order.

Akhmatova's poetry resembled a lively dialogue. The biblical and religious references   broadened the lyrical tenor of the poems. Slonimskii's musical setting underlined the romantic aspect of Akhmatova's poetic vision.[20]

Boris Tishchenko appreciated also the poetry of Anna Akhmatova. He felt a kinship with her poetic and human message and gave a powerful musical rendition in the *Requiem* based on the poem of the same name by Akhmatova. His former teacher, Dmitrii Shostakovich, commented favorably Tishchenko's composition. [21]

Soviet composers turned increasingly their attention to literary works of foreign writers. Thus, Sofia Gubaidulina composed the exceptional *Hommage a T. S. Eliot* in 1987. After reading Eliot's *Four Quartets* a year earlier, she found the poetic metaphores as well as the metrical structure to provide an easy bridge to music. The unusual opulence of the melodic flow and ingenious instrumental treatment testifies to Gubaidulina's mastery of the creative and compositional metier.

The interpretation of neoclassicism remained to influence the Soviet musical practice utilizing a wide range of musical sources including the orthodox Chant—*znamennoe penie*. The preparations for the celebration of the Millennium of Christianity in Russia in 1988 gave an impetus for the increased interest in the liturgical Chant. The composers of choral music were among the first to point to the tradition of the Russian Chant and the choral music of the XVIII century: the *kant* and *partesnoe penie*. As it may be expected, these vocal musical traditions were closest to the Ukrainian and Russian composers.

---

20. Porfir'eva: "Russkaia poeziia . . .," p. 45.

21. *D. Shostakovich o vremeni i o sebe,* Ed. M. Iakovlev, Moscow, Sovetskii kompozitor, 1980, p.333.

Rodion Shchedrin's *Zvony (Chimes)*, subtitled *Concerto No.2*, for orchestra, conjured the sound of chimes of ancient Russia. In addition, Shchedrin introduced reminiscences of the old church chant written down with ideographic neumatic signs. Since the neums gave indication of the direction of the melodic line but not the accurate pitch, Shchedrin used aleatoric devices as elements of improvisation inherent in the old liturgical practice.

Moreover, Shchedrin composed an oratorium, *Poetoria*, for a narrator, soprano, choir and orchestra. Shchedrin was inspired by the poetry of Andrei Voznesenskii and the Russian choral tradition. He updated the choral treatment by using a lively musical dialogue between the vocal and instrumental performers. This work brought accolades to the composer: Dmitrii Shostakovich wrote about the strong impression that the work left on him. Although Shchedrin was appreciated from the beginning of his career as a composer of great musical talent, his earlier works seemed to suggest a lightness of musical treatment and lack of a serious involvement in the compositional process. The composition *Poetoria* pointed to his sudden artistic growth and deepening of musical expression. Shostakovich thought that this composition marked the turning point in Shchedrin's creative path.[22]

Several compositions reminiscent of the liturgical musical practices need to be mentioned: the *Concert* by I. Karabitsa for the choir, soloists and orchestra was based on the text of G. Skovorody. The *Concert* reminded of the old choral concertos, although expressed in the contemporary musical language. Similar musical references were incorporated in the *Cant Vivat* by Iu. Falik for the choir based on the verses of A. Sumarokov. V. Kalistratov's *Russkii kontsert* made generous use of the Russian religious choral repository.[23]

The *Choral Concerto* by Al'fred Shnitke displayed the simplicity, and austerity of his musical language turning away from complexities and saturations of compositional means. The poems of the Armenian poet Grigor Narekatsi from the 10th century served as the textual basis of the composition. Shnitke acknowledged many sources of his inspiration, most of all, the influence of the baroque masters Heinrich Schütz, and Jochann Sebastian Bach, in addition to the Russian chant *znamennoe penie*.

---

22. *D. Shostakovich o vremeni i o sebe*, p. 314.

23. Kon'kova, "Nekotorye tendentsii . . .," p. 21.

Moreover, Shnitke included in the fourth movement, as an episode, a romance in Chaikovskii's style. He also included melodies with the augmented second reminding of the Armenian folk idiom. All these influences pointed to a polystylistic amalgamation inherent in Shnitke's musical language.[24]

Elements of neoclassicism were used selectively in operatic and ballet genres. In the ballet *Anna Karenina* by Rodion Shchedrin neoclassical elements occur in the scene depicting the Italian opera. Very seldom the main concept and style of an operatic or ballet score was rooted in the neoclassical model. A noted exception presented the ballet music *Caleidoscope* by F. Karaev based entirely on the themes of the Scarlatti sonatas.[25]

During the late 1970s the music theater attracted steadily the attention of Soviet composers, performers and the public alike. The staging of new and old opera- and ballet performances gained widespread popularity. However, the national operatic genre of epic proportions was poorly presented in the repertory save for the Prokof'ev's opera *War and Peace* and *Dekabristi* by Iu. Shaporin.

The opera *Petr I*, written by the composer Andrei Petrov, seemed to have filled this void and was received as a creative success. The libretto was written by N. Kasatkina and V. Vasilev covering the time between 1689 and 1703. This period of Russian history was marked by many uprisings and gradual disappearance of the ancient Russia of the old believers and the subsequent formation of the new government. The scenic design projected monumentality, invention and an impressive imagination. The opera was staged at the Kirov Theater in Leningrad.[26]

Interestingly enough, the story of Peter's life was not examined before by the Russian or Soviet composers. The beginning of Peter's rule was presented in the opera *Khovanshchina* by Mussorgskii, although Peter, as a historic figure, was not featured. Petrov's opera portrayed not only the commanding role of Peter, but equally the heroic efforts of the people. The opera was divided in ten scenes dubbed as 'frescoes.' Each scene

---

24. L. Kirrilina, "Ravno dlia malykh i velikikh," *Sovetskaia muzyka*, June 1987, p. 37.

25. Kon'kova, "Nekotrye tendentsii . . .," p. 21.

26. V. Rubtsova, "Opera rozhdena dlia stseny. Petr Pervyi A. Petrova," *Myzyka Rosii*, Sovetskii kompozitor 1978, p. 146.

presented a complete dramatic plot with its protagonists, the conflict and the subsequent solution. Such a concept enabled the presentation of a large number of personalities and overlapping events leading to Peter's ascent to the throne. Other episodes portrayed Peter's difficulties with the feudal chiefs, and the lyric interlude with Katerina.[27]

Petrov succeeded in a believable projection of this historic period populated by its main protagonists. The choral parts included a wide range of expressive devices ranging from whisper, rhythmical declamation, exclamations, and onomatopoeic effects of the bells ringing. The dramatic highlights were enhanced by the large choral scenes depicting the suffering of the people. Like in *Khovanshchina*, the sympathy of the viewers remains on the side of the tragically doomed population. The choral scenes conducted on a dimly lighted and bare stage underlined the oppressive and heavy feelings shared by many.

Petrov collected in this opera a wealth of musical repositories which helped to enhance the musical and dramatic conflicts and stage action. Some music material was newly composed and some presented a selection of old Russian music. The operatic score reminded of a unique musical documentary *(muzykal'naia dokumental'nost')* juxtaposing the liturgical chant *(znamennyi raspev)*, the spirited soldier songs and folk tunes *(chastushki)* with the contemporary musical language. Petrov used in this opera the melody of the old believers*(starovercheskii raspev)* "Kak na nas Gospod' razgnevilsia", in addition to the religious songs *kanty*, as essential dramatic elements in the context of the opera. The short and brisk idiom of *chastushka* genre was often used as a poignant characterization of a social group.[28]

The critics believed that this lively and impressive musical score affirmed the justification of the opera genre. Petrov succeeded in what he wished to achieve by creating, ". . . the authentic national, heroic and patriotic composition for the Soviet opera theater, and to accomplish this with the contemporary musical means."[29]

---

27. Rubtsova, "Opera rozhdena dlia stseny . . .," p. 146.

28. V. Zarudko, "Tipy vokal'nogo melosa i ikh prelomlenie v sovetskoi kamernoi i oratorial'noi opere 60–70 godov," *Muzykal'naia kul'tura bratskikh respublik SSSR, Muzychna Ukraina*, 1982, p. 45.

29. Rubtsova, "Opera rozhdena dlia stseny . . .," p. 165.

At the beginning of the 1970s a number of composers initiated a change by introducing lyricism, and a flowing melodic line. The former subdued musical reflections were often devoid of emotions and neglected the playful exuberance expressed in the topos of "homo ludens". In addition, the lyrical and romantic overtones enriched the evolving neobaroque development. Such was the lyrical elegy of the violas and cellos "O, Del'vig, Del'vig" in the *14 Symphony* by Dmitrii Shostakovich. Similar features shared the barcarole in the Finale of his *Second cello concerto*. The romantic notion in the neobaroque style was introduced also in the *Concerto for two violins* by Al'fred Shnitke and in the *Concerto for two violins* by Arvo Pärt. E. Tamberg's *Concerto for trumpet* presented a fusion of the percussive qualities of a baroque toccata with an expressive, lyrical content.

The *Piano concerto* by B. Chaikovskii included next to the thematic material associated with the toccata style expressive themes reminiscent of Chopin. Chaikovskii composed also a poetic and emotionally charged *Violin concerto*. The soft and gentle beginning of the introduction gradually leads to an impressive dramatic climax. The *Violin concerto* was based on several musical themes and their respective transformation. Moreover, Chaikovskii understood and used well the contemplative role of the monologue of the soloists in the musical and formal shaping of the concerto style. In his *Second Symphony* the monologue of the flute and the subsequent monologue of the solo viola lead to the finely wrought *Largo* movement. *Concerto for Viola* by D. Finko displayed even a greater affinity with the intonational associations of the language of romanticism, and equally in the dramatic and formal concepts.[30]

Stravinsky's early works based on the folk themes were well received from the very beginning and remained on the repertory of the Soviet orchestra. Stravinsky's profound knowledge of the Russian musical folklore, his appreciation of the inherent modality of the folk idiom, variable metrical schemes and shifting rhythmic and accentual organization served as an inspiration for many Soviet composers. Rodion Shchedrin wrote his *Ozornye chastushki (Mischievous songs)* with the subtitle *Concerto No. 1 for Orchestra*, under the influence of the ballet score of *Petrushka*, tempered by the inflections of the *chastushka* genre. Shchedrin's work became well known and often performed.

---

30. Utkin, "Kontsertirovanie kak muzikal'no-dramaturgicheskii metod," pp. 75–81.

During the 1960s and 1970s, several genres of vocal music were greatly influenced by the musical folklore pointing to yet unused repositories of this autochthonous tradition. In particular the folk songs from the northern region were introduced as well as the ritual melodies of the calendar cycle, ancient lamentations *(plach)*, and various ritual tunes associated with initiations. The folk songs of the 19th and 20th century, the musical commentaries of the village life *chastuski*, became very popular in the course of the 1960s and later on.

It is interesting to note a similar interest for the village life in literary works written in the early 1960s. Many Soviet writers started exploring the seemingly slow pace and unperturbed, placid existence in the villages only to discover the rich, and often intense human experiences. Many novels were written about the inhabitants of the villages marking the beginning of the flourishing genre of the village prose *(derevianskaia proza)*.

In the musical field, the beauty and uniqueness of the rich folklore tradition was showcased by Georgii Sviridov in his cantata *Kurskie pesni (Songs from Kursk)*. The inflections of the Russian folk melodies were used by Valerii Gavrilin in his vocal cycle *Russkaia tetrad' (The Russian Notebook)*. Gavrilin received the Glinka State Prize for this exceptional composition. The musical folklore inspired the creation of several ballets and operas. Thus, Sh. Chalaev, composed the ballet *Gorianka (The Girl from the Mountains)* and *Laskie pesni (Love Songs)*, using the folklore idiom from the Dagestan region. M. Kazhlaev composed his opera based on the folk tunes *Gortsy (Mountaineers)*.

Sergei Slonimskii used the musical idiom close to folklore for his first opera, *Virineia,* produced almost simultaneously in Leningrad and Moscow in 1967, marking the anniversary of the 1917 Revolution. The libretto, by Lydia Seiafullina, was based on a novel about a peasant woman emancipated by the Revolution. Slonimskii's skill in choral writing made the mass scene very impressive yet vaguely reminiscent of Mussorgskii's folk drama.[31] Slonimskii composed another opera based on the Russian choral tradition. The libretto was based on one of the censored masterpieces of Russian literature: the famous drama by Mikhail Bulgakov *Master and Margarita*. Slonimsky chose the style of the choral monody in order to highlight the unusual beauty of Bulgakov's phantasmagoric

---

31. Schwarz, *Music and Musical Life . . .*, p. 471.

prose.[32] The opera was staged in Moscow in 1991 at the newly founded theater Forum.

Moreover, folklore was not used only as a local color in order to lend authenticity and to freshen the composition. Folk creations were interpreted as complex musical and semantic systems comprising epic or lyric texts, a repertory of melodic inflections, modal and rhythmic patterns, and suitable musical instruments. These expressive elements evolved in the process of repeated performances within the various folk customs. The composers approached these traditional repositories in a variety of ways. Sometimes, the indigenous melodic material was used as a straight quotation while preserving the mode, and performance manner. At times, the composers intervened to a great extent by changing the idiomatic inflections of the selected folklore material or even assimilating simultaneously different temporal layers and geographic regions of folk art.

These creative efforts produced exceptional results and a fresh reading of the national folk idiom. Dmitri Shostakovich commented, in an interview conducted in 1968, about the influx of folk music in the newly composed works comprising a variety of approaches and genres. The composers utilized folk melodies from unused rich ethnic repositories of Russia, Ukraina and the Baltic countries, including the distant regions of the Asian republics, in particular Armenia, and Georgia. Moreover, these works reflected the style of the individual composer and the preference for a distinct folk song genre. As an example, Shostakovich posited that Rodion Shchedrin preferred contemporary folk songs like *chastushki*, while Sergei Slonimskii often used old folk songs. Shchedrin's *Ozornye chastuski* and his *First* and *Second Piano Concerto* had a style of their own and could not be mistaken with the *Pesniami voljnitsi (Capricious Songs),* and *Golosom iz khora (Choral Voice)* by Slonimskii. Shostakovich stressed that the respective compositional treatments of folk material had a marked individual style. Very likely Shostakovich remembered that until recently the folk melodies were "translated" and "homogenized" into an unambiguous tonal and melodic mold with a regular harmonic and rhythmic periodicity. The new approach emphasized a flexible musical

---

32. V. Zak, G. Grigoreva, "Simfoniia i problemy stilia," *Sovetskaia muzyka*, April 1987, p. 31.

phrase resulting from an asymmetrical harmonic and rhythmic articulation
with a chromatic, or modal melodic invention.

Shostakovich singled out the composers who used well the folklore
idiom such as Valerii Gavrilin, and Boris Tishchenko from Leningrad,
Iaan Riaets from Estonia, Miroslav Skorik and Leonid Grabovskii from
Ukraina, Giia Kancheli and Nodar Gabuniia from Georgiia, Edgar
Oganesian and Dzhivan Ter-Tatevosian from Armenia, Roman Lednev and
Aleksei Nikolaev from Moscow.[33]
However, some composers wrote new music while preserving the
authentic folk texts. The ethno-musicologists I. Zemtsovskii introduced a
new terminology for this phenomenon "the composers' folklore"
(kompozitorskii folklorizm). The composers aimed to interpret the
original folk texts in their own way. The newly composed music was
reminiscent of the indigenous folklore idiom, although it was an original
musical composition.[34]

In some compositions, a new synthesis of folklore elements was
achieved by incorporating several musical sources from different regions.
The composer Boris Tishchenko used in his ballet *Iaroslavna* the ritual
folklore of the northern Russian region in addition to the South Slav folk
songs. Shostakovich was so impressed by this composition of his former
student that he attended Tishchenko's ballet performance three times in a
row. Evgenii Stankovich used a similar approach in the ballet *Ol'ga*. In
order to recreate the atmosphere of medieval Russia, Stankovich combined
the ancient Russian epics — *bylini*, the songs of the medieval jongleurs —
skomorokhi, the ritual incantations, and the old Russian chant *znamennii
raspev*.[35]

During the late 1960s the rift between the serious and popular music
became intensified. Soviet musicologists, composers and music educators
pointed to the growing polarization in the musical field: the carefully
nurtured tradition of serious music was loosing its primacy and the
popular musical genres were taking an unprecedented upper hand. This
radical shifting towards popular musical genres changed to a great extent
the established structure of the Soviet musical life.

---

33. *Dmitrii Shostakovich o vremeni i o sebe*, 1926–1975, Ed. M. Iakovlev, Moscow,
Vsesoiuznoe izdatel'stvo, 1980, pp. 305–306.

34. Kon'kova, "Tendentsii razvitiia . . .," p. 11.

35. Kon'kova, "Tendentsii razvitiia . . .," p. 10.

The bridging of the existing gap between the popular and serious music could not be easily achieved. However, the concerto form offered a possibility for a synthesis of these two musical styles. The jazz- and popular music as well as the concerto share the instrumental dialogue, contrasting tone colors, virtuosity of instrumental improvisation, and aleatory elements. All these components allowed fluctuations of nuances of expressions in the melodic, rhythmic and harmonic flow. Thus, several Soviet composers believed that the concertant dialogue could solve the problem of alienation of the serious and popular musical cultures. The synthesis of the innovative musical semantics of the contemporary music with the jazz- and popular idiom became a reality in the musical practice.

Again, it was Stravinsky who set an example earlier, in this context, by composing his *Histoire du Soldat* in 1918, *The Ragtime* for eleven instruments in 1918, the *Piano Rag-Music* in 1920, and *Ebony Concerto* in 1945. Stravinsky's *Ebony Concerto* was not condoned by the ideologists of socialist realism and was not performed in Soviet Union, due to its official rejection. The *Ebony Concerto* was listed in the *Bol'shaia Sovietskaia Entsiklopediia* of 1956 as an example of moral laxity of the composer who would lower himself to compose besides the *Ebony Concerto* even polkas for a circus. In this context the *Ebony Concerto* and the music for the circus were obviously treated as a lesser genre of mass entertainment. This entry in the prestigious *Entsyklopediia* showed a surprizing elitist attitude: the composing of music for mass entertainment was beneath a composer of stature. Moreover, the mentioned entry was, in its essence, contradictory to the Soviet cultural policies since the circus was recognized as an artistic form in its own right and subsidized by the government. The circus performers were often awarded with high decorations and honorary titles as any other prominent artists in various fields of artistic endeavors.

However, the composers and musicologists, following Stravinsky's creative path, knew this witty musical score. In the changed cultural atmosphere of the 1960s the score of the *Ebony Concerto* provided the starting point for innovative explorations. In the wish to gain a wider acceptance and win over the young musical public, Soviet composers tried to establish closer ties between the serious and popular musical genres. The composers introduced in some genres of classical music the elements of jazz rhythm, harmonic patterns, and musical instruments previously used mostly in popular music. The composers were motivated by the wish to introduce an accessible musical form, and gain a greater impact on the listener. The efforts resulted in works of different profiles. Andrei

Eshpai composed his *Concerto for Orchestra* using skillfully the jazz idiom. Eshpai used a similar compositional approach in his *Fourth symphony*. Rodion Shchedrin's *Second Piano Concerto* introduced jazz improvisation in addition to the nostalgic reminiscences of the balalaika sound.[36]

Sergei Slonimskii composed several works using the popular musical genres. In his *First Symphony* he used the rhythmical pattern of the dance fox trot. Slonimsky also composed the *Concerto for a jazz ensemble* of three electrical guitars, saxophone, percussions and piano. In his *Concert-buffo* Slonimskii interspersed Latin-American popular music and Russian songs — *chastushki*, in addition to the application of the contrapuntal technique and improvisation. His *Fourth symphony* has a recurring musical theme based on a rock Leitmotif.[37]

A number of composers mixed the elements of serious and popular music creating a polystylistic approach. Sergei Slonimskii composed the *Exotic suite* for two violins and the beat ensemble. *Concerto for two violins and orchestra* by Al'fred Shnitke could serve as an interesting example of a polystylistic concerto grosso. A similar approach was used in large instrumental or operatic works. The *Rock-Symphony* by M. Kalnyn', and the rock-oratorio *Bread and work* by G. Kupriavichius used musical themes of contrasting nature combining the serious and popular musical idiom. The film-opera *The Devil's bride* by V. Ganelin, enhanced the dramatic conflict by juxtaposing the different psychological traits of the main characters projected in music with the use of popular melodic and rhytmic inflections. The song-opera *Orpheus and Euridice* by A. Zhurbin used the elements of serious and popular genres to conjure the fight for supremacy of opposing forces.[38]

The fusion of styles and genres created a lively musical discourse and included, in some compositions, different time planes and formal approaches. The introduction of popular genres helped in the clarification of complex ideas by reducing the complexity to the intelligible level of easy understanding in the manner of a newspaper article, commercial advertisement or poster art.

---

36. Utkin, "Kontsertirovanie kak muzikal'no-dramaturgicheskii metod," p. 73.

37. V. Zak, "Vyiti navstrechu slushateliu," *Sovetskaia muzyka*, April 1987, pp. 29–30.

38. Kon'kova, "Tendentsii razvitiia . . .," pp. 16–17.

The discussion of the emerging changes in Soviet musical culture clearly benefitted from the introduction of the *glasnost'* doctrine. At first, the ensuing clarifications in the musical journals reiterated to a great extent the well known and worn out criteria established by the doctrine of socialist realism. The art work, even if belonging to the sphere of entertainment and featured on popular TV shows, should, most of all, be in compliance with the established ideological, ethical and social standards. The artists and critics should interpret the established ideological postulates and functions that an art work should perform in a socialist society, fostering primarily education of the masses. The critics repeated that the socialistic musical culture was most of all founded in an unified and universally shared reception of musical works. The ideological and artistic requirements, formulated by the doctrine of socialist realism, should help the composers to produce works that would be accepted and understood by all the members of the Soviet society. The development of pluralism was alien to the basic democratic character of the socialist society. The ideological function of music, as the basis of the humanistic education of Soviet youth, should instill the spiritual strongholds opposed to the bourgeois world. However, the goals and aspirations of the Soviet youth seemed to be changing due to the influence of the popular music modeled mainly after Western genres. This perilous situation should be corrected and the youth should be able to recognize the proven musical values.

On the other hand, the composer Rodion Shchedrin spoke on several occasion about the importance of a dialogue between the younger and the older generation. During a special meeting in the concert studio Ostankino, Shchedrin stressed that attention and tolerance should be shown to the young audiences respecting their musical tastes. Shchedrin formulated a new point of view considering the role of the arts in the Soviet Society: Art should not be considered only and always as a tool or means for education.[39]

Several composers and musicologists supported the proposition that the future development of Soviet popular music should be enriched with the treasury of musical folklore. A number of vocal-instrumental groups: *Pesniary, Verasy, Ialla,* have chosen this approach and enjoyed success. The ensemble *Giunesh* from Turkmenistan introduced interesting

---

39. Igor' Kon, "Nuzhny ponimanie i terpimost", *Sovetskaia muzyka,* June 1987, p. 20.

combinations of national rhythmic patterns, and specific timbres of their instruments combined with elements of jazz and rock music. In addition, a number of folklore groups have lately intensified their efforts in explorations of folk song tradition such as the ensemble of D. Pokrovskii, the folklore group at the Leningrad Conservatory and others.[40]

In the course of the 1980s, the once dependable concert public seemed to have lost interest in the performances of serious music. The composer Al'fred Shnitke discussed some of the problems facing Soviet musical life while addressing a selected audience of the friends of chamber music. He pointed out that the current situation in the musical field gave cause for concern. The public did not show up at the performances of symphonic or operatic music. The loss of interest for the works of composers presented a loss of a vital support for any artist. Shnitke posited: "The misfortune of our time is the rift between Soviet art and Soviet public." ("Beda nashego vremeni razryv mezdu sovetskim isskustvom i sovetskoi publikoi"). However, Shnitke stressed that one should not think that only the commercial success and sold out performances could provide a satisfactory answer. He suggested a new approach: the creative artist should explore the commonly shared ideas and interests with the fellow man leaving the present time and place. Therefore, he advocated a courageous departure into the past: "Take a risk and try not to be contemporaneous."[41] Shnitke was aware that the explorations of the distant musical and literary past were shared by a number of composers in his country and elsewhere. He obviously identified with this quest and turned his attention to the old musical repositories. The result was the mentioned *Choral Concerto*, a work of epic clarity devoid of colorful descriptiveness found often in choral composition. The *Four Hymns for Chamber Ensemble* by Snitke shared a similar interest for the musical treasury of the past. The *Four Hymns* were based on the liturgical chant although translated into an instrumental idiom. The *Hymn IV* included reminiscences of the ostinato figures of percussive chords suggestive of the dance rhythm in Stravinsky's *Rites of Spring*.

Following the historic decisions formulated in the resolution of the 27th Congress of the Communist Party USSR, in April of 1985, the

---

40. Igor' Leont'evich Nabok, *Ideologicheskaia funktsiia muzyki*, Leningrad, Muzyka, 1987, pp. 67, 70.

41. L. Kirillina, "Ravno . . .," *Sov Muzika*, June 1987, p. 36.

ideologies of *glasnost'* and *perestroika* were introduced into the life of the Soviet society at large. The spirit of greater freedom was compared to the gentle spring breeze transforming the Soviet land. The ruling ideology of socialist realism did resemble the icy covers of winter halting the germination of a new life reflecting fresh points of view.

The Union of Composers passed its own Resolution that was published in the musical journal *Sovetskaia muzyka,* in the June issue of 1987. The composers expressed firm support for the 27th Congress, the Resolution of the Plenum of the Central Committee of the Communist Party of the Soviet Union and the restructuring proposition. The Union of Composers acknowledged the importance of *perestroika* and planed to implement restructuring in all of its activities. The Union urged all composers' organization to introduce radical changes and to disclose openly the official policies concerning organizational questions. The Unions in various Soviet Republics should show greater care concerning the gifted individuals and support all serious creative efforts.[42] The resolution acknowledged that Soviet composers have produced a considerable number of talented works. However, some newly composed works, in particular the works addressing patriotic themes, showed lack of desired quality. The flashy titles of such works concealed a drab content that, in fact, discredited the validity of important themes.

The resolution discussed also the issues facing popular music. The composers, members of the Union, were urged to explore the possibilities of creating a national style of music for entertainment. The vacuum created by the lack of musical taste of the young generation was replenished by the examples provided by the Western popular culture. Recently, such music showed poor quality, catering to primitive instincts, egocentrism, and "aggressive individualism". Therefore, the sociologist should urgently conduct research of the musical preferences of the young. In addition, the necessary recommendations for the betterment of musical education should be vigorously supported.[43]

The spirit of openness introduced a candid discussion about many problems facing the musical life. The editorials and articles published in

---

42. "Reshenie rasshirennogo zasedaniia sekretariatov pravlenii SK SSSR i RSFR, Moskovskoi kompozitorskoi organizacii i partkoma soiuza kompozitorov SSSR," *Sovetskaia muzyka* 1987, No. 6, pp. 11–12.

43. *Sovetskaia muzyka,* June 1987, pp. 11–12.

the journal *Sovetskaia muzyka* discussed the shortcomings never discussed before. In the course of time, the journal became a forum for an open exchange of views. The composers and musicologists addressed, most of all, the reinstitution of the once censored musical heritage of prominent composers unduly omitted from the concert repertory. Previously, many musical works that did not fulfill the requirements of the doctrine of socialist realism were declared as undesirable, and banned from performances and publication. These works remained for a long time suppressed and unpublished, nonexistent in the Soviet musical fond.

The composers Karim Khachaturian addressed the readers of the journal *Sovetskaia muzyka* in an editorial outlining his concerns and new aspirations. However, Khachaturian framed his grievances within the established context of reverence for the leadership of the Communist Party. Khachaturian quoted the following abstract from the Resolution of the 1987 January Plenum of the Central Committee of the Communist Party of the Soviet Union, as a motto for his article,:

"... *The debt of the artistic intelligentsia* ... *(is) to enrich the spiritual life of the fatherland* ... *produce talented and truthful works that reflect our reality in all its multitude and grandeur, to counterbalance decisively the ideological and cultural aggression of the imperialism striving to impose upon our people, most of all upon our youth, alien values to humanism."* [44]

Even two years after the announcement of openness and democratization, Khachaturian acknowledged the Party's leadership as the primary source of reference. The world was still perceived divided in two halves: the West and the East. The Western culture was accused of harboring imperialistic tendencies. At this point, the autocratic power of the Party continued to exert its influence in the decision making processes and evaluations of the present realities. Clearly, this assessment of the current situation perpetuated the worn out interpretations of the past era.

Khachaturian must have considered these words as truthful, and therefore decided to quote this paragraph from the Resolution as the motto for his article. He might have also followed an established pattern since the custom of quotations of resolutions issued by the Communist Party was a common practice and a proof of loyal support of the Party's policies.

---

44. K. Khachutarian, "Vremia sprosit strogo." *Sovetskaia muzyka,* April 1987, p. 6.

In the principal part of his article Khachaturian concentrated mostly on immediate goals in the musical field. He saw as the urgent priority the correction of narrow minded evaluations of a number of valuable yet forgotten composers and their works. The literary and artistic journals were ahead in their literary revaluations publishing the works that have been unjustly forgotten or because of various reasons were not published before. He noticed the abundance of verses, stories and novels that have enriched the Soviet literary fond. Khachaturian thought that this was a salutatory effort since every culture has its strength in its roots and in its memory.

The musical life in the past suffered from sclerotic conditions failing to acknowledge important composers and their works. Very seldom the symphonies and quartets of N. Miaskovskii were heard and likewise the works of masters such V. Shcherbachev, V. Shebalin, G. Popov, Iu. Kochurov - the former valiant builders of Soviet musical culture. Therefore, some young composers were 'discovering' what was known long ago. The preparation for the celebration of the 70th anniversary of the October Revolution should hasten the change and show a broader concern about the riches of this valuable heritage.

Khachaturian reminded the readers that Nikolai Iakovlevich Miaskovskii was dubbed "the conscience" of the Soviet music. His inquisitive mind followed the creative efforts in progress, the performances of new compositions, major concerts and publishing events. No one seemed to be able to emulate his example. Miaskovskii offered advice and steady support to his students and friends. Unfortunately, his works were seldom performed and he remained largely unknown to the Soviet public at large. Miaskovskii's deserving contribution as a prolific composers and his selfless patronage of the young were not remembered often enough.

Moreover, Khachaturian noticed a surprising lack of discussion among composers evaluating the new works. The composers seemed to be divided in groups pertaining to the genres of their works. Thus, a composer writing symphonies would not criticize a vocal composition — as if he was not qualified enough and would not be able to understand the specifics of genres others than his own.[45]

---

45. Khachaturian, "Vremia sprosit strogo.", p. 6.

Khachaturian believed that the restructuring in the field of music would also benefit from an open and just criticism. In addition, the ideological principles of a socialistic musical culture should help to produce the music of higher artistic and ideological standards, instilled with humanism, and social justice. He repeated the well known formulation that the main stronghold of the Soviet musical culture was the awareness of the powerful ideological foundation coupled with the support of the national musical tradition.

Khachaturian addressed also the established rituals of official national celebrations of important events. At such occasions the representatives of various republics were introduced, as well as the composers whose compositions were featured in the program. Khachaturian suggested that at similar celebrations the music alone should be heard and not the ceremonial announcements of many honorary titles of the chosen composers. The performed music should speak for itself, without elaborate introductions refering to the historical events. The music should be able to impress the audience by the token of its artistic distinction and true mastery without any verbal clarifications.

The discussion about the inadequacies of popular music remained the topics of many conferences and newspaper articles. The composer Giia Kancheli discussed in 1987, in the musical journal *Sovetskaia muzyka,* the poor quality of the compositions of popular music. However, he stressed that the compositions of serious music showed also a lack of desired quality.

During the past two years the two thousands members of the Union of Composers have produced a great number of new works. Kancheli thought that, unfortunately, many of these compositions showed a considerable lowering of aesthetic criteria and poor taste. Among a thousand newly written songs and as many sonatas only about ten in each category could be considered as successful. As a solution to the existing situation Kancheli suggested that the requirements for the membership in the Composers' Union should be scrutinized. The relatively large membership of the Union was in contradiction with the assumption of the innate uniqueness of creative talent. On the other hand, if the requirements for the membership became too demanding, the vital stream of young members might be cut off. Therefore, he suggested that the preparatory affiliation, described as the "candidate's stage" *(kandidatskii stazh),* should be lengthened. The composers were achieving full command of their faculties later than it was the case two hundred or even hundred years before. Kancheli pointed out that his thoughts about the reorganization of the Union of Composers caused dissatisfaction of many members, although in private talks nobody denied the validity of his assessment of the situation or the justification of his statement.[46]

The music critic V. Zak discussed in a lengthy article the necessity of a fresh approach in dealing with the public attending concert performances. The recitals of serious music in Soviet Union were often preceded by a lecture. The aim was to explain the musical program in order to enhance the appreciation of the performance. The lecturer aspired also to advance the musical education of the listeners elucidating important facts about the featured compositions. However, Zak noticed that these lectures often bored the public. Young people were denouncing the programs of serious music featuring such classics of Soviet music as Dmitrii Shostakovich or the dated popular programs with the compositions of Solov'ev-Sedoi. They shouted often denigrating slogans, and such an attitude distressed the performers and the concert public: "Do not interfere with our entertainment"*(Ne meshaite veselit'sia)*, or "We do not need Solov'ev Sedoi"*(Nam ne nuzhen Solov'ev-Sedoi);* "Shostakovich to the dust heap"*(Shostakovicha na svalku).*[47]

It became a rule when explaining a musical work to the public to use an academic approach, remote and measured. The lecturer would present the facts in a methodical fashion and such a presentation did not produce the wish to learn more or establish a dialogue with the public. The public often lost interest for the lecture and the musical work that was discussed. Young people, in particular, felt bored and often left the auditorium during the musicological analyses. Zak thought that such an unfavorable reaction discredited not only the lecturer but also the musicological discipline as a whole. He suggested a new format of music lectures by establishing a lively dialogue with the public. In the era of *glasnost''* it would be better to use an engaged and dynamic presentation in order to animate the audience and improve the reception of serious musical works. The role of a straight forward and lively oral communication has always a special appeal: such an address should help to overcome the indifference of the young.

---

46. G. Kancheli, "O budushchem—dumat' segodnia", *Sovetskaia muzyka*, June 1987, pp. 7–8.

47. Zak V., "Vyiti navstrechu slushateliu," *Sovetskaia muzyka*, April 1987, p. 24.

While discussing the importance of music education of the Soviet youth, Zak pointed out that the influence of rock music must be acknowledged. Otherwise, the attitude of the music educator would resemble the ostrich with its head in the sand. Rock music has taken a prominent place in the Soviet musical life. The task facing Soviet composers should be to to chart the goals and the creative transformation of this genre in order to serve better the needs of the young. Most of all, the rich folklore tradition should be used to enrich the rock music, instead of imitating Western canons. Several composers of popular music have used such an approach with favorable results, such as G. Garnian, A. Kozlov, D. Tukhmanov, E. Dogi, A. Rybnikov, Iu. Saul'skii, M. Minkov and M. Dunaevskii. Zak was obviously convinced that music making for the merriment of the youth should be regulated from above: the composers should try to promote the national tradition in a clever amalgamation with the Western rock music. The preference of the young for the rock music should be acknowledged, yet the newly composed rock music should also enrich their knowledge of the national music idioms.[48] Even in the heat of the discussions about new trends in musical practice, the critics and composers praised the proven value of folk music as the desired foundation of both popular and classical music.

The prevailing tendency in Soviet music during the 1960s, 1970s, and 1980s was a novel treatment of genres and musical forms. By and large the composers rejected the stringent canons and aimed for atypical solutions. Therefore, each work was observed as an unique creative task that required a special solution. It seemed that all the questions of musical genre, texture and structure had to be considered anew with a fresh point of view. All these tendencies did not develop in all Soviet republics at the same time and with the same intensity.

The Soviet musical scene in the era of *glasnost'* resounded with new musical voices. Many music historians, performers and composers alike became acutely aware of the importance of the musical heritage. Most importantly, a number of outstanding compositions of prominent composers, until recently neglected, were returned to their just place in the musical fund.

---

48. Zak, "Vyiti . . .," pp. 20–21.

CHAPTER VII

SOVIET RUSSIAN MUSICOLOGICAL REVALUATION OF STRAVINSKY'S NEO-CLASSICAL PHASE

The Soviet musicological literature devoted to the interpretation of neo-classicism in Russian, Soviet and consequently European music has introduced a pertinent and novel evaluation of the emergence of this stylistic formation. The depth and validity of musicological contributions of several Soviet music historians, published in the course of the 1960s and later on, merits a closer scrutiny due to the acuity of their findings elucidating in particular the compositional output of the neo-classical phase of Igor Stravinsky.[1] During this period, the distinguished musicologist Mikhail Semenovich Druskin devoted a number of his studies, including most of all an exceptional monograph, to Stravinsky, the man and his art, proclaiming at one point that Stravinsky spent his long life dedicated to Music, spelled with capital M, serving well this noble cause.[2] Thus, in spite of previous severe criticism in the course of the 1930s, 1940s and 1950s, Stravinsky's artistic legacy was powerful enough to ascertain a renewed acceptance in his native country.

After the gradual changes of the cultural policies and consequent introduction of the postulates of socialist realism in the course of the 1930s, Stravinsky's position was that of a prodigal son. Boris Vladimirovich Asaf'ev's monograph *Kniga o Stravinskom (A Book about Stravinsky)*, published in Leningrad in 1929, presented one of the last

---

1. B. Iarustovskii, *Igor' Stravinskii*, Moscow, 1963 and 1969. M. S. Druskin, *Igor' Stravinskii*, Leningrad, 1974. V. Kholopova,"O ritmicheskoi tekhnike i dinamicheskih svoistvakh ritma Stravinskogo", *Muzyka i sovremennost'*, Moscow, 1966. V. M. Blok, K. P. Portugalov, Ed., *Russkaia i Sovetskaia Muzyka,* Moscow, 1977, Prosveshchenie, pp. 80-91.

2. Druskin, "Igor' Stravinskii", *Muzikal'naia zhizn'*, Vol. 18, 1967. Quoted after *Russkaia i Sovetskaia . . .*, p. 83.

musicological writings displaying an effort at objective evaluation of Stravinsky's contribution.[3] As late as 1935, *Petrushka* was performed in Leningrad. For this performance, program notes were provided by Mikhail Druskin, a former student of Asaf'ev.[4] Subsequently Druskin's comments appeared revised, in form of a booklet entitled *"Petrushka" Igoria Stravinskogo*, published in Leningrad in 1935.[5]

Prior to the official acceptance of the doctrine of socialist realism at the First Congress of Soviet Writers in 1934, party leaders, writers and artists held discussions concerning the essential characteristics that an art work should embody. Lenin's principle of acceptance of the party ideology (partiinost') was acknowledged as fundamental, as well as his interpretation of the art work as emanation of folk and national spirit, in content and in form (narodnost'). Furthermore, an art work should present a truthful reproduction of typical characteristics and typical circumstances (tipichnost'), a requirement derived from Engels' explanations of inherent qualities of an art work. Andrei Aleksandrovich Zhdanov's contribution was contained in the assertion of the educational and propagandistic role of the arts, thus reinterpreting an typical "the reality in its revolutionary development". In addition, the art work should exercise an uplifting attitude and therefore comprise optimism and a positive outlook.[6]

These discussions in the political and literary field concerning the role of the arts were reflected in the changes of the ideological policies of various influential music organizations. Thus, the former Russian Association of Proletarian Musicians as well as the Association of Proletarian Writers were liquidated in April of 1932 following the resolution of the Central Committee "On the Reorganization of Literary-Artistic Organizations". The ideological policy of these associations was

---

3. Asaf'ev's book was reprinted 48 years later in Leningrad, in 1977.

4. B. Schwarz, *Music and Musical Life in Soviet Russia 1917-1970*, New York, Norton,1973, p. 354.

5. Schwarz, *Music and Musical Life* . . ., p. 128.

6. H. J. Drengenberg, *Die Sowjetische Politik auf dem Gebiet der Bildenden Kunst*. Forschungen zur Osteuropäischen Geschichte, Osteuropa-Institut an der Freien Universität Berlin, Historische Veröffentlichungen, Vol. 16, Berlin, 1972, pp. 319-323. Compare also: M. Owsjannikow, Editor, *Marxistisch-leninistische Ästhetik*, Berlin, 1976, pp. 336-339.

perceived, even in retrospect some twenty years later, as consisting of "nihilistic and formalistic distortions".[7]

In addition, a decisive break was announced against alien ideological influences, formalism and reactionary bourgeois tendencies. The influence of "modernistic music" was declared as pernicious, "defective" and "vulgarizing" for the ensuing development of Soviet music. Furthermore, it was stated that the role of classical heritage seemed to be debased. The implementation of so-called "theories" that were "excusing the confusion and cacophony in music" were severely criticized.[8] Another powerful revision of the ideological and creative postulates occurred in 1948. These changes were officially proclaimed in the resolution of the Central Committee in February of 1948. The resolution was declared as the "decisive blow to formalism" in the creative approach and artistic attitudes. Similarly, it was stated that the party guidance in ideological matters helped the musicologists in "eliminating their mistakes in order to find the right road in solving most important problems."[9]

The compositions Stravinsky created during his neo-classical period seemingly relinquished the Russian folk music idiom and did not fulfill other requirements postulated by the Soviet art doctrine of socialist realism, rigidly interpreted at one time. In particular, his abandonment of the Russian folk music idiom was repeatedly criticized. His polytonal harmonies and "constructional manner of arbitrary melodic and rhythmic configurations" marked him "as one of the leading representatives of modernism in music."[10] Save for sporadic visits to the Ustilug estate in the vicinity of Kiev prior to World War I, Stravinsky did not return to his homeland after emigrating to Switzerland in 1912 until some fifty years later, in autumn of 1962. He alienated himself from the Soviet government although his alienation from Russia itself was only superficial. Even when seemingly embracing the different and multifaceted human and cultural experiences elsewhere, he remained spiritually anchored in the orbit of his youth and formative years of early adulthood. In his own words Stravinsky felt that: "During my whole life I talked Russian, thought

---

7. *Bol'shaia Sovetskaia Entsiklopediia,* 2nd Edition, Vol. 28, Moscow, 1954, p. 514. Compare also Schwarz, *The Music and Musical Life* ..., p. 110.

8. "Muzykoznanie", *Bol'shaia Sovetskaia Entsiklopediia,* 2nd Edition, p. 533.

9. *Bol'shaia Sovetskaia Entsiklopediia,* 2nd Edition, p. 533-534.

10. *Bol'shaia Sovetskaia Entsiklopediia,* 2nd Edition, Vol. 41, 1956, p. 57-58.

in Russian and have a Russian style . . . . Perhaps it is not immediately evident in my music, but it is ingrained in it in its hidden nature."[11] To this effect one episode described by Craft in his conversations with Stravinsky was in particularly poignant. Commenting about his need to leave a light burning while asleep, Stravinsky felt as if an "umbilical cord of illumination" was perpetually tethered in his memories. As a boy, Stravinsky became accustomed to sleep, in his parents residence on the Krukov Canal in St. Petersburg, with a street light in front of his bedroom window as if guarding his dreams.[12]

In addition to this metaphorical source of strength rooted in the safety of childhood, Stravinsky retained to a large degree his creative and personal identity as shaped by his thorough and rigorous apprenticeship in the compositional class of his mentor Rimskii-Korsakov. By the very nature of his truly noble personality, and his dedicated and professional attitude in setting high standards for himself and his students, Rimskii-Korsakov stood as a formidable example to be followed. Stravinsky remembered with gratitude the guidance of Rimskii-Korsakov that surpassed in time the student-teacher relationships, since Rimskii-Korsakov became a paternal figure after the death of Stravinsky's own father.[13]

Mikhail Druskin stated in his monograph that it was Rimskii-Korsakov who introduced Stravinsky to the ancient layer of Russian peasant culture, folk rituals accompanied by ceremonial folk songs. These preoccupations found their reflection in the compositions of the 1910s: *Le Sacre du Printemps, Le Renard, Saucer Songs, Les Noces* and others.[14] In addition, Druskin emphasized the significance of Mussorgskii's operatic scores that provided Stravinsky with a glimpse of the old Russian way of life, the chant of the Orthodox Church, the well loved 'bell sonorities' and the archaic songs of the Old Believers (Raskol'niki). Chaikovskii's music with the "power of melody" exercised another lasting and even stronger impact

---

11. Druskin,"Igor' Stravinskii i Rossiia", *Muzikal'naia Zhizn, 1972*. Quoted after: Blok, Portugalov: *Russkaia i Sovetskaia Muzyka,*Moscow, 1977, p. 82.

12. Quoted after G. Seferis: Preface to the New Edition of the *Poetics of Music,* Cambridge, Massachusetts, Harvard University Press, 1970, p. IX.

13. Druskin,"Igor' Stravinsky ...", p. 82.

14. Compare Stravinsky's use of folk melodies: Richard Taruskin, "Russian Folk Melodies in *The Rite of Spring." Journal of the American Musicological Society*, Vol. XXXIII, No. 3, 1980, pp. 501-543.

on Stravinsky.[15] Druskin, as an eminent authority of Stravinsky's oeuvre, justly pointed out that the Russian characteristics in Stravinsky's music, in particular in their seemingly "hidden form" were mainly analyzed in the works of his first creative period. This period encompassed some fifteen years starting with *Feu d'artifice*, the ballet music *L'Oiseau de feu* inclusive with the comic opera *Mavra* and the choreographic cantata *Les Noces*. According to Druskin, the consequent evolution of Stravinsky's creative path brought new musical works that were only superficially discussed, stressing mainly, as it were, their apparent anti-national characteristics.[16]

With the change of cultural policies following the death of Stalin in March of 1953, a new and more liberal spirit emerged. The ensuing development during the period 1953-1962 was fittingly described as the *Thaw*. A fresh evaluation of the ruling art ideology of socialist realism was reflected at first on the pages of literary journals. The publication of Erenburg's short novel *Otepl (The Thaw)* in the May 1954 issue of *Znamia* became the literary highlight of the year and a topic for many clarifications. The novel's title became symbolic for the *thaw* in literature and the arts. Most importantly the novel was preceded by an authoritative article in the main newspaper *Pravda* in November 1953 that gave encouragement to re-examination of the ideological concept of socialist realism. The article stated that this doctrine offered "boundless vistas" and greatest freedom to the creative artists for the expression of their personalities and for the development of diverse art genres and styles: "*Hence the importance of encouraging new departures in art . . . of recognizing the artist's right to be independent, to strike out boldly on new paths.*" [17]

While the writers shortly after the publication of this article were in the vanguard, the composers and music historians eventually followed. Shostakovich composed his *Tenth Symphony* during the summer of 1953. The role of this remarkable work in Soviet music was comparable to the impact produced by Erenburg's novel *The Thaw* in literature.

---

15. Mikhail Druskin, *Igor Stravinsky,* Cambridge, Cambridge University Press, 1983, pp. 30-31.

16. Druskin, "Igor' Stravinskii i Rossiia", *Muzykal'naia Zhizn'*, 1972, No. 12. Quoted after *Russkaia i Sovetskaia Muzyka,* p. 83.

17. Schwarz, *Music and Musical Life* ..., p. 272-273.

Soviet musicologists in the late 1950s were predominantly centered on Russian and Soviet issues.   In the early 1960s Boris Schwarz quoted that the main topics of Soviet musicological research and specialization still showed an enormous preponderance of projects on Russian and Soviet music with barely any interest in foreign music.   Schwarz explained this lack of research in foreign music as resulting from a scarcity of primary sources on Western music in Soviet libraries.   As a rule, the Soviet libraries had strong archival holdings in the field of Russian music and hence their musicological research concentrated on related topics.[18]

Yet even the Russian and Soviet topics were at times severely censored. In a collection of musicological studies published in 1986 in Moscow, I. V. Nest'ev traced the prevailing attitude of official circles towards Prokof'ev's works.   Even after his return to the Soviet Union in 1932, Prokof'ev had been sporadically a target of criticism due to his "cosmopolitan" or "western" tendencies.   In this volume, Nesteev included an interesting summary of a speech delivered by Prokof'ev at the conference of Soviet composers on April 9, 1937 in which Prokof'ev refuted the critics charging him with "western" attitudes.   Prokof'ev pointed out that there existed a lively interest in the West for contemporary Soviet music citing the performances of works of Soviet composers abroad.   Yet the expectations were addressed to the novelty of the compositional approach, since the public in the West believed that the new Soviet society encouraged the creation of new music.   However, these expectations were not answered.   Prokof'ev concluded with a characteristic remark summing up clearly his attitude: "USSR - the new world, yet the composers are asserting the old".[19]

A decade later, similar criticism of Prokof'ev's cosmopolitan position was even more prevalent after the Party's resolution of 1948.   His compositions were not performed as often, and his works were not discussed in scholarly papers or monographs.   According to the testimony of Soviet musicologist G. Sh. Ordzhonikidze, there was an astonishing absence of musicological studies on Prokof'ev.   Shortly after his graduation from the Moscow Conservatory in 1952, Ordzhonikidze tried

---

18. Schwarz, *Music and Musical Life* ..., p. 374–375.

19. S. S. Prokof'ev, "Konspekt rechi na sabranii aktiva Soiuza Sovetskih kompozitorov 9 aprelia 1937 goda," I. V. Nest'ev,*Vek nyneshnii i vek minuvshii*, Moscow, Sovetskii kompozitor, 1986, p. 95.

in vain to learn more about Prokof'ev and his work. He visited many specialized music stores only to conclude that there was not even a slim volume dealing with Prokof'ev's compositions. He felt ashamed that, as a graduate student of music, he had not heard "one note of Prokof'ev's music" during his studies in Moscow. Ordzhonikidze also stated that he could not find explanatory musicological treatises dedicated to the compositions of this great artist.[20]

Most importantly, the ruling ideology, with its stress on cultivation of national values, discouraged musicological investigations of so called modernism, "cosmopolitan" and "decadent" musical styles of Western Europe. Suffice it to examine the entry on Stravinsky in the *Bol'shaia Sovetskaia Entsiklopediia (Great Soviet Encyclopedia)* published in 1956 displaying a persistence of such attitudes. His early compositions *Feu d'artifice* (1908), *L'Oiseau de feux* (1910) and *Petrushka* (1911) were described as positive achievements: "characterized by their splendor of orchestral color ... that with some other of Stravinsky's compositions entered into the repertoire of the symphony orchestras around the world". However, already *Petrushka* and in particular *Le Sacre du Printemps*, decisively showed "elements of aestheticism, acute stylization and violent polytonal harmonies". His later compositions like the vocal miniatures and pantomimes *Renard* and *Les Noces* showed "primitivism with decadent deformations". Compositions created after emigration to America "reflected the American bourgeois culture". Stravinsky composed without discrimination as if guided only by current demands: "*He fulfilled most different demands - from the Catholic mass to "Circus polka" (1942) and "Ebony Concerto" for clarinet and jazz orchestra (1945)*".[21]

Interestingly enough, some twenty years later, traces of similar evaluations of avant-garde tendencies were still present in articles written for the *Great Soviet Encyclopedia*, published in Moscow in 1976. Avant-gardism was declared as an expression of "the mood of petit bourgeois individualism, anarchism or political indifference." In contrast to such deviation of the musical art in the West, the Soviet and other socialist musical cultures were defined as displaying "a consistently democratic, popular character . . . (that) distinguishes socialist musical culture from

---

20. G. Sh. Ordzhonikidze, I. "Nest'ev — uchenyi, critic, publitsist", I.V. Nest'ev, *Vek nyneshnii . . .*, p. 3.

21. *Bol'shaia Sovetskaia Entsiklopediia,* 1956, p. 57-58.

other musical cultures." In addition, the well established criteria of socialist realism were reiterated as the utmost requirements in the pursuit of creation of accepted artistic values: "partiinost'" interpreted as party spirit and "narodnost'" manifested as close tie with the people. The doctrine of socialist realism was declared as "the method" that together with "narodnost'" and "partiinost'" presented the "artistic foundation of Soviet music".[22]

While similar evaluations reflected the ideologically sanctioned yet retrogressive platform of Soviet musicology apparently still persisting among some circles, a number of musicological studies of the 1960s brought a remarkable change. The keenness of observations and broad concepts of evaluation were launching Soviet musicologists in the forefront of musicological research. The stereotyped formulas previously used in the interpretation of musical works gave way to a new and more balanced outlook. In pursuit of a fresh and truthful evaluation of creative men and women and their work, Soviet musicologists have apparently besieged the worn out postulates of socialist realism, thereby allowing for a broadening of chosen subject matters and avenues of research. These efforts were directed towards abandoning the imposed isolation on the cultural field that led to parochialism and stagnation. Therefore, this period could be linked to the spirit of Pushkin's verses describing the founding of Petersburg as a symbolic opening of a new window to Europe: "V Evropu prorubit' okno" (To hack a window through to Europe.)[23]

Interestingly enough, it was in the same city, today's Leningrad, that musicologists introduced in particular new topics and methods of research. At the very heart of these investigations is the musicological output of Mikhail Semenovich Druskin, written during the 1960s, which helped establish the novel tenor of Soviet musicology.

Druskin's efforts did not pass unnoticed: the breadth of his observations, the validity of his statements, notably concerning the contribution of Stravinsky, drew appreciation in his country and abroad. His studies on Stravinsky, the man and his music, published in Soviet music

---

22. A. N. Sokhor, "Music", *Great Soviet Encyclopedia,* London, 1980, Vol. 24, pp. 263-264. Translation of the Russian edition: Moscow, 1976, Third Edition.

23. *Mednyi vsadnik: Peterburgskaia povest';* *The Bronze Horseman: A Tale of Petersburg,* quoted after Walter Arndt, *Pushkin Threefold,* New York, Dutton, 1972, p. 400.

journals during the 1960s, led to the publication of the monograph *Igor' Stravinskii'* that appeared in Leningrad in 1974. The book was shortly afterwards translated into German, and published in East Germany in 1976 with a second edition following in 1979. Soon after Druskin prepared a second revised edition in Russian: *Igor' Stravinskii-lichnost', tvorchestvo, vzgliady,* published in Leningrad in 1979. The English translation of the second Russian edition by Martin Cooper appeared in Great Britain in 1983.[24]

In due time Druskin was honored by his colleagues as one of the leading Soviet musicologists. In a special volume published in 1981 under the title *Istoriia i sovremennost' (History and contemporaneity)* dedicated to the fiftieth anniversary of Druskin's professional activities, composer Andrei Pavlovich Petrov stated with pride that Leningrad has given to the Soviet culture exceptional representatives of the musical thought: B. V. Asaf'ev, A. V. Ossovskii and I. I. Sollertinskii.[25] Druskin's place was acclaimed right along with his illustrious predecessors.

In his introductory statement, Petrov described the 1960s as the years that resulted in an enhancement of international contacts in the cultural field as Soviet composers had opportunities to gain information about the achievements of musical development in West Europe. It was the period that introduced new compositional techniques. Yet, this innovations had first to be examined and modified in accordance with ideological requirements of Soviet art. At this point, the musicological work conducted by Druskin traced the general development of music created outside Soviet boundaries during the 20th century. His research corresponded to the essential need for orientation and comprehension of intricate qualities of contemporary music. Many composers and musicologists felt as if an imperative demand persisted for a new appraisal of Stravinsky's musical legacy. Druskin's evaluations apparently stirred up imagination and gave food for thought. Andrei Petrov, himself a practicing composer, felt that Druskin's work helped the composers to

---

24. Cambridge University Press, Cambridge, London, New York, 1983.

25. Petrov was born in 1930 in Leningrad. His compositional work encompassed several ballet scores, symphonic music, vocal cycles and music for the movies among others. Petrov acted also in the 1960s as a high ranking official of the Russian Soviet Republic. *Entsiklopedicheskii muzikal'nii slovar',* Second Ed., Moscow, 1966, p. 391.

clarify their own compositional task within the framework of contemporaneity.[26] Petrov praised Druskin's monograph on Stravinsky as his best achievement. Druskin's book discussed issues that were on the mind of each and every composer: such as the consequent development of music in general, the evolution of the musical language, the influence of music on the public and the professional goals of the composer. The spiritual world of Stravinsky had succeeded in projecting its imprint on contemporary compositional issues. Stravinsky's artistic credo and general points of view presented, in a mutually interdependent fashion, a phenomenon of great interest. Stravinsky's creative thought, its essence and its multitude captured in his compositional work, coincided at times with artistic attitudes of many of his colleagues be they Soviet, French, Polish or American composers. Therefore, Druskin's book elaborated the position of Stravinsky and, the almost universally shared artistic outlooks of contemporary composers elsewhere. Stravinsky embodied in his complex and contradictory human and artistic personality many of these postulates due to the strength of his genius, intellect and general culture. That is why Druskin's book, due to its outstanding understanding of the cultural climate of the 20th century, presented as well the continuation of the impending discussions about the artist and his time. Druskin succeeded in grasping the psychology of the creative process of music composition. In other words, Druskin was not satisfied with an analysis of the compositional techniques and characteristics of the compositional score, but also tried to examine the higher categories of creative thought. He analyzed the compositional process while stressing the introspective monologue of the composer in the evaluation of possible choices. Druskin aimed to clarify, with great insight, the yet unexplained secrets of creativity.[27]

Druskin elucidated in particular Stravinsky's role in the formation of the neo-classical style. Druskin argued that Stravinsky succeeded in adapting chosen ancient musical models and accomplished their creative rebuilding within a contemporary musical idiom. This re-creation was not based on a stylized approach but rather directed to the radical adaptation of models while using new musical means. Although, kindred ideas were at

---

26. Andrei Petrov, *Muzykant, Pedagog, Uchenyi, Vmeste predislovia*, in *Istoriia i sovremennost'*, Leningrad, Sovetskii kompozitor, 1981, p. 4.

27. Petrov, *Muzykant, Pedagog, Uchenyi*, p. 5–6.

the time in abundance, Stravinsky remained a neo-classicist for a longer period and with greater consistency than any other leading artist of his day.

Yet Druskin had a predecessor for his splendid research: Boris Vladimirovich Asaf'ev published in 1929 an inspired and valuable study on Stravinsky. In this book written in the course of the 1920s, Asaf'ev was among the first to point out Stravinsky's innovative attitude towards the folk music idiom. According to Asaf'ev, Stravinsky did not use a stylized approach in compositions of his first creative period. He treated the folk melodies not as an archaic layer but rather as a living language. Stravinsky himself expressed that he intended "to rework the art ... created by the people's genius" ("pererabotat' iskusstvo ... sozdannoe geniem naroda").[28] This tendency came to full fruition later on, in the radical adaptation of various older models used in the creation of his neo-classical works. Thus Asaf'ev pointed out the *Serenade for Piano*, composed in 1925, as an example of the neo-classical method of model adaptation. Stravinsky embodied in this work all the lyrical elements associated with this form and succeeded in projecting a universal and all embracing range of contents. He managed to depict the enchanting inflections of lute and guitar music and all the lyricism underlying the exalted, romantic mood, yet translated in a concise, even laconic, contemporary piano style. In a similar vein, Stravinsky presented the *Royal March* from the *Soldier's Story* as a typical military march, summing up this genre in its rhythmical and intonational essence, but expressed in a contemporary idiom.[29]

Druskin, starting from Asaf'ev's analytical judgments, came to a similar conclusion in his subsequent studies dedicated to Stravinsky. In the process of clarification of Stravinsky's compositional style, Druskin also explained his understanding of the term "adaptation" of a model:

"All that fascinated him . . . or for some reasons interested him, he studied and adapted, changing it after his liking and suitability. In adapting

---

28. Lev Raaben,"Eshche raz o neoklasitsizme", *Istoriia i sovremennost'*. Ed. A. I. Klimovitskii, L. G. Kovnatskaia, M. D. Sabinina, Leningrad, Sov. kompozitor,1981, p. 201.

29. Boris Vladimirovich Asaf'ev, *Kniga o Stravinskom*, Leningrad, 1977, p. 250.

the creative models, Stravinsky typified its structure — melodic, rhythmic, textual, compositional."[30] During the same period, on a broader scale, the development of European music was reexamined. The neo-classical period itself was scrutinized in Soviet musicological writings published during the 1960s and consequently continued to attract further attention. In addition, several monographs and studies were published dealing in particular with Igor Stravinsky and some other composers, such as proponents of neo-classical stylistic formation.[31]

Still another leading musicologist from Leningrad, Lev Raaben, observed that the emergence of neo-classicism played an important role in the "revolution" of the musical language (znachenie neoklassitsisma v iazykovoi revolutsii) of the 20th century.[32] The harmonic innovations of Skriabin's *Prometheus* and the polytonal and polymodal harmonies of Darius Millhaud, Arthur Honneger, Francis Poulenc and others evolved previously out of a rampant need for radical change. Further enrichment came from the inclusion of modal idioms contained in folk music as in compositions of Zoltan Kodaly and Bela Bartok. Bartok's compositions revealed an intricate relationship of atonal and modal means, underlying the expressionistic qualities of his musical language. Another source of inspiration was the music of non-western nations, in particular India, as in the case of compositional work of Albert Roussel, Andre Jolivet and Olivier Messiaen. Raaben linked the emergence of neo-classicism along with other innovations in the development of contemporaneous musical language.

Pierre Boulez attributed the radical change and the emergence of "the new music" of the first half of the 20th century mainly to Arnold Schoenberg and Igor Stravinsky. Raaben thought it unjust to underline only the technical aspects of these changes, displaying in fact a biased and tendentious attitude. Furthermore, Raaben disagreed with Boulez' interpretation of Stravinsky's contribution since Boulez declared Stravinsky's compositional invention as entirely limited to the domain of

---

30. Mikhail Semenovich Druskin, *Igor Stravinsky, His Life, Works and Views*, Cambridge, Cambridge University Press, 1983, p. 86.

31. B. Asaf'ev, *Kniga o Stravinskom*, Leningrad, 1977. T. Levaia, O. Leont'eva, *Paul' Hindemit*, Moscow, 1974.

32. Raaben, *Eshche Raz o Neoklassitsizme*, p. 197-198.

rhythm while still preserving the classical tonal relations of the tonic, dominant and subdominant. Boulez, therefore, explained as faulty Stravinsky's retention of harmonic progressions already established by the composers of the classical era.

Raaben declared Boulez' findings about Stravinsky's contribution as one-sided mainly due to the reduction to one compositional aspect of rhythmic configurations, even if presented as the most important. Raaben stated with a degree of indignation that, in the course of time, the apostles of the New Viennese school elaborated further on their own importance and negated the historical role of other contemporary movements as well as of the contribution of Stravinsky.[33]

On the other hand, Raaben acknowledged both Schoenberg and Stravinsky as creators of compositional systems of importance for the consequent development of music. Raaben allowed the possibility of not accepting their individual compositional systems due to different aesthetic principles or acquired taste, but maintained that it would not be possible to deny their existence.

Raaben's commentary, as stated, reflected a defensive connotation while pleading for a more truthful recognition of Stravinsky's contribution. Raaben was obviously identifying Stravinsky's achievements as part of the national treasury of the Russian artistic thought, confronting the unjust promotion of Schoenberg's innovations with supercilious treatment of Stravinsky's achievements. Furthermore, Raaben's acknowledgment of different criteria directed towards the evaluation of Stravinsky's neo-classical phase attested to his knowledge of such persisting attitudes. Yet, in all fairness to different views, he acknowledged the reality of existence and creative impact of both Stravinsky's and Schoenberg's compositional systems, although he stressed that Stravinsky's contribution was unjustly slighted by the proponents of the New Viennese school.

In order to further emphasize the validity of Stravinsky's compositional credo, Raaben explained Schoenberg's dodecaphony, championed by his followers, as if in time overshadowing the innovations of Stravinsky. Raaben noted that Stravinsky developed his compositional system slowly, until it eventually crystallized in his works of the neo-classical period. His system was based on a special creative method rooted in the manifold modifications of varied genres and stylistic models contained in musical

---

33. Raaben, *Eshche Raz o Neoklassitsizme*, p. 198-199.

compositions of different epoches and national cultures. This method replenished and enriched in a fundamental way the musical resources of the 20th century resulting in a distinct aesthetic and stylistic formation known as neo-classicism.

Raaben's conclusions should be observed juxtaposed with the musicological exploration that followed the established guidelines of socialist realism in the 1930s, 1940s and 1950s. The studies and essays on music reflected rigidly, during that time, the observance of the postulates of socialist realism. Hence, musicological evaluations projected the neo-classical style as artificially constructed, severing all ties with the national musical traditions. The compositions showing an inclination towards neo-classicism were proclaimed as "decadent" or artificially constructed. Often it was stated that neo-classical compositions projected values of the bourgeois class serving its imperialistic goals. Arnold Al'shvang was among the first to introduce such an evaluation of Stravinsky in his essay entitled: *The Ideological Path of Igor Stravinsky*, published in the journal *Sovetskaia Muzyka* in 1933. Al'shvang stated in the opening sentence: *"Stravinsky is an important and almost complete artistic ideologist of the imperialist bourgeoisie."*[34]

Yet with acquired historical distance and due changes in the interpretation of the ideological doctrine of socialist realism, a more truthful evaluation emerged. The musicological research conducted in the late 1950s, 1960s, and later brought the necessary corrections. Neo-classicism, became recognized as one of the leading stylistic trends between the World Wars, and was repeatedly studied. Since the principle of *narodnost'* (national roots) was considered as one of the leading criteria safeguarding the validity of an art work, the Soviet musicologists brought this overlooked entity into the focus of their discussion. Druskin and Raaben were among the first to trace the influence of various national musical idioms in compositions of Stravinsky as well as of other leading composers who were also proponents of the neo-classical stylistic orientation.

According to the prevailing criticism in Soviet musicological literature during the late 1930s and 1940s, the major drawback of neo-classicism was its estrangement from the national spirit. Therefore, neo-classicism was declared as stilted and artificially created, lacking the essential national

---

34. Schwarz, *Music and Musical Life* . . ., p. 354.

denomination and identity. Even as recently as 1974, the evaluation of neo-classicism in the *Bol' shaia Sovetskaia Entsiklopediia* asserted that neo-classicism projected a dichotomy of both positive and negative qualities. On the one hand fostering clarity and orderliness in organization of ancient musical styles; on the other, leading frequently "to cold, formal imitation and artistic recreation of obsolete methods".[35] However, in their reexamination and closer scrutiny of this stylistic formation, a number of Soviet musicologists pointed to positive properties of neo-classicism. In their separate appraisals, Druskin and Raaben established that major composers of this trend drew often enough from the national tradition their source of inspiration. The stylistic models from their respective national past had provided, in the time of social unrest, the feeling of stability and affirmation of the continuity of existence.

Raaben further stated that the feeling of political and economic instability that permeated the period between the World Wars created a need for classical requirements of clarity and balance. Many composers found reassurance in the projection of orderliness and formal control typical of the compositions from the pre-classical and classical era. These were the reasons that helped to incorporate neo-classicism in the compositional schools of many countries. Neo-classicism consequently became the dominant stylistic trend in the period between the World Wars. Although it acquired a strong anchor in respective national traditions, neo-classicism reflected also some universal traits, such as the avoidance of exaggerated emotionalism of the late romanticism. Moreover, neo-classicism hastened the process of the necessary renewal of European music. Such a renewal of musical resources resulted out of an urgent need following the full course of development of the late romanticism and the consequent exhaustion of modes of expression.[36]

Raaben repeatedly stressed that neo-classical style often attained respective national connotations. The national tradition was in particular prominent in the compositions of French neo-classicists. Thus, the *First Sonata for Viola and Piano* by Darius Millhaud, based on the themes of French songs of the 17th century, was reminiscent also of another well known form of French music: the suites of Couperin and Rameau. Poulenc composed in the style of the celebrated French harpsichord

35. *Bol'shaia Sovetskaia Entsiklopediia*, 3rd Edition, Vol. 17, Moscow, 1974, p. 470.

36. Raaben, *Eshche raz o neoklassitsizme*, p. 207.

miniatures the *Three Pieces: Pastorale, Toccata and Hymn* in 1928, and in 1933 the *Album Leaf* comprised of *Arietta, Phantasy, Gigue*. Similarly, Poulenc's *Suite for Two Oboes, Two Bassoons, Two Trumpets,Two Trombones, Percussions and Harpsichord* presented in a stylized manner such French dances of the 16th century as pavane, the branle and others. In order to further enhance his *Suite*, Poulenc used the old instrumental setting of the wind ensemble and employed modal harmonies. As a result, Poulenc's *Suite* is one of his most accomplished neo-classical works. Some compositions of Albert Roussel showed both impressionistic and neo-classical characteristics, in particular his *Suite en Fa*. Similar features were expressed in the ballets music for *Bacchus et Ariadne* and *Aeneas* composed in the 1930s.[37]

Raaben agreed with Druskin's statement, expressed with forthright admiration, confirming that neo-classicism became only truly universal in the compositions of Stravinsky. Stravinsky's neo-classical compositions presented a tribute to his musical erudition and revealed his comprehension of many stylistic epochs and national styles. Due to the strength of his compositional capacity Stravinsky included in his neo-classical idiom, the national and cultural traditions of many other countries, in addition to his Russian heritage.[38] Thus, during his residence in France in the 1930s, Stravinsky was very likely influenced by the prevalence of the Greco-Roman themes among various French composers attesting to the predilection for archetypes of ancient mythology. While in France, Stravinsky composed *Apollon Musagete, Persephone,* and *Serenade for Piano,* reflecting in part, the French preference - *le gout français* - for mythological themes.

Furthermore, Raaben acknowledged that Druskin traced justly the importance of the baroque era as another source of inspiration. This tradition, as exemplified in the works of Bach and Handel, was present in a number of Stravinsky's compositions: *Concerto for Piano, Symphony of the Psalms,* and *The Dumbarton Oaks Concerto*. The latter was dubbed as the seventh *Brandenburg Concerto* due to its closeness in spirit to its baroque model. Similar stylistic features characterized *The Symphony of Psalms* and *Oedipus Rex*. *Concerto for Violin* showed Vivaldi's influence as well. The spirit of classicism was present in the *Symphony in D-major*

---

37. Raaben, *Eshche raz o neoklassitsizme*, p. 209–210.

38. Raaben, *Eshche raz o neoklassitsizme*, p. 209.

pointing to Haydn while the *Symphony in three Movements* showed the influence of Beethoven. The closeness to the models of romanticism was noticeable in *Capriccio for Piano and Orchestra,* and in the ballet *Baiser de la fee.* [39]

In his further discussion of neo-classical tendencies Raaben thought that social turmoil was directly reflected in the prevailing attitudes of some artists as speakers of their time. He pointed out that the expressionists of the New Viennese school have projected chaotic comprehension of the social reality by means of deformation of form-building musical components. However, even the rational dodecaphonic constructivism of such compositions did not evoke, during performances, a feeling of stability. In contrast, the musical art of past centuries seemed to provide the needed stability with its balance of form and content, tonal centricity, devoid of false sentimentality and pathos. Most importantly, Raaben stated that neo-classicism did not present a flight to the proverbial ivory tower, as it was sometimes declared, since it introduced means for active participation in the struggle for salvaging ethical and moral values in times of general turmoil.

With this statement Raaben effectively discredited earlier postulates of Soviet musicologists about the isolationism and decadence of composers espousing neo-classical tendencies. Raaben succeeded in presenting a new and positive aspect of neo-classicism that was previously overlooked in Soviet musicology. In the time of economic crises and political upheaval the composers were relentlessly searching for renewed order and stability trying to uphold the serenity and dignity of creative endeavors. The neo-classical idiom served well in the achievement of this goal.

Furthermore, Raaben asserted that neo-classicism did not cease to exert its propitious influence after the end of World War II. Neo-classicism was not only limited to the music of the bourgeois society: witness the multitude of partitas, toccatas, cycles of preludes and fugues, suites and concertos with baroque traits written by Western as well as Soviet composers. Raaben singled out Shostakovich for the presence of neo-classical elements in his compositional oeuvre. Shostakovich's cycles of preludes and fugues, chorales, toccatas, partitas, symphonies and chamber ensembles testified to the many faceted modes of neo-classical influence. However, Raaben was careful to point out that Shostakovich's ideological

---

39. Raaben, *Eshche raz o neoklassitsizme,* p. 199.

and semantic attitudes displayed remoteness to neo-classicistic aesthetics. Most of all, neo-classicism introduced a new phenomenon, dubbed by Raaben as 'poly-stylistics', in lieu of a more suitable terminology. Neo-classicism implemented the creative method of contemporary adaptation of models from different styles and epoches. In other words, this style presented the idea of superposition of time: the past serving the present. Raaben concluded that more research would be necessary to elucidate neo-classicism as one of the most universal among the new systems of music of the 20th century.[40]

The noted musicologist, Nelli Grigor'evna Shakhnazarova, on the other hand, stated that neo-classicism pointed most of all to the domination of the intellect in the compositional process. Shakhnazarova expressed these thoughts in her book on the problems of musical aesthetics as discussed in the theoretical works of Stravinsky, Hindemith and Schoenberg. The strict organization and restraint in the outward presentation and the absence of open emotionalism expressed a defined rationalistic tendency. In her opinion, dodecaphony presented the consequence of the one sided development of the same rationalistic tendency. This attitude derived from the assumption that the composer could only induce order into the existing chaos by introducing a rational approach. She stated that she felt that the theoretical works of these composers were inadequately presented in Soviet musicology. However, these composers influenced and even formulated some of the most important tendencies of the contemporary music. In her concluding chapter, Shakhnazarova pointed to the important role that Hindemith played in the formation of neo-classicism as a phenomenon of importance in the development of contemporary music. However, in her opinion, Stravinsky with his best compositions, notably *Le Sacre du Printemps,* embodied one of the noblest achievements of the artistic consciousness of the humankind.[41]

Leonid Arnol'dovich Entelis explained the occurrence of neo-classicism as a reaction to the hypertrophied modes of expressions and perilous fragmentations of musical form. The longing for orderliness and repose led many composers to accept different aspects of neo-classicism in accordance with their different needs. Entelis in particular discussed the

---

40. Raaben, *Eshche raz o neoklassitsizme,* pp. 213–214.

41. Nelli Grigorevna Shakhnazarova, *Problemy muzykal'noi estetiki v teoreticheskih trudah Stravinskogo, Shenberga, Hindemita,* Moscow, Muzyka, 1975, p. 233 and p. 237.

compositions of Stravinsky, Hindemith and Orf pertaining to neo-classicism. Entelis noted that Stravinsky projected in his neo-classical works an epic serenity, while safeguarding his own distinctive compositional style. Entelis book presented an outline of the development of music of the 20th century by centering attention on prominent composers and their contributions. In the foreword, Entelis mentioned that his book comprised selected lectures that he delivered to his students at the Conservatory in Leningrad.[42]

The attention bestowed on Stravinsky's heritage during the 1960s and later brought about the reprinting of Asaf'ev's *Kniga o Stravinskom (Book on Stravinsky)* whose first printing appeared in 1929. This second edition was published in 1977, almost fifty years after its first publication.[43]

The introduction to the second edition by Boris Mikhailovich Iarustovskii deserves special attention due to the candid evaluation of changed ideological postulates. At the height of his musicological career and fame, Iarustovskii openly discussed the one time silent banishment of this book due to its favorable presentation of Stravinsky's compositional achievements. Asaf'ev book was not readily mentioned or quoted in various studies or reference material pertaining to Stravinsky's life and work. Iarustovskii stated that the book slowly resurfaced during the decade preceding its recent appearance. Although it presented until recently a bibliographical rarity - it was nevertheless repeatedly studied, discussed and quoted.

All of this testified to the lively influence of the composer of *Petrushka* and *Sacre du Printemps*. His visit in the early 1960s further stimulated the growing interest for his compositional legacy. As a consequence of the attention bestowed on Stravinsky and resulting musicological studies dealing with his work, Iarustovskii pointed out with a note of sarcasm, Asaf'ev's book was again "remembered" and prepared for reprinting. According to Iarustovskii, Asaf'ev's monograph had been, discredited by

---

42. Lev Arnol'dovich Entelis, *Siluety kompozitorov XX veka*, Leningrad, 1976, p. 13.

43. Asaf'ev's *Kniga o Stravinskom*, was translated into English by Richard F. French in the late 1950s. However, this translation was published only in 1982 by UMI Research Press, in the series *Russian Music Studies*, No. 5, Ed. Malcolm Hamrick Brown. Therefore, Iarustovskii's Introduction to the second Russian edition of 1977 was not included in the 1982 UMI edition.

the followers of the ideology of the Russian Association of Proletarian Musicians and then repeatedly in the late 1930s and 1940s by the apparent heirs of these ideologists. Iarustovskii described these critics as if condoning simplification in explanations of complex issues of the world's artistic scene and therefore not in favor of books written from another viewpoint.[44]

In conclusion, Iarustovskii reminded the reading public that Asaf'ev correctly stated that the final and crucial acceptance of Stravinsky's work and a true comprehension of his human nature remained to be pursued by Soviet composers. Iarustovskii completed this thought by suggesting the inclusion of Soviet musicologists in the achievement of this formidable task. Furthermore, Iarustovskii noted that the latest works of Soviet musicologists as well as the statements of prominent composers like Shostakovich and Khachaturiian were published only after a long delay. Some of these works were able to project the complete evolution of Stravinsky's creative path, by including the latest compositions of the old master. The distinguished authors of these books elucidated the early works of Stravinsky that were previously discussed with great insight in Asaf'ev's book. Iarustovskii concluded that essentially all those studies attested to the lasting influence of Asaf'ev's pioneering work. The published works of M. Druskin, I. Vershinina, V. Smirnov, Iu. Kholopov, V. Kholopova, A. Shnitke, L. D'iachkova, S. Savenko, G. Alfeevska and many others have already created a solid foundation of the Stravinskyian research *(Fond nashei Straviniadi)*.

In his introduction to Asaf'ev's *The Book about Stravinsky*, Iarustovskii discerned one common denominator in all recent publications by Soviet musicologists dedicated to the preservation of Stravinsky's heritage. The majority of the mentioned authors approached Stravinsky not only as one of the great figures of the contemporary scene, but equally referred to "his primeval (stihiinoi) Russian nature" confirming Asaf'ev's earlier pronouncement. Iarustovskii concluded that Stravinsky was indeed accepted by his compatriots and that this acceptance spurred the dedicated preservation and renewed research of his heritage. Again Iarustovskii stressed that Asaf'ev was first to voice his view on the importance of such an acceptance.

---

44. B. Asaf'ev, *Kniga o Stravinskom*, p. 3.

It should be added that Iarustovskii's own introduction to Asaf'ev's book had a special importance of a testimony of an informed contemporary. Iarustovskii, born in 1911, witnessed the Proletkult ideology and the emergence of socialistic realism as the leading art doctrine. Unfortunately his introduction to Asaf'ev's book was one of the very last works that he published during his lifetime. He died in 1978 shortly after its appearance.

Iarustovskii himself was obviously aware of the immense richness that Stravinsky's message was able to bestow to his fellow men and in particular to the members of the Soviet society. By trying to elucidate the complex contribution and understand Stravinsky's unique vision a splendid beacon was lighted illuminating creative vistas until then not fully explored. The very process of acceptance of Stravinsky's invaluable heritage must have served as a breaking point of the new ideological path. *The Message of Igor Stravinsky*, to paraphrase the title of Theodore Stravinsky's book on his father, was perpetuating his Russian and at the same time his unique human and artistic bequest. Stravinsky's work, in its magnificent versatility, shall remain as a monument of perseverance and integrity of a Russian artist living abroad yet continuing to "think in Russian." It behooves to repeat with Pushkin:

> Ia pamiatnik sebe vozdvig nerukotvornyi
> K nemu ne zarastet narodnaia tropa . . .

> Unto myself I reared a monument
> A path trod by people shall never be overgrown with grass . . .[45]

---

45. Exegi monumentum, K. Bogdanova Ed., *Desiat' Russkih Poetov*, Moscow, no date, p. 50.

CHAPTER VIII

THE CHANGING ROLES OF POPULAR AND SERIOUS MUSICAL GENRES

In June of 1983 the Plenum of the Central Committee of the Soviet Communist Party addressed some of the issues relating to the purported pernicious influence of popular music. The fact that these issues were discussed by the highest echelons of the Communist Party testified to the importance that popular musical culture has achieved, permeating many aspects of everyday life. While the audiences and numbers of devoted fans continue to grow, the leaders of Soviet Society are obviously troubled by this development. This situation prompted the Plenum of the Central Committee to pass a resolution calling for the necessity of rectification of the existing situation in the field of popular music.[1]

Consequently, the Ministry of Culture of the USSR, in compliance with the resolution of the Central Committee of June 1983, introduced a number of measures that were expected to produce positive results. Necessary steps were planed in order to raise the professional standing of popular stage performances. In particular, attention was directed to the importance of the ideological role of the arts. It was expected that a greater mastery of the performing abilities, coupled with clearly understood ideological and aesthetic principles, should prevent further proliferation of mentioned productions described as primitive and stereotyped. Most importantly, the corroboration of the truthful aesthetic and ideological aspirations, as established by the Soviet cultural reality, should lead the musicians on a fruitful creative path.[2]

The doctrines of *perestroika* and *glasnost'*, aiming for a broad democratization of Soviet society, produced a number of interesting studies which discuss the implications of these changes including the emergence of popular music. The controversy centered around the varied interpretations

---

1. *Communist,* 1983, No. 9, pp. 28-29, quoted after Igor' Leont'evich Nabok, *Ideologicheskaia funktsiia muzyki,* Leningrad, Muzyka, 1987, pp. 66-67.

2. Ibid., p. 67.

of Soviet popular music, shortly before and after the introduction of *perestroika* and *glasnost'* doctrines, projected the diachronic continuity of the cultural policies: the awareness of the established canon of socialist realism in contrapuntal dialogue with current innovations. While the existing diachronic continuity was primarily manifested in the adherence to the platform of socialist realism, the search for artistic novelty pointed to a synchronic juxtaposition to artistic development elsewhere, uniting creative minds amid diversities of their respective national, social, and political vicissitudes.

The Soviet perception of the pernicious influences posed by Western models of light musical genres is rooted, to a large extent, in the history of ideas centered around the emergence of the artistic doctrine of socialist realism. Literary discussions, in the late 1920s and early 1930s, often focused on the examination of the social and political role of literary and artistic works. Maksim Gor'kii, with a number of writers, artists, and political leaders, supported the introduction of a realistic stylistic orientation. Gor'kii understood the ensuing doctrine of socialist realism as a method and technique of literary creations, as aesthetics and ethics of Soviet art, fostering the socialistic and revolutionary comprehension of the world.[3] This didactic and socially engaged artistic perspective was favored because it resembled the to traditional role of writers and their works in Russian society. In addition, socialist realism introduced the criteria of "partiinost'," interpreted as party spirit, and "narodnost'" manifested as a close tie with the people.[4]

Gor'kii was also concerned about the current development of the musical scene in the Soviet Union, in particular with the trends of popular music genres introduced by the newly formed jazz bands in the course of the 1920s. These bands were performing new dance forms that enjoyed great appeal. The sound of the jazz bands was even spreading its influence to the realm of serious music. Many prominent composers around the world, including Claude Debussy, Maurice Ravel, George Gershwin, Paul Hindemith, Igor Stravinsky, Darius Milhaud, Aaron Copland, among others, have used jazz in their compositions. The composers aimed to

---

3. Aleksandr Ivanovich Ovcharenko, *Sotsialisticheskii realizm*, Moscow, Sovetskii pisatel' 1977, p. 81.

4. M. Owsjannikow, Ed., *Marxistische-leninistische Ästhetik*, Berlin, 1976, pp. 336-339.

expand the tonal resources with the introduction of new melodic inflections, compositional techniques, instrumentation and sound organization. Igor Stravinsky was among the first to incorporate such an influence in his compositions of the 1920s. The composers were looking for new sources of melodic and rhythmic wealth. The jazz idiom was one of the possibilities to this end.[5]

In the mid-1920s the Soviet jazz bands were formed and attracted lively attention. Several bands were established and led, respectively, by V. Ia. Parnakh, A. N. Tsfasman, G. V. Lansberg and L. Ia. Teplitskii. The State Variety Stage Band which was organized in 1929 by L. O. Utesov and played in the course of its existence an important role in the formation of the Soviet jazz style.[6] Parnakh, as the founder and leader of the first Soviet jazz band, was particularly successful. His musical performances and views on the jazz music delighted the painter Pablo Picasso, among others, who drew a portrait of his young friend in 1922.[7]

The music of these bands was not appreciated by all segments of the population and equally by the officials of the government. In particular, Anatolii Vasilevich Lunacharskii, the first Commissar of Education, criticized the introduction of jazz music. He disliked the repertoire of the jazz bands that included the new dances such as the fox trot and Charleston. These dances presented, he wrote, a degenerated attitude fostering promiscuity. The dance halls of Berlin, Paris and New York proffered well this bourgeois style of entertainment:

"The dancing rooms show at its best the post-war bourgeois world. I was intrigued to watch unobserved what was happening there. The dead, wooden beat of the jazz-band, and the roar and moaning of the saxophone, kicking and jerking, an

---

5. Stravinsky used again jazz inflections during the 1950s and these compositions were subsequently criticized in his native country. The brief article in the *Bol'shaia Sovietskaia Entsiklopedia* (2nd Ed., Moscow 1956, Vol. 41, p. 58), pointed out that Stravinsky accommodated the wishes of the Western bourgeois society composing even for the circus *(Circus Polka)* or jazz performances *(Ebony Concerto)*.

6. Ibid.

7. The portrait was included in Lunacharskii's book, *O massovyh praznedstvah, estrade, tsirke*, "U zvuchashchego polotna," Moscow, Iskusstvo, 1981, p. 271.

unpleasant crowd of people as if seized by a convulsion and nobody smiling. The women with heavy make-up, with lots of rouge on their faces that look like masks."[8]

Lunacharskii thought that the popularity of the fox trot was mainly due to the simplicity of its movement: everybody can easily learn the dancing steps. However, this dance form also served well to introduce the frivolous encounters between sexes. Another more difficult dance form, the Charleston, contained even uglier, more lascivious movements. The dancers did not seem to enjoy each other, they moved in a mechanical manner, "as if obediently kneading an invisible dough with their feet". According to Lunacharskii, these dances resembled "the last ball of the capitalistic Satan". Yet worst of all, the people on the street reflected the same listless attitude, they hurried in a daze, as if they have "lost their souls".[9]

Furthermore, Lunacharskii disclosed that during a conference of the Communist Party the question of "syncopated music" was raised. This musical style comprised mainly the dances fox trot, and tango, as the main entertaining genres of the American and European bourgeoisie. Lunacharskii reiterated his opinion about the undesirable erotic qualities of these dance forms. However, in the ensuing discussion, some comrades expressed concern in the case of a sudden banishment of these dances in various clubs. They pointed out that there were numerous reasons to rejoice and enjoy the life. The young people achieved great victories in the past and very likely will achieve extraordinary deeds in the future. They should feel happy and free to dance as they choose. Lunacharskii agreed with this assessment although he further stressed that the fox trot should not be the only dance form performed by young adults. He even proposed the creation of a special "proletarian dance":

> "Let us have Apollonian music generated from the reason, energy, vigor; our music should be erotic, but not lecherous. Such music should express the feelings of a young man approaching a young woman, the mother of future children (as Chernyshcvskii once wrote)."[10]

---

8. Lunacharskii, "Tanets na estrade,"*O massovykh . . .,*, pp. 296-297.

9. Lunacharskii, "Tanets. . .", p. 297.

10. Lunacharskii, "Tanets. . .", p. 301. All translations from Russian are my own. J. M. Dj.

Lunacharskii's own attitude was well expressed in this assessment of the current situation. He obviously favored a conservative point of view, fostering traditional family values. Even when allowing social contacts among young people that contained erotic overtones, he reminded of Chernyshevskii's admonishment that young girls, as future mothers, should be respected. Most of all, Lunacharskii considered the music an important tool for education capable of instilling desirable social and moral qualities. Lunacharskii's views on education, ethos, and cultivation of fine arts were influenced by the cultural legacy of ancient Greece and its ethical education which fostered moral rectitude permeated with Apollonian spirit. He even envisioned the creation of new syncretic art forms that would recreate the antique ideal uniting drama, recitation, dance, pantomime, instrumental and vocal music and film.[11]

Maxim Gor'kii was equally opposed to the newest trends in music entertainment. Gor'kii wrote with eloquence in the 1930s about the "chaos of convulsive sounds" of the jazz music. He preferred the music of Beethoven and Mozart, the dance music of the minuet or the waltz. Interestingly enough, his formulation of the degradation of Western popular music persisted in the interpretation of the doctrine of socialist realism in literature and the arts. His pronouncement about the debasing influence of the jazz idiom was still accepted as a truthful evaluation of this genre even as late as 1952 and quoted anew in the *Bol'shaia Sovetskaia Entsiklopediia*:

"This is the music of the gross . . . . It presents the evolution from the serenity of the minuet and lively passions of the waltz to the cynicism of fox trot and convulsions of the Charleston, from Mozart and Beethoven to the jazz band of the Negroes who very likely chuckle in private at the sight of their white overlords turning into savages while the American Negroes have left such a state and moving from it further away."[12]

The above quoted entry on jazz in the mentioned *Bol'shaia Sovetskaia Entsiklopediia* of 1952 was in agreement with a similar pronouncement

---

11. A. N. Lunatscharski, *Die Revolution und die Kunst*, Dresden, VEB Verlag der Kunst, 1974, p. 28.

12. *Bol'shaia Sovetskaia Entsiklopedia*, 2nd Ed., Moscow 1952, p. 200.

formulated by V. Gordinskii. In 1950, Gordinskii published a booklet under the title: *Muzyka dukhovnoi nishchety (Music of Spiritual Poverty)*, which fittingly summed up his negative evaluation of jazz, perpetuating Gor'kii's legacy. In the same entry, jazz was declared as the product of the bourgeois culture. Jazz borrowed from the music of the American Negroes some typical characteristics of the rhythm such as syncopation, tonal patterns, and instrumentation, although these elements were distorted in the process.

Parallel to the gradual introduction of the realistic stylistic orientation and the abandonment of the avant-garde experimentation in literature in the course of the 1930s, similar efforts existed in the field of music. The new sources of enrichment, previously sought by the composers of serious music, were reexamined and often gradually suppressed, aiming for clarity of expression. The composers often acted as their own censors putting aside compositions that did not correspond to their changed ideological and artistic credo. The new realism in music was manifested in a predominantly tonal harmonic language and melodic inflections instilled with the folk music idioms. In addition, vocal and vocal instrumental forms were favored, coupled often with poetic texts that expressed a similar ideological outlook. The composers introduced these changes in order to facilitate the comprehension of their music and seeking acceptance by the broader segments of the public.

However, the sound of the jazz bands was not forgotten and in particular after the end of World War II became attractive again to the youths in the Soviet Union. In the early 1950s, following the proliferation of popular music genres in the West, small instrumental ensembles were formed in the USSR. These ensembles often specialized in improvisation.[13] However, the followers of this musical style, as well as Western fashions in clothing, were branded as "stiliagi" (the teddy-boys) and criticized as admirers of Western culture. In the Soviet press, these young people were often depicted in a derogatory manner. Satirical feuilletons under titles such as "Pleseni" ("The Scums") alluded to the young adherents of Western styles, the mentioned stiliagi, in a scornful manner. Even the writers of the popular genre of couplets commented the

---

13. *Great Soviet Encyclopedia*, Vol. 24, Moscow 1976, English translation 1980, p. 548.

occurrence of *stiliagi* and suggested the necessity of proper education of the young generations.[14]

The gradual liberalization brought a reexamination of the early 1950s and several literary works depicted this period with a fresh insight. The literary works written in the 1970s and 1980s brought often recollections of the 1950s. The theatrical play *Vzroslaia doch' molodogo cheloveka (The Grown-Up Daughter of a Young Man)* discussed the generation coming of age in the 1950s. The play was written in 1979 by V. Slavkin, and it established him as a promising new playwright. The play was subsequently produced on the stage of the prestigious Stanislavskii Theater in Moscow, and established also the director A. Vasil'ev, who never before directed in Moscow theaters. The plot centered around the reunion of former close friends after a long separation. The now middle-aged heroes of the play were exchanging memories of their generation coming of age in the early 1950s. They shared a modest meal in the privacy of an apartment of a friend. Their recollections of the past and their assessment of the present were entwined in a lively discussion, and as the conversation grew more intense they danced to the musical tunes of their youth. They talked about the passage of time by tracing the growth and education of their children.

The play developed on two time planes contrasting the past with the present. The present life was filled with the worries of the forty-years old people, while the past was dominated by brave efforts to put the mind over matters. Such an attitude helped to overcome the sufferings during the World War II, and the hardships immediately after the end of the War. The characters in the play remembered their youthful openness and curiosity about the human experiences elsewhere: their search for different ideas and happenings far from their immediate surrounding, ready to explore the unknown. They remembered the sounds of the trumpet of Louis Armstrong, the songs and improvisations of Ella Fitzgerald, the surprizing visual and musical imagery of the composer-painter Chiurlenis, the literary thought of Hemmingway.

Summing up the impact of the play, the critics noted the utter simplicity in the portrayal of the characters embroiled in the web of the everyday life. Although the play gave an impression of loosely connected fragments, the presentation of events and characters was truthful and

---

14. G. K. Terikov, *Kuplet na Estrade*, Moscow, Iskusstvo, 1987, p. 151.

believable. The former accusations of the "Western attitudes" of the onetime young people, branded as *stiliagi*, were declared as unjustifiable and unfortunate.[15]

Interestingly enough the Soviet film *Jazzman*, released in 1983, criticized the Soviet official renouncement of jazz in the late 1920s. The plot followed a student at the conservatory, Kostia, who left his studies of classical music in order to promulgate jazz among people. Kostia declared jazz as the people's music because its origins were in the folk songs of black American slaves, and he opposed Lunacharskii's views inferring that jazz manipulated sexual and savage impulses. In order to change the negative attitude toward jazz, Kostia organized a jazz band that enjoyed great popularity. However, the local authorities opposed Kostia's views and even initially cancelled one of the arranged concerts. The band sought help from another jazz supporter and eventually staged the concert in front of a sold out hall.[16]

The evolvement of rock and roll and the various light music derivatives of this genre in the course of the 1970s were met with serious concern by the Soviet cultural and political leaders. The strongly formulated opinions against rock and roll, reminded of similar criticism of jazz music and dance music of the 1920s and early 1930s. In addition, rock music was even understood as a form of subversive power capable of introducing the "westernization" of the Soviet youth.[17] Many musicologists, composers and sociologists tried to explain the seemingly unjustified popularity of some rock groups. These critics stated that the musical repertoire of these groups lowered the professional and aesthetic standards as well, aiming mainly towards greater popularity. An example of such deliberations, centered around the ideological function of popular music, presented the study *Ideologicheskaia funktsiia muzyki (Ideological Function of Music)* by the musicologist Igor' Leont'evich Nabok, published in Leningrad in 1987. Nabok discussed popular groups that showed the mentioned lack of necessary professional requirements. According to Nabok, these explicit

---

15. *Istoriia russkogo sovetskogo dramaticheskogo teatra*, Iu. A. Dmitrieva, Ed., Moscow, Prosveshchenie, 1987, Vol. 2, p. 158-159.

16. David A. Cook, "Socialist Realism", in *An Introduction to Soviet Cinema*, Special Report, Kennan Institute for Advanced Russian Studies, Washington D. C., 1987, p. 27.

17. Igor' Leont'evich Nabok, *Ideologicheskaia funktsiia muzyki*, Leningrad, Muzyka, 1987, p. 4.

changes in the realm of light music in the USSR took place roughly during the last fifteen years. Starting from the early 1970s, new musical ensembles were formed under the influence of the Western rock groups.[18]

Nabok conducted a thorough research of the evolution of rock music in Western societies. However, his presentation of the selected source material primarily centered around the negative aspects of light music in the West. He seemed to assume that rock music was an organized activity with clearly defined goals of propagating bourgeois ideology and promulgating the "westernizations" of Soviet youth. He stressed the imperialistic qualities of Western societies and projected an aggressive attitude underneath the façade of entertainment.[19] The youth was sadly deprived of the authentic values of the traditional treasury of folklore idiom that was substituted with cheap commercial products capable of social manipulations.

Nabok also gave an analysis of the Soviet popular music and suggested guidelines for future development. He stressed the existence of a variety of musical genres and the long and valuable tradition of light music, yet he thought it ludicrous that the present expansion of rock, in the contemporary bourgeois culture, managed to influence all genres of mass culture. The aggressive aspect of western rock music was a potential danger threatening other genres of light music, even the serious music, and the classical heritage.

This pernicious influence was characteristic not only of the products of Western popular music, with its large following in the USSR, but equally in the development of the Soviet youth music. In the West, rock music aspired to achieve an universal appeal to the youth population, independent of national and class differences. The rock music showed orientation towards dynamic behavior and self assertion providing in addition emotional compensation. It served also as an aspect of communication of the youths within their own age group. Therefore, rock music presented an escape from the alienation of the social and economic reality of the bourgeois society, and the existing conditions of life. It was a remedy, a "medical prescription", from the pains of growing up that soothed the feeling of apparent uselessness to the society. This escapism had sometimes the form of an anarchistic confrontation due to the social and psychological

---

18. Nabok, *Ideologicheskaia . . .*, p. 57.
19. Nabok, *Ideologicheskaia . . .*, p.4.

poles of contra culture: The music adopted the strong rhythmical beat, low melodic registers, and hypertrophy of dynamics. The vocal soloists developed a particular style of ecstatic and forceful singing. Nabok understood all these innovation as oppressive and superfluous. In fact, these styles of performance had nothing to do with the authentic and true music performances. The hard rock contained emotional overtones that included explicit aggressiveness towards bourgeois culture and way of life.[20]

Nabok was obviously concerned that the copying of the Western rock performances will cause harm to the Soviet youth. The attitude of independently aggressive behavior was based on the social myth about the eternal animosity of generations, the younger and the older, that was steadily preached by the bourgeois ideologists and theoreticians of contra culture. Nabok stressed that such confrontations and circumstances were foreign to the social reality in USSR. This statement projected an idealized assessment of human relations glossing over the existence of difficulties, if any, in the idealized socialistic society.

In his classification of Western popular music Nabok placed the musicals as the most prominent form safeguarding the established characteristics of the bourgeois culture. The musical folklore and its role in the national musical tradition was singled out as the second large area, including the rich heritage of the Negro music. The third entity comprised the pure jazz, without the proliferation of its commercial forms. The fourth group included the music as a form of political protest, most of all as a reflection of the values and world views of the youth contra culture originating in the late 1960s and the beginning of the 1970s, and producing the protest songs. The fifth group resulted as a product of deterioration of rock music under the influence of the commercialization and "ideological brain washing" by the domineering bourgeois culture. This last phenomenon, Nabok described as the "pop-music". Nabok pointed out that the suggested classification, in spite of its simplification, may help to project the ideological genesis of musical mass culture.

Nabok stressed that there existed a radical difference between the rebellious rock of the 1960s and the disco and punk rock of the 1970s. The rebellious rock originated mainly in a spontaneous manner, disco and punk were supported by the ruling culture. The late 1970s witnessed the

---

20. Nabok, *Ideologicheskaia* . . ., p. 48-49.

appearance of the eclectic style "pseudo-rock", closely associated with the
enterprising show business variety. This musical style could be associated
with various musical groups and styles, starting with the the old rock and
roll, on one side, and on the other with the numerous groups playing music
described as hard rock and heavy metal. The 1970s brought the return of
rock and roll close to the style of country music. Nabok concluded that
rock music as an expression of the youth protest did not cease to exist
completely. The continuation of its influence was manifested by the
participation of rock musicians in the peace movement. Such was the
coalition "Rock against Nuclear War", as well as the occurrence of the
"black rock" and whose representative was Steve Wonder.

Nabok's evaluation displayed as well a thorough knowledge of the
theoretical body of works that helped establish the doctrine of socialist
realism. It is characteristic that Nabok based his evaluations of popular
music on a well known and often quoted study: "Krizis burzhuaznoi
muzyki i mezhdunarodnoe revolutsionnoe dvizhenie" ("The Crisis of the
Bourgeois Music and the International Revolutionary Movement") by L.
N. Lebedinskii. Lebedinskii's study was published in 1933 in the leading
Soviet musical periodical *Sovetskaia muzyka*. This journal presented the
official platform of the Union of Soviet Composers. Nabok quoted
Lebedinskii's statement already at the beginning of his own study. He
obviously thought that Lebedinskii's evaluations were still pertinent and
applicable even to rock and roll, and all other popular musical styles
inclusive disco music, as much as once before Lebedinskii's arguments
were valid in discussions about the perils of the notorious dance fox trot.

Lebedinskii discussed often the ideological role of the arts in society
and he advocated the acceptance of the doctrine of socialist realism in
musical arts. Very much like Lunacharskii, Lebedinskii saw the situation
on the cultural field in the West as a reflection of a decaying and decadent
bourgeois society. The mentioned study by Lebedinskii pointed out the
negative and stereotyped presentation of the musical scene in the West, in
compliance with the official critical attitude towards Western bourgeois
culture in general. Lebedinskii devoted part of his study to the
development of popular music genres and to the much criticized dance fox
trot:

> ". . . ideological and emotional content of fox trot is contained in the reduction of
> all the varieties of movements, as existing in the nature and in the society, to the
> mechanical form only . . . (Fox trot) induces the training of subordination of

thoughts, and will power of men by introduction of mechanical automatism, and causes the general debasement and enslavement of the psychological life of men. This diversion is reflected in the breaking of human intellect from the fresh and clear comprehension of reality and from the independent relation towards it."[21]

Nabok endeavored as well to present the ideological and socio-cultural role that the rock music had held in the Western bourgeois society. Therefore, he offered an historic digression elucidating the evolution of this genre within the realm of light music. On one side there existed an obvious link with the ideas and practices of the contra culture, while on the other side rock displayed a steady connection with the established forms of musical entertainment. The early forms of the rock and roll of the 1950s presented an eclectic mixture of different musical styles: blues, country style, jazz, and traditional music for entertainment. In addition, rock and roll corresponded to the psychological needs of the teenage population in creating their own music that was different from the music of the adults. In addition, Nabok thought that rock and roll served well the show business establishment looking for new sources of revenue. The 1960s presented the flowering of rock music, in connection with the rise of the youth movement. Nabok stressed the evolution of the theory and practice of the contra culture, embracing not only music but equally other forms of art. This period was tied to the appearance of the *Beetles* and varied versions of the "rebellious rock" (buntuiushchii rok). The new rock that emerged at the end of 1960s and early 1970s proved to be a contradictory appearance, as the contra culture itself that produced it. The process of commercialization was caused not only by the bourgeois ideologists and show business establishment but equally by the discrepancies in esthetic and ideological views and the weakening of the youth movement. The products of the fragmentation of the rock music in the 1970s were the disco style, with its expressed commercial aspect, the "new wave", and the punk rock.

While analyzing the Soviet rock music, Nabok described several ensembles cultivating the undesirable new style of entertainment. He singled out the Moscow vocal-instrumental group with the pretentious name *Poslednii shans (The Last Chance)*. This group used the traditional

---

21. *Sovetskaia muzyka*, "Krizis burzhuaznoi muzyki i mezhdunarodnoe revoliutsionnoe dvizhenie", 1933, No. 4, pp. 101-102; quoted after Nabok, *Ideologicheskaia*, p. 7.

musical instruments such as the violins and guitars, in addition to various children's toys, rattles, and percussive instruments. This instrumental selection alone should have helped to impart to the audience the elusive "return" to the worry-free childhood and its perceptions of the world. According to Nabok, the intentional primitivization of the musical expression and the absurdity of the instrumental selection did not, in reality, project the hoped for effects. More specifically, it projected an infantile attitude and passivity to an already exhausted and tired audience very likely previously repeatedly exposed to the overpowering sounds of *rock and roll* concert performances or recordings.[22]

The stage setting and visual impact of rock concerts very often reminded of well known western models. The audio-visual effects and other extravagancies, presented another matter for concern. According to the comments of reviewers of such presentations, these concerts were closely associated with artistic kitsch and poor taste. The reviewers also described the outward appearance of the musicians, their behavior while interpreting the songs, as well as the general concept of such predictably choreographed musical performances. A. Troitskii stated that there existed a great conformity among young Soviet musicians with the Western rock and roll practices:

> "The staging of rock groups consists of a stricter or freer imitations of standard concert tricks established by foreign artists. These imitations include falling on the knees, the splits (considered as high class), a jump on the last chord (or as a variant: a jump on the first chord), minute runs while holding the instruments, synchronized hopping, formation of lines of players holding the guitars as if ready to hit it off."[23]

Soviet performers have acquired the casual style of behavior (raskovannost') that often crossed over to vulgarity and debauchery under the influence of bourgeois mass culture. The utter simplicity of performance practices bordered on primitivity and non-professionalism. The stark uniformity of lyrical texts aimed at discrediting the established values, showed lack of responsibility, and moral laxity where everything is permitted. This aggressive behavior was concealing an infantile world

---

22. Nabok, *Ideologicheskaia* . . ., p. 66.

23. A. Troitskii: "Puti nelegkogo zhanra," *Muzykal'naia zhizn'*, No. 15, 1983; quoted after I. Nabok, *Ideologicheskaia* . . ., p. 61.

outlook, social passivity, and a false contemporaneity. Finally, the throbbing effects of the amplifiers drowned the melodic and intonational expressiveness of the songs.[24]

Nabok declared that these attitudes were not in agreement with the desired behavior and optimistic outlooks of the Soviet youth. The atmosphere of emotional ecstasy, provoked and intensified by sound and visual effects, in particular in discotheques, could manipulate dangerously the behavior of the audience. The influence of popular music was facilitated by the availability of technical means for recording of performances and dissemination of recorded material. Nabok feared that, in the long run, such methods may enable Western bourgeois ideologists to pursue the "westernization" of Soviet culture. Therefore, the analyses of ideological aspects of the musical art presented an outstanding task for the Soviet aestheticians and musicologists. The genres of popular culture were not sufficiently studied as if these works did not present an object for serious analysis, in spite of the huge followings of young audiences. Nabok warned that these entertaining and easy going productions often harbor artistic and ideological principles not compatible with the Soviet reality. Equally the audio-visual effects invented for rock performances proved to elicit outbursts of emotional responses, overwhelming the audience with unexpected, unusual and extravagant.[25]

Many musical groups have flooded the musical scene, cultivating programs that were declared by some critics to be of dubious quality and therefore liable to produce ideological harm to the young audiences. However, the concerts featuring rock groups were usually sold out in advance. Soon enough the television stations introduced rock music programs that quickly became established by creating their own audiences. Some television programs asked the audience to participate in the evaluation of performances, which caused concern among the professional music critics and music theoreticians. Nabok cited, as an example, the popular television show from Leningrad "Muzikal'nyi Ring" (Musical Ring). This show encouraged viewers to express their opinions about the featured programs, "as if everybody's judgment was correct, be it professionals or dilettantes". Nabok pointed out that such an attitude

24. Nabok, *Ideologicheskaia* . . ., p. 65.

25. Nabok, *Ideologicheskaia* . . ., p. 4-5.

deprived the professionals to define the objective ideological, artistic and educational aspect of an art work, and fostered a pluralistic outlook.[26] Clearly, this explanation about the role of music criticism adhered to the dogmatic rules of socialist realism. The art work, even if belonging to the sphere of entertainment and featured on popular TV shows, must be in compliance with the established ideological, ethical and social standards. The artists and critics should interpret the established ideological postulates and explain the functions that an art work should perform in a socialist society, enhancing primarily the education of the masses. The ideological and artistic requirements, as formulated by the doctrine of socialist realism, should help the composers to produce art works accepted and understood by all segments of the population. The development of a pluralistic attitude was alien to the basic democratic character of the socialist culture and the ruling ideological platform.

A number of theoreticians commented on the evaluation of popular musical genres by various audiences. The musicologist Galina Ignat'evna Pankevich, pointed that simple answers of liking or disliking a musical composition could not suffice. The evaluation should be based on a thorough analytical understanding of an art work, its form and content. Furthermore, such an evaluation should not present an emotional response only: it should refer equally to the relationship between an art work and its social obligations within general human existence. Such comprehension should develop from the proper aesthetic education offered at state schools and dedicated to the education of the people in USSR. Yet, Pankevich bemoaned the apparent lack of sufficient musical education among large segments of Soviet population.[27] She furnished statistical data that showed three quarters of the technically educated intelligentsia and two fifth of intelligentsia with liberal arts degrees without elementary musical education. Even the majority of members of the numerous vocal-instrumental ensembles did not have the regular elementary musical education.[28]

The musicologist and senior council to the Ministry of Education Nelli Shakhnazarova shared a similar view and advocated the necessity of improved musical education. Shakhnazarova warned that the musical

26. Nabok, *Ideologicheskaia* . . ., p. 70.
27. Galina Ignat'evna Pankevich, *Iskusstvo muzyki*, Moscow, Znanie, 1987, p. 98.
28. Ibid., p. 105.

education of the young should never start from the premisses of popular music. She stressed that the popular music should not be considered as an introductory phase in the general musical education, following the approach from simple to complex. Shakhnazarova was also convinced that popular music and discothecs cannot serve as a bridge to the proper understanding of the classical musical literature such as Beethoven's symphonic music. As an example of the futility of such an approach she pointed out that for the performers in pop ensembles, without musical education, the classical musical heritage presented a closed book. On the other hand, the players with some musical education appreciated both the serious and popular music repertoire.[29]

Most importantly, during the course of the 1970s and 1980s, the deepening of the emerging polarization of the serious and popular musical genres took place. The musical language of the rock genre deepened the break between the rock music and other manifestations of musical culture. While in the 19th century the serious and light genres of music used similar musical sources, and it was not hard for the listeners to comprehend the musical expressions of both styles, the situation has changed in the 20th century. In addition, Nabok saw the experiments in serious music with the new compositional techniques of the avant-garde composers, as another source of this division. In spite of the fact that in the socialistic musical culture this confrontation has not taken ultimate forms, one should not ignore existing tendencies. The existing confrontation between the serious and light music was opposed to the spirit of the socialistic musical culture. In his conclusion, Nabok stressed that the process of *perestroika* and the broad aspects of democratization in the USSR will need serious and complex measures pertaining to the musical culture. The simple emphasis on classical music and the enhancement of such a repertory would not suffice. These measures should include the restructuring of the whole system of the musical life, starting with the music and aesthetic education in public schools, and comprising equally the professional music education. Finally, the organization of the musical life should be restructured. Nabok stressed the need for serious musicological and sociological research of the contemporary musical life. *Perestroika* should not allow rock music to further evolve on its own accord. The

---

29. N. G. Shakhnazarova, *Problema narodnosti v Sovetskom muzika' nom iskusstve na sovremennom etape,* Moscow, Muzyka, 1978, p. 78.

restructuring of music education should be able to help the rock musicians to find their place in the Soviet culture, to overcome the narrow stereotypes and obtain a truly creative input in the field of popular music.[30]

Many popular musical genres were steadily gaining the upper hand enjoying wide spread popularity while the concerts of serious music gradually lost their steady public support. This change became a matter of great concern for serious music performers and composers alike. The composers of serious music, members of the Union of Soviet Composers, discussed this development during the 7th Composers' Conference of the USSR in 1986. The well known composer Rodion Shchedrin criticized the present situation in his speech, pointing to the mistakes that caused the loss of prestige of serious music in the present day Soviet society:

"Obviously the guilty ones are the composers: they ignored too long the people's requests, exploring the impenetrable thicket of technical possibilities, while forgetting that music is the same as the everyday bread. At present, they wave their hands and declare that the people have lost the interest in contemporary music, and some are trying to justify this occurrence as a consequence of the proper development in time."[31]

Shchedrin's criticism pointed to the knowledge of the preponderance of popular music genres. In addition, he disapproved the position of composers of serious music espousing avant-garde tendencies. He described such music as mostly centered around "technical difficulties" and thus deprived from a sound musical content. His statement, in fact, reiterated the well known official position disapproving of artistic experimentations while departing from established realistic concepts.

The composer Andrei Pavlovich Petrov discussed, with a fresh insight, the changing position of serious music in Soviet society. His views were presented in numerous articles and interviews that were subsequently collected and published in 1987 in Leningrad. Petrov, music educator and a well known composer, recipient of the coveted title People's Artist, and long time president of the Leningrad Composers Association, presented this development in a more objective way, trying to understand the recent development as part of the changes in the life style of Soviet citizens. He

---

30. Nabok, *Ideologicheskaia* . . ., p. 71.
31. Nabok, *Ideologicheskaia* . . ., pp. 57-58.

pointed out that the disproportion that existed between the serious and popular musical genres did not develop overnight. Very likely a larger audience always existed for traditional vocal songs and dances than for symphonic and operatic performances. However, this disproportion became enlarged in the recent time. The musical language of the contemporary compositions increased in complexity and became too difficult for many to be fully appreciated. At the same time, the popular music gained tremendous ground among the young listeners presenting even new themes not discussed previously in the light musical genres. The newly composed rock-oratorios and rock-operas introduced often pertinent philosophical themes and their musical language approached the level of symphonic eloquence.

Although further evolution of popular music was fruitful, it pointed as well to its own limits. The supporters of this style tended to perpetuate the same musical style that depleted its own resources and led to stagnation. Petrov noted that the serious music, in turn, experienced a form of democratization. The symphonic and operatic works approached the melodic inflections of popular musical genres in an effort to facilitate the understanding and capture the attention of the broad public.[32]

Petrov mentioned the improved recording techniques and availability of record players that enabled the listeners to enjoy music in the comfort of their own homes. Speaking from his own experience, Petrov stated that the recorded music became an accepted substitution for the live music performances in concert halls. He also stated, with a measure of reassurance, that good recordings of serious music found quickly their buyers and did not stay long on the shelves of music stores.[33]

Petrov was aware that the serious music was loosing its established priority in the cultural life. Many excellent concert performances and operatic productions were conducted in front of a handful of true fans: the concert halls and operatic theaters in many cities were often filled only to one half of the available capacities. In particular, the Soviet operas have lost their public and the accustomed polished style of performances. The operatic productions were arranged hurriedly, with too little attention to the proper staging. The performances were not rehearsed enough and the

32. A. Petrov, *Vremia, muzyka, muzykanty*, Leningrad, Sovetskii kompozitor, 1987, p. 12-13.

33. Petrov, *Vremia . . .*, p. 18.

modest costumes and stage design left a lot to the imagination. The leading roles were given to less known artists whose names the public did not recognize. These artists had not yet achieved the ability to attract new audiences. However, Petrov acknowledged the emergence of popular music as an established genre. The large audiences, gathered at concerts of popular music, spoke clearly about changed attitudes. Never before musical performances enjoyed such popularity. He compared this new entertainment form with the popularity of soccer games generating in a similar fashion great many fans. Interestingly enough, the concerts of popular music had even larger audiences than the soccer games. Petrov tried to determine the reasons for the success of popular music. Speaking as a professional musician, Petrov singled out the simplicity and accessibility of popular songs. As an example he quoted the repertoire of the well known group *The Beatles*: all their songs can be easily performed by others promoting the feeling of personal participation and an easy recognition of musical patterns. Such an acceptance was not possible even with the jazz music idiom, not to speak about the complexities of the music of Bach or Beethoven. Therefore, Petrov argued that popular music could be compared to the musical folklore, since these new songs have acquired the likeness and function of urban musical folklore. The role that the folk songs had in the 19th century resembled the role of popular music in the present. The melody of popular musical genres was based on the same underlining principle established by the folk songs, most of all due to its aphoristic quality and brevity of the musical themes. Such melodic idiom was suited for an expressive and pointed rendition without elaborate details. In addition, the harmonies contained in the accompaniment were based on the natural tonal base, almost without any chromatic alterations of seventh- and ninth chords.[34] Petrov himself composed, in addition to symphonic and operatic works, music for many cinematic productions and eventually turned his attention to vocal music, especially to the genre of popular solo songs with instrumental accompaniment. Petrov reminded his readers that vocal songs with instrumental accompaniment had great followings in the 1930s and 1940s. He singled out several Soviet composers of this genre that produced unforgettable compositions that enjoyed great approval.

---

34. Petrov, *Vremia* . . ., p. 16-17.

Petrov concluded that contemporary composers had to acknowledge the popular music as a widespread phenomenon. Soviet musicians should realize that popular music can reach millions of people and possibly influence equally the dissemination of political and social ideas. Petrov stated gingerly that caution should be exercised and not everything from the West should be assimilated.[35] Petrov, was aware of the growing demand for various forms of popular music in the Soviet cultural scene. Thus, as a noted educator, professor of composition at the Leningrad Conservatory, Petrov suggested a change in the academic curriculum. He thought that the students at the Conservatory should be introduced to various compositional styles, including the popular music. This would prepare the future composers for different tasks, even if they do not chose to devote their life entirely to light music.

The popular music idiom left its permanent mark on the contemporary musical life. Petrov observed that some composers of serious music were changing their artistic credo aiming for democratization of their musical language. The folk songs of the villages and cities, the romances, the author's songs, the songs from variety shows, brought the gradual transformation of the contemporary musical language. Some of these melodic inflections were utilized in the compositions of several leading Soviet composers. Andrei Eshpai, Giia Kancheli, and Rodion Shchedrin, engaged in similar creative exploration. Petrov used this approach in his compositions as well. He advocated the necessity of a thorough knowledge of the "whole arsenal" of the devices of genres of mass communication.[36]

The future goals of the Soviet music were discussed at the 7 Conference of Composers Unions USSSR. The composers convened in April of 1986, three weeks after the adjournment of the 27 Conference of the Communist Party of the USSR. The composers evaluated the conclusions reached at the Party's congress and confirmed their conviction that the Soviet composers were not only witnesses and chroniclers of the life of their contemporaries, but equally active participants in the all encompassing process of perestroika. The composers proudly acknowledged that the Communist Party entrusted them with the realization of the goals established by the 27 Party Congress. *Perestroika* was taking place in the musical life itself guided by the highest leadership: the Central Committee

---

35. Petrov, *Vremia* . . ., p. 17-18.

36. Petrov, *Vremia* . . ., p. 13.

of the Communist Party in conjunction with the Council of Ministers USSSR issued the Resolution in September of 1986 about the necessity of improving the concert organizations in the country and upgrading the material and technical conditions of the concert agencies.[37]

The secretary of the Board of the Composers Union, the composer Andrei Eshpai reported that the composers issued their own Resolution summing up the clarifications reached during the Conference in April of 1986. Most importantly, the composers acknowledged the doctrine of socialist realism as the continuing guiding ideology. The Resolution stressed that "the democracy and the ties with life itself sustained the socialistic realism". The fundamentals of socialist realism were as ever firmly founded in Lenin's principles of close ties with the party *(partiinost')* and folk spirit *(narodnost')*. On the other hand, the composers emphasized the uselessness of the preoccupations with compositional techniques, "abstract plays with sound formations", and unjustified complications of musical expression. Very often such devices were used in order to hide the creative inability or escapism from life itself. The truly great musical works should be created inspired by great goals and great ideas. The composers concluded that the 27 Congress of the Communist Party has established a new rhythm and tempo guiding the renewal of the musical development.[38] Thus, the Resolution confirmed the official conservative position that the leadership of the Union of Composers has been upholding since its very foundation.

Describing the future plan of action, the composers' Resolution of 1986 pointed to the necessity of active and organized promotion of classical compositions of Russian, Soviet and foreign composers. Only the musical works with high ideological and artistic qualities could provide the necessary enrichment and instill truthful criteria for evaluation of contemporary musical productions. Such works could also help to establish a strong ideological immunity towards the alien influence of the bourgeois "mass culture" and popular music genres.[39]

The lowering of criteria in the evaluation of musical compositions was discussed in the 1987 Resolution of the Union of Composers. The

---

37. Andrei Eshpai, "Kniga i muzyka", *Kniga o kul'turnoi zhizni Moskvy*, Moscow, Moskovskii rabochii 1987, pp. 127-128.

38. Ibid.

39. Ibid.

Resolution was published in the musical journal *Sovetskaia muzyka*, in the issue that appeared in June 1987. In the very first paragraph of this Resolution, the composers reiterated firm support for the 27 Congress and the resolution of the Plenum of the Central Committee of the Communist Party of the Soviet Union. The Union of Composers was expected to introduce serious changes, voicing openly the official position in all creative and organizational questions.[40]

The Resolution stated that Soviet composers have written numerous fine works that were well received by the puiblic and critic alike. Recently, some newly composed works, honoring important events, showed lack of quality casting a shadow on the reputation of the Union of composers and its members. The Resolution discussed also the issues facing popular music. The composers were encouraged to explore the possibilities of composing popular genres of music for entertainment permeated with the national music idiom. Regretfully, the lack of musical taste of the young generation enabled the proliferation of music imitating the examples provided by the Western popular culture. As a rule, such music showed poor quality, catering to aggressive instincts, and egocentulsm. In conclusion, the betterment of musical education of the young was declared as an urgent task.[41]

The discussion elucidating the emerging changes in the field of Soviet musical culture benefitted from the introduction of the *glasnost'* doctrine. The Soviet musicologists, composers and music educators, were able to formulate freely the growing polarization in the musical field: the carefully nurtured tradition of serious music was loosing its primacy and the popular musical genres were taking an unprecedented upper hand. This radical shifting towards popular musical genres were changing the established structure of Soviet musical life.

However, the ensuing clarifications reiterated to a great extent the criteria established by the doctrine of socialist realism. The art work, even if belonging to the sphere of entertainment and featured on popular TV shows, should, most of all, be in compliance with the established ideological, ethical and social standards. The artists and critics should

---

40. "Reshenie rasshirennogo zasedaniia sekretariatov pravlenii SK SSSR i RSFR, Moskovskoi kompozitorskoi organizacii i partkoma soiuza kompozitorov SSSR", *Sovetskaia muzyka* 1987, 6, pp. 11-12.

41. Ibid., p. 12.

interpret the established ideological postulates and functions that an art work should perform in a socialist society, fostering primarily education of the masses. The critics repeated that the socialistic musical culture was most of all founded on an unified and universally shared reception of musical art works. The ideological and artistic requirements, as formulated by the doctrine of socialist realism, should help the composers to produce art works accepted and understood unequivocally by all the people alike. The development of a pluralistic attitude was alien to the basic democratic character of the socialist musical culture. The ideological function of music, as the basis of the humanistic education of Soviet youth, aimed to instill the spiritual strongholds of a socialistic world view opposed to the Western bourgeois postulates. This approach seemed to be threatened by the introduction of popular music modeled mainly after Western rock music genres.

Several musicologists proposed, as the way out of this situation, that the future development of Soviet popular music should be enriched with the treasury of musical folklore. A number of vocal-instrumental groups: *Pesniary, Vorasy, Ialla* have chosen this approach and enjoyed success. The ensemble *Giunesh* from Turkmenistan introduced interesting combinations of national rhythmic patterns, and specific timbres of their instruments combined with elements of jazz and rock music. In addition, several folklore groups have lately intensified their efforts in explorations of folk song tradition such as the ensemble of D. Pokrovskii, the folklore group at the Leningrad Conservatory and others.[42]

An interesting clarification took place at the 27 Congress of the Communist Party. The general secretary of the Communist Party Gorbachev found it necessary to reassure the public that there existed no foundation for the exaggerated fear of the bourgeois propaganda from the West. However, Gorbachev stated in his report that the Soviet people knew well the prize of certain prophecies, its prophets, and the subversive goals of monopolistic powers. Therefore, the Soviet people should never forget that the "psychological war" was in reality the fight for the influence on the human mind, and thus the conceptualization of the world. It presented a fight for the framework of references pertaining to the sustenance of existence, social and spiritual orientations.[43]

---

42. Nabok, *Ideologicheskaia* . . ., pp. 67, 70.

43. Nabok, *Ideologicheskaia* . . ., p. 4.

The ideology of *glasnost'* did establish the importance of a free exchange of ideas. The critics believed that, in the field of music, the restructuring would benefit most from open and just criticism. Such criticism should lead the musicians on the right path and eliminate the irrational thirst for popularity and questionable "glory", opposing ideological sabotage, apolitical attitudes, social passivity, and irresponsibility. The ideological principles of a socialistic musical culture should aim to produce the music of higher artistic and ideological standards, imbued with humanism, and social justice. The awareness of the established ideological foundation coupled with the support of the national musical tradition presented the sanctioned strongholds of the Soviet musical culture .[44]

The reiteration of lofty ideals that should continue to guide the artists in creating art works of general import based on national music idiom, propagating socialistic ideology, was contrasted in the reality of daily life with the preponderance of genres of popular music. The many thousand of professional Soviet rock groups and disco clubs presented a cultural phenomenon that transcended the boundaries between the USSR and the the West. The youths were stubbornly forging their own vernacular and the fresh yet often crude utterances spoke loudly about the many commonly shared aspirations of the young generations around the world.

---

44. Nabok, *Ideologicheskaia* . . ., p. 67.

CHAPTER IX

SOVIET SYSTEM OF EDUCATION IN THE 1980S: THE OBJECTIVES OF RESTRUCTURING PROPOSITIONS

The existence of undesirable and negative attitudes among the Soviet youth was an often debated issue in the course of the 1980s. In addition, the increased spreading of the Western mass culture projected, in the view of some educators, a pernicious attitude and loss of humanistic ideals. To this effect the popularity of western movies, in addition to the expansion and growing popularity of rock music *(rokovaia ekspansiia)*, testified to the "frightening ideological and artistic ignorance of the young generation" [1]

Many educators, political leaders, cultural historians, writers and concerned citizens alike proposed solutions to existing problems. In 1986 the general secretary Mikhail Gorbachev discussed some of the problems facing the young in USSR. In an interview for the French newspaper *Humanite*, he spoke about the necessity of overcoming the existing insufficiencies while underlying the urgency of improving the ideological and scholastic potentials of young Soviet citizens. Gorbachev thought that the youth displayed "lack of responsibility, consumerism, bad taste, narrowness of spiritual horizons, and insufficient knowledge of cultural heritage". Gorbachev's candid assessment of the shortcomings of the Soviet youth stressed the need for eradication of these inadequacies while improving the Soviet educational system.[2]

The noted academician N. Ia. Bromlei shared the concern for the Soviet youth. He pointed out that the process of socialist transformation, in the sphere of spiritual culture, should not be considered as fully

---

1. E. Nozhin, "Bor'ba idei — vazhnaia kharakteristika dukhovnoi sfery sotsialisticheskogo obshchestva", *Dukhovnaia sfera sotsialisticheskogo obshchestva*, Moscow, Mysl', 1987, pp. 360–364.

2. *Kommunist*, No. 3, p. 17, 1986; quoted after Nabok, *Ideologicheskaia funktsiia muzyki, Problemy estetiki*, Leningrad, Muzyka, 1987, pp. 64–65.

completed. The existing traditional values showed great perseverance. Bromlei quoted N. I. Konrad who declared that the sickle can be substituted with a combine, but in his view it would be 'mechanically' impossible to change from an epic tale to a 20th century novel. The time span from the beginning of the socialist government corresponded roughly to the life span of two to three generations: this period was too short to warrant a complete transformation of the social and individual characteristics of various segments of the population. The undesirable qualities alien to the socialist morality reoccurred persistently such as drunkenness, hooliganism, parasitism, theft of socialist property, bribery, money grabbing, and similar amoral attitudes.[3]

Bromlei noted that already the Plenum of the Central Committee in June of 1983 discussed the anti-social behavior and shortcomings of Soviet citizens. It would be wrong to understand these occurrences only as the leftovers from the past, still alive in the mind and attitudes of people. The reasons for the distorted behavior were rooted in the difficulties of present day realities and absence of proper education and upbringing. In addition, this behavior influenced the amoral actions of some workers, and perpetuated difficulties that the life brought on. The lack of education worsened the situation.[4]

Having in mind the existing problems, the 27th Congress of the Communist Party suggested concrete goals of improvements for those in need of assistance. The Party suggested the radical uprooting of all that interfered with the formation of the new man. The Congress recommended a struggle against unearned incomes and installed "additional measures against parasites, pilferers of state property, bribers, and those taking the road alien to the work-loving nature of our country."[5]

In addition, the 27th Congress pointed to the necessity of a thorough reexamination of the goals, plans and past achievements of the educational system. The resolution of the Plenum reiterated that the Soviet government aimed to provide for its citizens favorable conditions for a

---

3. N. Ia. Bromlei, "K voprosu ob obshchem i osobennom v dukhovnoi kul'ture stran sotsialisticheskogo sodruzhestva," *Sovetskaia kul'tura, 70 let razvitiia,* Moscow, Nauka, 1987, p. 282.

4. Materialy Plenuma Centralnogo Komiteta KPSS, Moscow, 14–15 June 1983, p. 30; quoted after Bromlei, " K Voprosu . . .," p. 282.

5. Bromlei, "K Voprosu . . .," p. 272.

steady intellectual and creative growth, and for the improvement of professional qualifications. These measures required, in turn, the growth of all aspects of education and most of all pointed to the necessity of radical changes in the education and upbringing of Soviet youth. It was expected that these reforms will produce trained personnel that will implement Party's plans towards acceleration of social and economic development.[6]

Furthermore, the Central Committee of the Communist Party, in conjunction with the Council of the Ministers USSR, issued in March of 1987 a restructuring recommendation of the higher, secondary, and vocational-technical education (*Osnovnye napravleniia perestroiki vysshego i srednego spetsialnogo obrazovaniia v strane.*) It was expected that the restructuring will enhance the education of specialists in conjunction with the radical improvements of their future places of employments in the people's economy. These measures were expected to enable a far reaching scientific, technical and social progress. All these efforts should result in the blossoming of the new type of spiritual culture, and an authentic humanistic ideology. The ultimate perfecting of socialism, will depend on the development of the man himself and his command of professional knowledge and socialist ideology. The strengthening of the collective spirit and collaboration will provide additional help towards achieving this goal. The Soviet experience has proven that education presented one of the most reliable ways of bestowing high cultural values to the workers.[7]

From the very beginning of the Soviet state the newly appointed authorities strove to show that the education actively influenced the life of all categories of population, young and old alike. The existing statistical data showed that before the Revolution three fourth of the population could not read or write. Already in 1939, 87.4 percent of the population was literate. At the end of the 1930s, the seven year education was gradually implemented. In the early 1950s, the seven year education became obligatory, and in large cities the ten year education was introduced. By the end of 1950s, and the beginning of the 1960s, the eight year education was made possible, and at the end of 1970s the ten year

6. T. A. Kudrina, "Puti sovershenstvovanniia narodnogo obrazovaniia," *Dukhovnaia sfera sotsialisticheskogo obshchestva,* Moscow, Mysl', 1987, pp. 181–202.

7. Bromlei, "K Voprosu . . .," p. 272.

education became a rule everywhere. In 1960, the higher institutions of learning had an enrollment of 2.3 million of students, while in 1984 the number of students was increased to 5.2 million.

Great attention continued to be directed to the workers' education in various professional and general studies programs. In 1985-1986 there were more than three million of workers enrolled in general studies programs taught in the evening classes. Around ten million were enrolled in the classes for professional, economic and political education. Bromlei pointed out that in USSR three to five times more workers were able to enhance their education compared to the situation in capitalistic countries.[8]

The proposed educational reforms, outlined in the mentioned resolution of 1987, were closely tied to the restructuring of the secondary and higher education. The restructuring of secondary education was singled out as the most important factor in the long ranging development of the Soviet society since it pointed to the importance of nurturing the 'human factor'. These changes were aimed at the general educational and cultural level in order to hasten the eradication of differences between the academia and labor, village and urban communities, while promoting friendly ties with all peoples and nationalities in USSR.[9]

The educators thought that *perestroika* should change the undesirable attitude of institutions of higher learning that has developed in the recent past. Many universities were not actively engaged in updating their curricula in order to provide the theoretical and practical training of specialists in the field of national economy. Therefore, these institutions should strive to elevate necessary material and technical capabilities in order to accommodate the new needs introduced by the scientific and technical progress. The total integration of higher learning with the industry, should result in the radical improvement of the preparation of trained personnel. To this end, the restructuring of the university administration would contribute to the overall success. In addition, the dedicated and goal-oriented attitude of the students coupled with the Marxist-Leninist education, should help to produce future specialists. Equal attention should be given to the improvement of scientific and pedagogical skills of the faculty. All these efforts should bring the

---

8. Bromlei, "K Voprosu . . .," p. 271.

9. Kudrina, "Puti. . .," p. 186.

intensification of the scientific and technical progress of people's economy.[10]

While discussing the goals of restructuring, the noted educator T. A. Kudrina reminded that the Soviet educational system was developed in compliance with the Constitution of the USSR. This system provided the educational and professional preparation of the citizens, enabling as well the communistic education. The educators aspired to encourage the intellectual and physical growth of the the young generation and prepare them for work, civic responsibilities, and protection of the homeland.

The educational system presently comprised the preschool, elementary, secondary and professional education, as well as the college education. In addition, the educational system included the *(vneshkol'no vospitanie)* out-of-school educational and recreational activities provided by various clubs, and athletic competitions. In 1985 the cost of Soviet education amounted to 38.4 billion rubles, which represented more than 6 percent of the national income. According to the official sources, in 1985 there were 5.1 million of students enrolled at Soviet universities. The secondary and vocational schools were attended by 44.4 million of pupils.[11]

At the beginning of the 1980s a number of shortcomings became apparent. The scholastic aptitude tests of the pupils of urban and country schools, as well as of the pupils from various republics and regions, reflected different achievement levels pointing to the inequality in scholastic standards and academic preparations of students. These disparities were very likely the result of the differences in approaches to teaching, and in social conditions. The analysis of these problems hastened the reforms of the secondary and vocational schools. The needed reforms were also conducted in order to fully realize Lenin's postulate of a necessary unity between the academic learning and practical work. The aim was to improve the efficiency of education in order to prepare the young generation for a chosen field of work and an independent life.[12]

The preschool centers, in order to continue to function even better, should improve existing conditions in order to strengthen the health of the children while pursuing the general comprehensive development and

---

10. Kudrina, "Puti. . .," p. 187.

11. *Narodnoe khoziaistvo v SSSR v 1985,* Moscow 1986, p. 496, quoted after Kudrina, "Puti sovershenstvovanniia Narodnogo Obrazovaniia", p. 182.

12. Kudrina, "Puti. . .," p. 183.

teaching of various skills. The budget for preschool education was generated for the most part by the government, and also by participating social and professional organizations. The cooperatives, kolkhozes, and other professional organizations contributed their fair share. Plans have been prepared for the allocation of funds in order to establish a new network of nurseries *(iasle)*, and kindergartens *(detskie sadi)*. In addition, these funds provided opportunities for improvement of the professional knowledge of the personnel, and the enhancement of methods of children's care and upbringing.

In compliance with the master plan of the Basic Economic and Social Development in the USSR for the period 1986–1990, and leading to the beginning of the new century, the problems of pre-school education should be gradually eliminated. The master plan called for additional three million preschool centers which would provide improved conditions for the education and upbringing of the young children. The programs for education of children were presently developed in accordance with the psychological and physiological needs, respecting the important input of the various national cultures and traditions.[13]

The basic link in the system of Soviet education presented the secondary school of general educational or vocational training. The implemented educational reforms have directed the attention to the societal needs that the school system should try to fulfill. Most importantly, the new generation of Soviet citizen should gain command of the basic body of knowledge, and develop habits of individual studies in order to keep abreast with the latest development. It was expected that the school should equally promote the desired high moral principles and help to instill the materialistic philosophy and humanistic point of view.

The secondary school included, at present, four years of general education. After the ninth year the students had to accomplish two additional years of specialized education directed in three areas: the area of general studies of secondary education, the vocational-technical curriculum, or specialized studies offered at an appropriate educational institution.[14]

However, the scholastic curricula of secondary education and even of university education were mostly concerned with the transmission of a sum

---

13. Kudrina, "Puti. . .," p. 184.
14. Kudrina, "Puti . . .," p. 184.

of knowledge and to a lesser degree with the development of skills of self instruction. Many educators contended that the current situation required a continuous acquisition of new informations due to the steady pace of scientific and technical progress. Even the modernized forms of production needed updating and rebuilding after some five or seven years. The only solution for this rapid development was to teach the students to keep up with the flow of new knowledge. The teacher should present the students with necessary skills that would enable them to assimilate new knowledge that should be self taught. The students should be able to analyze various sources in the assessments of political situation, economy, or culture. In order to achieve the desired goals the students should also know how to prepare reports by using the primary sources, special reports, photo-documentation, films, or press releases.[15]

In the final analyses, Kudrina stressed, the further perfecting of socialism and the building of communism would be impossible without the numerous improvements of cultural standards, education, social responsibilities and inner maturity of Soviet citizens. The education of young men and women was influenced by an additional number of factors, such as the family, and the character of the immediate environment. The contacts between the family and school, working collectives and public life, should be enhanced in order to broaden the ideological and political, moral and aesthetic education of the young students. One should not forget that the young people of today are the future parents, and the degree of their education will influence the education and upbringing of their own children.[16]

Many educators believed strongly that the studies of humanities influenced the improvements of the intellectual abilities. However, the existing courses in humanities were not fully appreciated. The abbreviation of previously allocated teaching hours for literature, history, music, and arts in secondary education, caused already great worries among the teachers, writers and concerned citizens. The present reforms have influenced changes in teaching of history in secondary schools. Many teachers believed that the knowledge of national history, and of the

---

15. Kudrina, "Puti . . .," p. 190.
16. Kudrina, "Puti . . .," p. 189.

October Revolution, provided inspiration for the young generations by developing a healthy feeling of patriotism.[17]

Iu. S. Kukushkin, corresponding member of the Academy, advocated the importance of historical knowledge in the general and communistic education of the Soviet youth. However, Kukushkin thought that the present teaching of history gave cause for great concern. The students used to receive basic knowledge of history in the schools of secondary education. During the last twenty years the number of hours set aside for history has been reduced to 140 hours, roughly 30 percent of the previous allocation. Earlier, 400 hours have been planed for teaching of history. Kukushkin posed the question about the justification of this reduction. He tried to answer this puzzle and thought that very likely the teachers did not protest the cut. Due to the changed textbooks, the teachers were unable to explain to the pupils the most important concepts of historical processes, without references to concrete data: "History without facts, without names and biographies, is only a bare scheme *(golaia shema)*."[18] Therefore, Kukushkin pleaded that the program for teaching history in secondary schools should be seriously reconsidered. In 1986 the history examination was dropped for the entering freshmen in the College of Humanities. Since the history examination was dropped, the interest for this subject declined and the prestige of the historical studies, in general, was lowered. This situation also hampered the selection of history majors among the best students entering the university.

At the present, national histories, as an important scholastic subject, were taught in the secondary schools of all Soviet republics. However, the time for teaching respective national histories in single republics was in disproportion with the time allotted to the studies of Soviet history. Kukushkin thought that this phenomenon presented a matter for serious concern. He reminded of Gorbachev's speech, delivered at the 27 Congress of the Communist Party, that discussed difficulties of solving national policies. Gorbachev stressed that the various republics should continue to have a healthy interest in the best achievements of their respective national cultures. Yet, this interest should not produce the

---

17. Kudrina, "Puti . . .," p. 188–189.

18. Iu. S. Kukushkin, "Rol' istoricheskih znanii v kommunisticheskom vospitanii molodezhi," *Sovetskaia kul'tura, 70 let razvitiia,* Moscow, Akadamiia nauk SSSR, Nauka, 1987, p. 323.

partition and estrangement from the "objective processes of collaboration and rapprochement of national cultures" as the foremost aspiration of the Soviet political, cultural, and economic policies.[19]

The remedy for the unsettling nationalistic question was sought in improved education and strengthening of the desired balance between the dialectical relationship of nationalism and internationalism. To this effect, the writer Chingiz Guseinov discussed the undesirable outbursts of nationalistic sentiments. The destructive actions of huligans and disturbances of the social order incurred by the teenagers, working class youth, and students at the universities reflected the existing dissatisfaction. In May of 1986, the leaders of the Communist Party in Iakutsk debated the negative occurrences taking place in their republic. The implication of this issue was discussed in the report of the first secretary of the regional party organization Iu. N. Prokop'ev. Prokop'ev submitted his report entitled: "The international education — a concern for the regional party organization" (Internatsional'noe vospitanie — delo vsei oblastnoi partiinoi organizatsii). Prokop'ev reiterated Lenin's principle of the importance of the cultivation of national cultural tradition and, equally, of the culture of the all humankind. According to Prokop'ev, there was not enough attention directed towards elucidating the international cultural scene. On the other hand, the schools were not even providing sufficient knowledge about the past and the present history of the republic, its literature and culture of its people. These insufficiencies required attention and introduction of necessary measures for the improvement of the system of education.[20]

Although the study of history was acknowledged as a powerful source of education, the shortage of needed textbooks persisted. This issue was discussed in a meeting of the secretary Gorbachev with the heads of the mass media, ideological institutions and artistic unions held in January of 1988. The Editor-in-Chief of *Moskva* magazine, Mikhail Alekseiev observed that people in the Soviet Union knew more about the history of Britain, France or Germany than about their own historical events. He expressed his concern stating that it was virtually impossible to bring up conscientious young patriots by denying the knowledge to the people of

---

19. Kukushkin, "Rol'. . .," p. 323.

20. Chingiz Guseinov, *Etot zhivoi fenomen*, Moscow, Sovetskii pisatel', 1988, pp. 414–415.

their historical roots. Alekseiev suggested a new approach in solving the existing shortage of needed textbooks. He said that a decision was reached by the editorial board of his magazine to publish in full *A History of the Russian State* by Nikolai Karamzin. Alekseiev commented:

"We know the history of the Soviet period, but what is to be done about the other thousand years? From whose hands did we receive this one-sixth of the Earth bearing the brief name of "Rus"? What are we building our socialist homeland on? . . . We should not deprive history of its right to take part in our contemporary affairs, in educating our people."[21]

Mikhail Nenashev, chairman of the USSR State Committee for Publishing pointed out that previous mindless obedience has done the greatest harm to book publishing, in particular to the publication of books on Russian history: "There was a time when we published books on history, in such an inadequate manner, that people found themselves deprived of the opportunity to fully understand and dully assess Russia's socio-political thought." In the meantime, a new program has been worked out and an adequate number of history books will be published. The printing of Solov'ev's and Kliuchevskii's works shall be increased from 50,000 to 200,000 copies, but the demand is still far greater than that. Many demands can not be met, for the time being, because of the backward state of printing industry.[22]

The new educational plan was introduced on the 1 September 1986. The educator T. A. Kudrina discussed the new plan and defended the decreased number of teaching hours for several academic courses of studies. These cuts, she stressed, gave more time for socially useful work in the community, and gave additional opportunities to the upperclassmen for choosing their future professional course work. Social sciences have received additional 20 hours and new subjects were introduced such as: *Fundamentals of the world ecology, Basics of production, Choosing of a profession, Ethics and psychology of family life, Basics of information and computer technology.* [23]

---

21. M. S. Gorbachev: *Democratization—the Essence of Perestroika, the Essence of Socialism*, Moscow, Novosti Press Agency, 1988, p. 29–30.

22. Gorbachev, *Democratization . . .*," pp. 45–46.

23. Kudrina, "Puti . . .," p. 194.

However, some educators were not always ready to introduce major revisions of established and proven ways. Iu. S. Kukushkin, corresponding member of the Academy, pleaded that one should not forget the positive lessons from the past. Among the past achievements of the Soviet education, Kukushkin singled out the implementation of an important change in the history curriculum: In May of 1934, the highest echelons of the Party and government bodies issued the resolution "On Teaching Civil History in USSR Schools" *("O prepodavanii grazhdanskoi istorii v shkolakh SSSR")*. Kukushkin acknowledged the efforts of historians and political leaders who issued this resolution.[24] The resolution of 1934 formulated well the educational potential of teaching history in the formation of a Marxist-Leninist point of view. The resolution stated that it was necessary to abolish the abstract sociological, and historical deliberations in order to present the concrete events in their chronological succession. Furthermore, it pointed to ". . . the necessity of accessible, concrete historical material, on which basis the true examination and explanation of historical events should be conducted, leading the student to the Marxist understanding of history."[25]

Apparently, Kukushkin thought that this resolution was valid and important, in spite of the fact that it was issued during a difficult time of Soviet history at the beginning of Stalin's era. However, Kukushkin's decision to single out this resolution, as a possible model for improving the present teaching of history, presented an unusual approach since the criticism of the 1930s was widespread among the adherents of *perestroika*. In all probability, Kukushkin thought that the zeal of criticism impaired the judgment of some solid achievements accomplished previously by Soviet historians.

However, the plea of Iu. N. Afanas'ev, Rector of the State Institute for History and Archives in Moscow, for the abolishment of the deadly influence of Stalinist dogmatism in the historical science was fully justifiable. Afanas'ev stressed in particular the deplorable situation created by teaching courses under the heading "Marxism-Leninism," since these courses have, in fact, no relation to Marx or science. Thus, even presently almost 30 percent of the classroom time is lost by teaching dogmatism, in addition to influencing the formation of socially passive and creatively

---

24. Kukushkin, "Rol' . . .," p. 324.
25. Kukushkin, "Rol' . . .," p. 324.

fruitless individuals. He thought that during Stalin's time history was not needed as an historical discipline: the role of history was degraded to the ancillary service of propaganda or to the justification of wrongdoings created by the regime.[26]

The efforts addressing the general improvement of the Soviet society should center, in the view of the educators and concerned citizens, on the urgent necessity for better professional and moral education. Having in mind the existing insufficiencies and shortcomings, the educational reforms became one of the central issues of *perestroika*. All these efforts should prompt the blossoming of the new type of spiritual culture, and an authentic humanistic and moral ideological basis.[27]

The restructuring of education was indeed welcomed by many. Thus, the noted dramaturge, film director, and theoretician S. A. Gerasimov wrote in one of his last articles, under the characteristic title "Tochka Otscheta" ("Point of Reference"), his personal recollections of the historical events that took place during his long lifetime. He remembered the difficult days of World War II and the siege of Leningrad. The hardship of the battle for survival brought people together and, at this point, he and his wife joined the ranks of the Communist Party. While reminiscing about the past, Gerasimov was also aware of the current situation, and the introduction of the doctrines of openness and restructuring. He commented, with obvious satisfaction, the implementation of school reforms that were "anticipated for a long time." He stressed that the role of the teachers should be strengthened since the moral and aesthetic education of the coming generations depended to a great degree on the skills and abilities of the teachers. Gerasimov thought that the teachers of literacy and literature played a decisive role in the process of the formation of young generations. The principal changes of the mentioned school reforms, he thought, should be implemented in the teaching of literature. Gerasimov was very likely referring to the introduction and rehabilitation of some writers and their literary works that were until recently censored, and although valuable, remained unpublished. Gerasimov also pointed out that in the past many famous writers testified, with due gratitude, to the beneficial influence of their

---

26. Iu. N. Afanas'ev, "Istoriki i pisateli o literature i istorii", *Voprosy istorii,* 1988, No. 6, pp. 72–73.

27. Bromlei, "K Voprosu . . .," p. 282.

respective teachers. Among such testimonies, Gerasimov mentioned Pushkin's recollections of his own education. Pushkin singled out the influence of his college professor Kunytsin: He influenced strongly his ethical, esthetic and civic points of view and subsequent choices in life.[28]

Joining the plea for the recognition of the role of teachers, the writer Viktor Astaf'ev penned his recollections on the influence of his first teacher in the elementary school at Igarka, a township in the Arctic region of Siberia. He vividly remembered his teacher Ignatii Dmitrievich Rozhdestvenskii who taught Russian language and literature in an imaginative and interesting way. His teacher, a young poet himself, in the course of time, became one of the well known poets of Siberia. Rozhdestvenskii asked his students to read aloud the selected poems and prose works, in front of the class. Astaf'ev remembered the first praise that he received for reading "faster and better" than any other of his classmates. Rozhdestvenskii occasionally read to the pupils his own verses about Siberia, to the great delight of his pupils. His verses spoke about the well known landscapes of their native region. The transformation of these familiar sights into a poetic context impressed the young pupils and gave an added importance to the life in Igarka. Astaf'ev remembered the verses about the building of Siberia; the tracing of the planed highways and building of palaces and camps for recreation of young "pioneers" — all this in order to make life better for his generation of youngsters. Rozhdestvenskii described also the spring in the Arctic Polar region and the modest little tufts of flowers starting stubbornly anew their short life cycles. These flowers seemed different from the lush blossoms elsewhere:

> Oni mohnaty, kak zver'ki
> Tsvety vysokoi paralleli.

> They are furry like little beasts
> The flowers of the high parallels.[29]

---

28. S. A. Gerasimov, "Tochki Otscheta, *Kniga v Kul'turnoi Zhizni Moskvy,* Moscow, Moskovskii Rabochii 1987, p. 94.

29. Viktor Astaf'ev, "Rodnoi golos," *Vsemu svoi chas,* Moscow, Molodaia gvardiia 1985, p. 164.

Many years later, Astaf'ev still thought that reading to the children and encouraging children to read themselves were the best approaches to literary education. Rozhdestvenskii's classes presented a lasting influence on Astaf'ev's creative mind. However, Astaf'ev did not start to write immediately after high school, or pursue the study of literature. Born in 1924, he joined as a very young man the Red Army, and fought for his people in World War II. Yet, the first introduction to the literary word proved to be a memorable experience of lasting influence. Even during the war, he was deeply moved when reading to his fellow soldiers Rozhdestvenskii's poems published in military journals.

After the end of war, as a wounded veteran, he returned to Siberia. He had to overcome the haunting memories that the war events left imprinted on his young mind. He was biding his time in a Siberian factory as a night watchman when he heard about a literary evening club and, on the spur of the moment, decided to join. From than on he was on his way to become eventually one of the best liked Soviet authors. He recalled, with great pleasure, that in 1953 his first book of collected stories *Do budushchei vesny (Until the next spring)* was published in Perm. The very first autographed copy was dedicated to his former teacher Rozhdestvenskii, who instilled in him the respect for the literary thought and awakened the will to write.[30]

However, the educators admonished the young generations to pursue goals of self perfection. The out-of-school education could help to generate enthusiasm for learning through the variety of activities. This additional system of people's education can instill interest for many areas of human endeavors and contribute to the general enrichment of one's personality. The many hundreds of camps, and homes for young children, the so-called "pioneers", provided many organized activities leading the young minds on the road to new discoveries of the world around them. The music schools for children, the art schools and sport clubs, the museums of natural history and technical sciences, the children's libraries, and movie houses, presented a host of outlets for enrichment of youngsters. The social significance of all these institution was to provide additional education, next to the time for studies allotted regularly in the classrooms. Most of all, these activities would contribute to the education

---

30. Astaf'ev, "Rodnoi golos," p. 9.

of the young by forming special interest groups and developing habits of rational use of free time.

The present-day secondary schools of general education and the vocational and professional schools have succeeded in combining the education with the work in the industry. The work associated with industrial production did not present only a subsidiary component of school education, but instead it had assumed an important role. According to the data provided by the Ministry of Education USSR for 1985, the teaching basis of industrial and professional education were expanded by 35 percent. This expansion enabled the practical training of 4.6 million of students. In 1987 the number of students participating in industrial and professional training was increased approximately to 5.4 million of students. Kudrina reiterated that there existed many possibilities for improvement, until each and every Soviet student has realized that it was necessary to work not only with one's head, but equally with one's hands as well. Therefore, Lenin's message to the young generation remained still relevant: Every young generation should organize their studies in such a manner to be able to contribute, on a daily basis, to the socially useful work in the community, even if these tasks seem slight or simple.[31]

In compliance with the mentioned school reform, it was planed to establish in every district a complex of institutions with a broad spectrum of activities. Local authorities have been advised to establish such centers in old as well as in new neighborhoods. Such improved centers would draw support of parents and working collectives. The children would enjoy the leadership of young komsomol leaders from the ranks of workers, kolkhozniks, or university students and from various specialists in the field of culture and economy.[32]

In addition, the present-day secondary schools of general education and the vocational and professional schools have succeeded in combining the education with the work in the industry. The work associated with industrial production did not present only a subsidiary component of school education, but instead it had assumed an important role. According to the data provided by the Ministry of Education USSR for 1985, the teaching basis of industrial and professional education were expanded by 35 percent. This expansion enabled the practical training of 4.6 million of

31. Kudrina, "Puti . . .," pp. 193–195.

32. Kudrina, "Puti . . .," pp. 185–186.

students. In 1987 the number of students participating in industrial and professional training was increased approximately to 5.4 million of students. Kudrina imported that there existed many possibilities for improvement, until each and every Soviet student has realized that it was necessary to work not only with one's head, but equally with one's hands as well. Therefore, Lenin's message to the young generation remained still relevant: Every young generation should organize their studies in such a manner to be able to contribute, on a daily basis, to the socially useful work in the community, even if these tasks seem slight or simple.[33] However, Kudrina noted that the schools have not yet overcome some immature and infantile outlooks, as residues of belated bourgeois points of view. In spite of all efforts, there existed even a lack of interest towards learning among some students.

Acknowledging the importance of education a special editorial board for scientific and educational literature *(Redaktsiia nauchnoi i uchebnoi literatury)* was formed in order to research the appropriate scientific and pedagogical literature. The board was established, under the auspices of the Academy of Social Sciences (Akademiia obshchestvennykh nauk). The Academy, in turn, was founded by the Central Committee of the Communist Party. The Academy comprised several scientific institutes dedicated to the research of varied aspects of social sciences. The board published the results of the research of its collective of authors in 1987, in the volume *Dukhovnaia sfera sotsialisticheskogo obshchestva (The Spiritual Sphere of the Socialist Society)*. In the Preface, the Editors stated that the dynamic development of the Soviet society was directed towards the restructuring of all aspects of societal life. The Editors considered this volume as the beginning of a major research project directed towards the study of tendencies of the intellectual development in the period of perestroika. Therefore, the Editors encouraged additional proposals and constructive criticisms that could improve their projected work.[34] Considering the political and social prestige that the members of this institution must enjoy, their bid for advice reflected well the new democratic spirit and respect for the opinions of readers.

---

33. Kudrina, "Puti . . .," pp. 193–195.

34. "Vvedenie," *Dukhovnaia sfera . . .*, Eds. Zh. Toshchenko et al., Moscow, Mysl', 1987, p. 5.

The Editors stated that the achievement of their goals would be hardly possible without a thorough analyses of the social awareness of the economic, social and political processes. The experience has shown that the intellectual factors can accelerate or slow down the solution of such problems as the organization and stimulation of planed work, the basic improvement of the management, self government, democratization of political processes, and socialist competition.[35]

The cultural progress remained the constant goal of socialism and the appreciation of cultural heritage became a highly characteristic aspect of Soviet life. The main function of cultural and educational institutions was to serve the special interests and needs of people. A. S. Zakalin examined the role of various educational and cultural clubs in the continuous efforts of furthering the edification of Soviet citizens. These clubs served well in the process of enlightening, and training of the people. The related activities were chosen as personal preferences and therefore helped to develop and strengthen initiative and self-reliance. Already at the very beginning of the new Soviet government, N. K Krupskaia had the foresight to ascertain that the clubs should present the focal point of workers' initiative towards goals of self-perfection.[36]

The new program of the Communist Party stressed the importance of the knowledge of cultural achievements and, therefore, encouraged artistic creativity. The aesthetic education and nurturing of inherent artistic talents, in the harmonious development of a personality, should help in the fight against the pernicious influences of the bourgeois mass culture. The various clubs can channel people's interests and attract the attention of workers to literature and fine arts by arranging reading conferences. Such sessions should analyze and discuss selected books. The fine arts clubs promoted successfully a better knowledge of music, theater, ballet, film, photography, and applied arts. There are many other clubs for interested individuals in the areas of political and social issues, or in the technical realm uniting the talents of inventors, teachers of technical studies and

---

35. "Vvedenie, *"Dukhovnaia sfera . . .,"* p. 3.

36. *Pedagogicheskie sochineniia*, Vol. 10, 1960, p. 131. Quoted after A. S. Zakalin, "Kul'turno prosvetitel'naia rabota i ee rol' v obogashchenii dukhovnogo mira sovetskikh liudei," *Dukhovnaia sfera . . .,* p. 224.

modelers. The clubs for athletics, sports, and recreation have enjoyed large memberships.[37]

Many workers have joined music clubs and organized orchestras of various instrumental groupings. The most popular ones often specialized in folk music. Some have attained a solid reputation and even travelled abroad for guest appearances representing their country at international festivals. However, the orchestral ensembles that have received a prestigious position, served often as a hiding place for certain organizers who did not want to engage in continuous work with new membership. They preferred to stay attached to one orchestra, than to continue training new members in other clubs. Zakalin mentioned this occurrence as an undesirable attitude that often caused speculations about the true motivations of the club organizers. Human beings enjoy sharing their talents and performing well, and Zakalin thought that there is hardly anybody without talent. Clubs serve as outlets for peoples talents, and therefore it is desirable to arrange for various competitions, and meetings with other groups. The club members should develop the feeling of identity with their respective clubs, and therefore start acting as hosts rather than as guests.[38]

The serious concern for the young generation, shared by many citizens and educators alike, instigated the support of the Communist Party in the educational restructuring. The general secretary of the Communist Party Gorbachev spoke about the renewal of ideology within the revolutionary restructuring at the Plenum of the Central Committee of Communist Party in February of 1988. The democratization of the public life, and the radical economic reforms required clear perspectives of future action. Therefore, this Plenary Meeting of the Central Committee was preparing, in fact, the platform of the XIX Congress of the Communist Party. Gorbachev stressed that the central issue shall remain the man himself, his political image and international orientation, his masterful skills, his patriotism and internationalism, his creative abilities, his civic participation and activities.[39]

---

37. Zakalin, "Kul'turno . . .," pp. 224–226.

38. Zakalin, "Kul'turno . . .," pp. 227–228.

39. M. S. Gorbachev, *Revolutsionnoi perestroike—ideologiiu obnovleniia*, Moscow, Politizdat, 1988, p. 3.

In his further assessment of the present situation, Gorbachev pointed out that the education was directly connected with restructuring. Education, he thought, presented the most important part of perestroika. Since education was already established as an essential category of Soviet culture, Gorbachev proposed that the authoritative role of the teacher should be recognized and duly stressed. The teacher, endowed with knowledge and pedagogical talent, was the "main link" (osnovnoe zveno) of the whole educational system. Therefore, Gorbachev declared that the teacher's participation was of central importance in the process of perestroika.[40]

Gorbachev drew a parallel with the early years of the emerging Soviet society. He reminded of Lenin's admonishments about the necessity of building the new Soviet school system as the basis of Soviet education. Lenin thought this task to be one of the most important responsibilities of the Party. Gorbachev agreed fully that Lenin's concern was understandable, since the future of socialism depended from the education and upbringing of the new man. Gorbachev felt that the present period dealt with the same situation: the Soviet society was approaching a revolutionary transition leading to a new phase. Therefore, the new concept of education should be quickly implemented and the new programs and technical aids, such as computers, should be introduced. The existing facilities of all institutions of higher learning, as well as schools for elementary, and secondary education, should be improved.

However, without the dedicated people who would guide the young, all these improvements shall remain only formal and expensive novelties without a real impact on the educational results. The Teacher, spelled with a capital letter, was virtually the most important person of the perestroika process. Such teachers, "with their knowledge and with their heart", were eminently suited to produce the new generations of able Soviet citizens. Gorbachev concluded that if the teachers decided to support the Party and if their support was convincing, vigorous and ardent, perestroika would receive many new sincere followers and fighters who will continue the revolutionary work. An indifferent attitude, or a formal and neutral support will not suffice: not partial improvements, not half measures but the full development of democracy.

---

40. Gorbachev, *Revolutsionnoi perestroike . . .*, p. 4.

Gorbachev was confident that there was much hope for a new and better life, since the language of perestroika was heard everywhere. This language spoke of honesty, openness and justice which is also the best social pedagogy. The hopes for the future are to a considerable degree tied with the activities of Soviet schools and with the internal perestroika of the schools under the guidance of the pedagogical talents of the Soviet teachers.[41]

Gorbachev asked for the swift and determined change in the attitudes towards the teacher. The teacher should be freed from the petty tutelage and given greater freedom. He should be not plagued with suspicions in regards to his various requests for necessary expenditures concerning the improvements of teaching aids. In addition, the teacher should be excused from unnecessary obligations that are not directly related to the teaching in order to preserve teacher's energy and the valuable time for his main purpose. Gorbachev suggested the elimination of all the barriers on the road to the new and inventive pedagogy as well as the introduction of increased salaries. All these tasks presented the obligation of the party and of the Soviet government. Gorbachev acknowledged that already many talented pedagogues worked in the multinational Soviet school system searching for new ways of teaching their pupils. Some of them were well known. By increasing the number of such teachers with high qualifications, Soviet schools will be quickly liberated from the routine, formalism, and spirit of retardation. The reforms of the schools of secondary education and institutions of higher learning should be followed through in order to achieve the new degree of perfection. However, Gorbachev thought that the Plenum should not determine all the concrete steps necessary to achieve the renewal of education. The public at large should have the opportunity to comment on the new educational goals. Most of all the specialists, the educators, should express their valuable input. The conclusions reached in 1987 at the January and June Plenums of the Central Committee of the Communist Party of the Soviet Union should serve as a recommendation to the Party's leadership of teachers unions. Gorbachev hoped that this recommendation would be carried out in the spirit of democratization and perestroika.[42]

---

41. Gorbachev, *Revolutsionnoi perestroike . . .,* p. 4.

42. Gorbachev, *Revolutsionnoi perestroike . . .,* p. 5.

Gorbachev's support for the restructuring of education pointed as well to the need of serious changes. In order to revive the stagnant economy, in addition to the political and the societal systems, a well trained manpower was needed to turn the wheel of historical changes. Therefore, the education presented the core of these aspirations. Gorbachev imported that the educators should strive to instill not only the technical or professional knowledge, but equally a well balanced humanistic, moral, and ethical upbringing of the Soviet youth.

Index